Jeremy Black is one of the UK's ... rians. He is Professor of Histor... renowned expert on the history ... *Brief History of Italy*, and *The W...* historian's perspective on the Bond novels and films. He appears regularly on TV and radio, including BBC Radio 4's *In Our Time*.

C000110974

A BRIEF HISTORY OF

SPAIN

······················

JEREMY BLACK

ROBINSON

For Taylor Downing

ROBINSON

First published in Great Britain in 2019 by Robinson

3 5 7 9 10 8 6 4

Copyright © Jeremy Black, 2019

Spain map © dikobraziy/iStock

A CIP catalogue record for this book is available from the British Library.

ISBN: 978-1-47214-168-2

Typeset in Scala by TW Type, Cornwall
Printed and bound in Great Britain by Clays Ltd, Elcograf S.p.A.

Papers used by Robinson are from well-managed forests and other responsible sources.

Robinson
An imprint of
Little, Brown Book Group
Carmelite House
50 Victoria Embankment
London EC4Y 0DZ

An Hachette UK Company
www.hachette.co.uk

www.littlebrown.co.uk

Contents

Contents

Preface

When Arthur Young visited the Catalan Pyrenees in 1787, he found hard beds, fleas, rats and mice in the unsatisfactory inns in which he stayed, but, in 1742, George Carleton provided a better indication of some of the pleasures of Spain when he recorded of Madrid:

> such variety of delicious fruit, that I must confess I never saw any place comparable to it . . . their rabbits are not so good as ours in England; they have great plenty of partridges, which are larger and finer feathered than ours. They have but little beef in Spain, because there is no grass, but they have plenty of mutton, and exceeding good, because their sheep feed only upon wild potherbs; their pork is delicious, their hogs feeding only upon chestnuts and acorns.

A sub-continent pretending to be a country, Spain, which dominates the Iberian peninsula, pushing Portugal to the margin, is at once an expression of Spanishness and a complex amalgam and interaction of distinctive environments and particular cultures. Its history reflects these tensions, a key theme of which has to be not just the history of Spain and its regions, but also of Spain in the world. Indeed, from Columbus's first voyage, in 1492, that history was central to Spain's global impact. Moreover, until the loss of Cuba, the Philippines and Puerto Rico in 1898, Spain's colonies continued to be very important to its domestic and European position. In addition, as this book will show, the history of Spain was far from inevitable: politics and warriors counted for much.

Spain's history is all too affected by 'history wars', the

interaction of the contentiousness of the present with the issues of the past. This is a theme that can be found throughout the book. It is important because it helps explain how the sites that survive are presented and also, to a considerable degree, what sites survive and are accessible. Guidebooks and other material should be read in the light of these 'history wars'. Far from new, they stretch back over two millennia, and notably influenced how the Roman conquest of Spain was to be treated, including by rivals of the successful generals. More recently, the Muslim conquest, the Christian Reconquista, Habsburg rule in the sixteenth and seventeenth centuries, Bourbon centralisation in the eighteenth, the responses to the French Revolution and Napoleon, the varied iterations of liberalism and conservatism between 1812 and the temporary end of the monarchy in 1931, the background to the 1936–9 civil war and the conflict itself, the Franco years (1939–75), and what came after, have each provided contentious contexts both for history as viewed from then and for subsequent accounts of it.

And so the process will continue. There is scant chance of a depoliticised account of Spanish history. This is not least because of the extent to which Spain has been shaped by its history. For example, the Reconquista helped lead to the conquest of the Americas, and the mining of silver and gold there contributed to economic stagnation in Spain, rather as oil wealth does in the Middle East today.

An invitation to write a brief history of Spain also provides an opportunity to return, thanks to hosts and to those with whom I have travelled there. My lecturing has led to visits to Barcelona, Bilbao, Cartagena, Ciudad Rodrigo, Corunna, the Escorial, Granada, Madrid, Málaga, Pamplona, Salamanca, San Sébastian, Santiago and Vitoria, and I would like to thank a variety of academics and others who were responsible for these trips and for providing hospitality. I have benefited from the most helpful comments of Simon Barton, Silvia Espelt Bombín, Sergio José

Rodríguez González, Enrique García Hernán, Richard Hitchcock, Nicholas Inman, Richard Kagan, Max King, Mark Lawrence, Nick Lipscombe and Heiko Werner Henning on an earlier draft, and share the sorrow of many that Simon, a colleague and friend of many years standing, has since died unexpectedly early. I would like to thank my parents for taking me to Alicante, and to Sarah for holidays in Córdoba, Madrid, Seville and northern Spain. This book is dedicated to Taylor Downing in friendship.

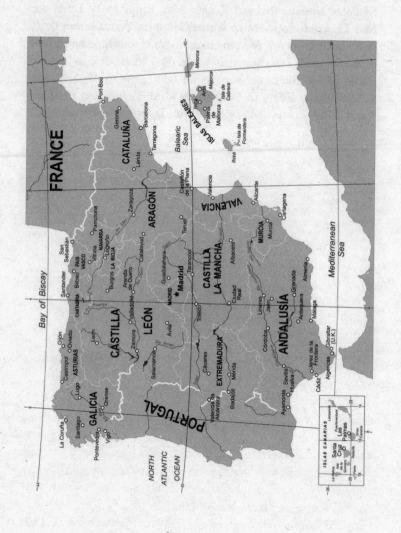

CHAPTER ONE

The Environment

'The rain in Spain stays mainly in the plain.' Well no, it does not, but this line, made famous by *My Fair Lady* (1956) and later ridiculed by comedy duo Flanders and Swann, captures the need to understand the environment of Spain. The phrase does not appear in George Bernard Shaw's original play, *Pygmalion* (1913), but was used in the 1938 film of the play and then more famously in the 1956 musical, with lyrics by Alan Jay Lerner. In Spanish, the phrase was translated as '*La lluvia en Sevilla es una maravilla*' (The rain in Seville is a miracle).

In practice, it is not a case of an environment, but rather of environments, for there are a great number of these and a complex variety for the traveller. This complexity is underplayed due to developments in transport in recent decades, notably the building of impressive high-speed rail links, in particular the 1900 miles (3100 kilometres) of the Alta Velocidad Española (AVE), which links Madrid to Barcelona and Seville, with extensions planned, including from Barcelona to Seville via Valencia and Granada. The first line, that from Madrid to Seville, was opened in 1992. In 2015, it was extended to Cádiz. In 2004, the AVE connected Madrid to Málaga in two and a half hours. Opened in 2008, the line from Madrid to Barcelona via Zaragoza covers the 386 miles (621 kilometres) in a similar length of time. There are AVE connections with France, and the Spanish train industry has a global reputation; train systems are being built elsewhere, for example between Mecca and Medina.

Motorways, now an extensive infrastructure, and internal air services have had the same effect in collapsing space, altering time, and speeding on over the terrain. They are also important economically, ensuring, for example, that in Madrid, far from the coast, it is possible to eat excellent fish that has been landed that morning. Indeed, inhabitants of Madrid will tell you that they have the best fish in Spain.

This, however, is all very recent. Before the use of high explosives from the late nineteenth century, to help tunnelling, Spain was a country defined and divided by its topography. Mountain ranges expanded distance and cut off regions, especially when the problems of terrain were exacerbated by bad weather. Travellers faced many difficulties getting to Spain and travelling within it.

In the first case, it was necessary to cross the Pyrenees, a task exacerbated by winter weather and the spring snow-melt that turned rivers into spate. The mountains rise to 11,168 feet (3404 metres). They have become the basis of a longstanding political boundary that bisects what were previously territories on both sides, notably Aragón and Navarre. Only recently have some of the physical barriers been overcome, for example by the *Túnel de Vielha* (1948) and the *Túnel del Cardí* (1984) in the eastern Pyrenees. In the western Pyrenees, the Somport road tunnel between France and Spain was opened in 2003. There are no tunnels in the central Pyrenees.

Travelling by sea was problematic until marine steam engines overcame the commonplace problems of winds (or lack of them), currents and storms. Such problems had been especially notable for voyages across the Bay of Biscay to Atlantic Spain.

Within Spain, Arthur Young in 1787 noted 'miserable roads'. William Stanhope, en route from Paris to Seville in 1729, complained that it was impossible to travel fast in Spain without going post on horseback, which was uncomfortable, and that, if mules were employed, the traveller had to use the same set for a hundred leagues. The particularism of Navarre and, even more, the Basque Country owes something to their physical separateness, although historically Asturias and Cantabria were more inaccessible. However much reduced by the train, the distance between Madrid and Barcelona is very important to their political antipathy.

Spain is not so much too big to be defined by a single geographical feature, although size is certainly a factor: the country is far larger than England. At 194,980 square miles (505,000 km²), Spain is the fourth largest country in Europe, after Russia, Ukraine and France. It is, rather, that there is no river basin that can provide such a single focus, and certainly none comparable in size to those of the Nile or the Mississippi, the Danube or the Yangtze.

Instead, the dominant feature is a high plateau, the Meseta, which contributes to the average altitude of the country being 2100 feet above sea level. The Meseta covers much of central Spain and is bracketed on most sides by mountain ranges, notably the Cantabrian Mountains to the north-west, the Sierra Morena to the south, and the Cordillera Ibérica to the north-east. Beyond the last two are major river valleys, those of the Guadalquivir and the Ebro, the key rivers for Andalusia and Aragón respectively, and, beyond them, are higher mountain ranges, the Sierra Nevada and the Pyrenees respectively. Between some ranges and the coast are coastal plains, which can swell in size and significance as important rivers, notably the Ebro and the Guadalquivir, make their way to the sea. The rivers Douru (*Duero* in Spanish) and Tagus reach the sea in Portugal, at Oporto and Lisbon respectively.

The coastal plains are far narrower to the north of the Cantabrian Mountains and to the south of the Sierra Nevada. Views there are framed, if not dominated, by mountains. Essentially, the Mediterranean, the Atlantic, the Portuguese border and the Pyrenees mountains, which provide the frontier with France, end Spain.

The coastlines are very different geologically, and in climactic and agricultural terms. In addition, the Mediterranean is far easier on the whole to sail than the Atlantic. Moreover, there were difficult links between the two, which affected navigation. In particular, a strong westerly current at the entrance to the

Mediterranean had an impact on ships trying to row or sail west. This current was in part circumvented by using an undertow along the northern shore. As a result, the Phoenicians were able to sail from the Mediterranean to Gadir (Cádiz).

There are also Spanish possessions beyond the sea, notably the Balearic and Canary Islands, but also the coastal enclaves of Ceuta and Melilla in Morocco. The latter two are Spain's equivalent of Gibraltar, an enclave in southern Spain that has been ruled by Britain since 1704, although Spanish governments do not accept any equivalence. Spain's empire elsewhere has gone, but, at one time, it was the greatest empire in the world as measured by size and global range.

Geological variety encourages the major contrasts in climate that reflect Spain's situation. Castile, the land of the Meseta, has cold winters and very hot and dry summers, creating a somewhat harsh environment for life and agriculture. In contrast, there are areas of Mediterranean climate along that sea, and also the Atlantic world of north-west Spain, Galicia. There are many similarities to Brittany and the West Country of England in Galicia, not least the role of fish in the diet and the extent to which rainfall encourages a wooded cover and dairy production not seen in most of Spain. The drinking of cider rather than wine is also striking.

The central Spain of the Meseta, notably Old (or northern) Castile, most of which is in the basin of the River Douru, focused on agriculture, especially wheat, and had a relatively low population. This was certainly so as compared to the Mediterranean coast where the presence of water could lead to highly populated irrigated areas. Intensively cultivated, the latter produced a range of crops, including citrus fruit and rice. The diversity of Spanish life is at once present in the range of environments: the difficult pastoral and arable life of the Meseta as opposed to the peasants working the fruit-laden *huertas* (irrigated farmlands) around Valencia, or the life in the cod-fishing communities scattered along the Cantabrian coast.

Yet, there have been fundamental changes due to technology. The muleteers, mentioned in Cervantes's *Don Quixote* (1605/1615), and who supplied Madrid with fresh fish, have become lorry drivers. The contrast between the landless *braceros* (labourers) working the great *latifundia* (large landholdings) of Andalusia and the peasants working *minifundia* (small landholdings) in Galicia has been eroded by agricultural mechanisation. The nature of rural life, however, still reflects far more than the machinery used. Environmental considerations remain very important.

FOOD

Food availability and cuisine are closely linked to the environment, but also to the impact of history, notably in terms of particular traditions. Religion is one, although the impact of the Muslim prohibition of pork- and ham is no more. Indeed, pig products are among the highlights of Spanish cuisine, and particularly so with *jamón Serrano* (Serrano ham) and with the pork- and bean-based casserole, *fabada*, of Asturias.

Abroad, Spanish food is generally treated as a uniform whole. There are Spanish restaurants, although far fewer than Italian, French, Indian, Chinese or Thai. Moreover, in recent years, there is a style of eating that is to the fore when Spain is discussed, that of *tapas*. In Spain, this means a small amount of food to go with a drink: a typical *tapa* is *tortilla Española*, also known as *tortilla de patatas*. In Britain, it is typically a restaurant meal in which a large number of small dishes are eaten to provide a number of different tastes.

Treating Spanish food as a uniform whole leads to an underplaying of regional differences. In the space available, it is only possible to offer a few highlights, but the key point is the appeal of pursuing variety, within and between regions, and within Spain as a whole. For example, tomatoes, peppers and paella are particularly noted for the Mediterranean coast. *Gazpacho* is the sole Spanish soup most foreigners know of, but it is best for the heat of the summer, and there are many other soups, most of which are far more appropriate for the winter, for example *lentejas* (lentil soup) and *sopa de cocido*. So also with other courses and types of food.

Wines vary greatly, the sparkling cava of Catalonia being a world away from the dessert wines of Andalusia or the reds of Rioja. They are best drunk at or near source – a marvellous excuse for travel.

The environment provided its own rigours and rhythms for Spain's history. For example, peasants were affected differently by the economy of proprietary wealth – the system built around rent and poor remuneration for labour in the context of a markedly unequal distribution of land, as well as by government intervention, for example in the shape of war and military service. Nevertheless, the peasants were all dependent on the environment.

In the twenty-first century, it is difficult for a predominantly urban readership to understand a world in which the calamities of environmental mischance were matched by the incessant pressures of trying to scratch a living (a reasonable remark given the nature of the ploughs of the past) in adverse circumstances. Electricity, the internal combustion engine, and selective crop and animal breeding, had not yet conquered the countryside and transformed both agriculture and agrarian life and, indeed, did not do so in much of Spain until the late twentieth century. This contributed greatly to the difficulties of life.

Power was largely limited to human and animal muscles, with milling performed by the aid of wind and water. Furniture, utensils and foodstuffs were basic and rough, while crop and animal breeds were improved only by the watchful care of generations. And everywhere the awful and unpredictable extremes of climate and disease could always lessen or annihilate the prospects of crops, livestock and the humans who depended upon them.

Traditional fiestas often keep alive a sense of the rural life of earlier days. In particular, they mark reliance on the seasons, fertility and the hungry gap of the year.

CHAPTER TWO

Origins to Fall of Rome, –410

Archaeological work in Spain has expanded greatly in recent decades, producing much of importance, for ancient as well as recent history, in a process that continues. Most of this work is undertaken by Spaniards, but there are also important contributions by non-Spanish scholars. As a consequence, the narrative of Spain's past is more textured than was the case at the end of Franco's long rule in 1975.

Early hominids lived in Spain, with finds of *Homo antecessor*, the archaic *Homo sapiens*, at a number of sites, notably in the Sierra de Atapuerca, and at Cova Negra and Lezetxiki. It is generally argued that these hominids reached Europe from Africa via the Middle East about 850,000 years ago. Indeed, ease of access from Africa was important to early settlement. They were followed by Neanderthals, and then by Cro-Magnon humans, the origins of modern *Homo sapiens*. In time, the latter became the sole-surviving human species, with the Neanderthals in Spain dying out about 27,000 BCE. Initially cave-dwellers, the Cro-Magnon humans were able to range widely, using stone and composite tools, not least as weapons, and developed skills accordingly. The later Neolithic period can be approached by visiting the caves at Cueva de los Murciélagos.

Spanish cave paintings are highly impressive, as natural pigments are used with great skill. Animals play a major role. Those in Cueva de la Vieja show men with bows hunting stags; those in Altamira depict bison as well as a wild boar; those in the Cueva de la Pileta near Ronda show panthers, goats and a large fish. This is an aspect of Spanish history that should not be forgotten, and these sites should not be omitted from tourist itineraries.

The ice ages provided major issues of adaptation, as the climate cooled, but the subsequent rise in the temperature saw more benign environments for plants and, in part as a result, for animal life. Humans benefited and the population rose. Larger mammals were badly affected by climate change and also hunted to extinction. Cereal cultivation spread, with the domestication of wild crops and their propagation, as did sheep and goat herding.

As a consequence, hunter-gathering was replaced by more sedentary lifestyles. Villages that were inhabited year-round were established, for example at Coveta de l'Or and Cueva de Nerja in the sixth millennium BCE. Such settlements saw the development of craft skills and trade, and had the manpower for establishing and maintaining irrigation systems. Social activities including rituals are increasingly evident in the archaeological record.

During the Copper Age (4500–2500 BCE), southern Spain was an important area of copper working. This produced prosperity in the form of the rich grave goods in elaborate tombs that suggest social stratification. Cereal cultivation increased. Important archaeological sites from the period include Los Millares near Almería. The site can be visited and it is possible to see the remains of walls and houses, as well as reconstructions of domed graves. Pottery from the site (and others) can be appreciated in the modernistic Museo Arqueológico in Almería. The extensive Museo Arqueológico Nacional in Madrid provides an impressive chronological cross-section, with the great majority of material coming from within Spain, including four-thousand-year-old pottery bowls found near Madrid. The museum is well worth the time for visitors to the capital.

The Bronze Age (2300–1500) saw tin come to the fore as it was crucial for the manufacture of bronze. Like copper, tin was found in Spain. Trade was enhanced as a result; there were valuable products to export and, with the resulting income, imports could be obtained. Meanwhile, as the population rose, there was an expansion of settlement. Major sites from the period include Cerro de Real and Cortes de Navarra. The three dolmens near Antequera are imposing. A Bronze Age settlement on the site of what became Córdoba traded on copper and silver from the nearby Sierra Morena. Stone monuments from the Bronze Age can also be found in the Balearic Islands.

Bronze Age cultures also left evidence of conflict, notably in the shape of weapons and fortifications, as at El Argar. The Bronze Age of south-eastern Spain was characterised by hilltop, stone-built settlements. Archaeological research has provided evidence of fortifications, for example at the site of La Bastida where, in 2012–13, masonry walls were discovered, which in part flanked an entrance passage, along with five solid square protruding towers resting on carefully prepared foundations to prevent sliding down the steep hill, a considerable feat. The close-backed towers provided an opportunity to throw objects, while the main entrance was protected by special defensive design measures that would have exposed attackers.

There was also a water cistern. While that was necessary for settlements, whether fortified or not, the presence of cisterns made it easier for defenders to sustain a blockade, and thus could encourage attackers to mount an assault.

Earlier fortified precincts in Iberia survive from c. 3000 BCE, in the Copper Age, usually with concentric walls to protect successive walled precincts, and an emphasis on defensive archery through loopholes in the walls. In contrast, in La Bastida, a centre of power, the location was in a mountain environment, and the settlement was probably more clearly military in purpose, with the emphasis apparently on close combat. It is unclear how far this different style of fortification, notably the solid square towers, reflects diffusion from the eastern Mediterranean where there are earlier examples.

There are still many stone-built settlements in the hills,

notably the so-called 'white villages'. The defensive character of these sites is readily apparent, not least in terms of visibility over valley routes into the hills, thus also providing warning against raiders, as well as in having only one entrance. This pattern continued with medieval Spanish villages such as Pedraza de la Sierra. Issues of visibility, surveillance and sightlines are all significant in terms of fortification, this being the case at every level and for all types. These issues help explain both the location of particular fortifications and the response to the possibilities and problems of the site. With reference to Julius Caesar's campaigns against Pompey's sons in Spain in 45 BCE, a Roman writer noted:

> The hilly type of country by no means unsuitable for the fortification of camps. In fact, practically the whole region of Further Spain, fertile as it is and correspondingly well watered, makes a siege a fruitless and difficult task. Here too, in view of the constant sallies of the natives, all places which are remote from towns are firmly held by towers and fortifications, as in Africa, roofed over with rough-cast, not tiles. Moreover, they have watch-towers in them . . . A large proportion of the towns are established in naturally elevated positions, with the result that the approach to them, involving as it does a simultaneous climb, proves a difficult task.

Fortified settlements were often located on hillsides so as to provide warning of raiders. This was especially the case to warn of raiders approaching from the sea, a pattern that was to be seen in southern Spain until the threat of North African Islamic raiders ended in the nineteenth century. Hilltop watchtowers were also built in coastal positions such as Castell de Ferro, a tower that may have Phoenician origins alongside its Arab features, on Spain's Mediterranean coast.

In turn, the Iron Age saw the development of strong maritime links in the form of Phoenician merchants who established their first base at Gadir (Cádiz), probably in about 800 BCE, and then founded settlements further east, including Malaka (Málaga), as far as Villaricos near Almería. The Phoenicians certainly got as far north as Galicia. The precious metals of Spain, particularly copper, tin, gold and silver, were their goal and well worth the journey. In return, the Phoenicians brought Mediterranean goods, such as wine and textiles. Thanks to minerals, Spain was very much integrated into a broader Mediterranean economy.

From the Greek settlement at Marseille in modern France, Greek merchants also played a role, notably in north-east Spain. Greek remains can be seen there at Empúries. The Greeks also reached as far as Andalusia. Trade became the means for technological and cultural transmission, including writing.

Within Spain, given the geography and the size, there was no one dominant state, a situation also seen in France and the British Isles. Tribal kingdoms were to the fore. There were also different cultural groups, although there was probably much overlap between these groups. An Iberian civilisation has been counterpointed with distinctive Celtic and Basque groups in northern Spain, and with a Celtiberian culture in north-eastern Spain. Alongside these differences between cultural groups, which are certainly apparent, it is important also to note the many difficulties involved in classification and in its application. There are, for example, many issues posed by the contrast between distinctiveness and overlap. Changes across time also entail questions about causation.

These cultures have left some remains, as with the Bulls of Guisando, figures carved out of granite that can be seen west of Madrid at San Martín de Valdeiglesias. Comparable figures are found across the province of Ávila. The archaeological museum in Seville holds gold jewellery from the Tartessos civilisation, the core area of which was around Huelva. This civilisation was active in the seventh to sixth centuries BCE and had links with the Phoenicians.

The nature of the available archaeological and, even more, written records direct attention to external links and foreign intervention in Spain, which can lead to a serious underplaying of indigenous developments. Phoenician influences came to be directed by Carthage, a Phoenician colony near modern Tunis, rather than more distant Phoenicia (modern Lebanon). Following defeat by Rome in the First Punic War (264–241 BCE), a struggle essentially for control of Sicily, and one that left Rome in control of Sicily and Sardinia, Carthage began to expand its power in southern and eastern Spain. This expansion, which included the industrialisation of mineral production, led to growing tension with Rome and in 218 BCE war began as Rome decided to oppose future expansion. Control over Saguntum (Sagunto), which the Carthaginian general Hannibal had captured in 218 BCE despite Roman protests, sparked the Second Punic War. Saguntum, where the men sortied out to their death while the rest of the population committed suicide, survives, with the ruins of the citadel reflecting the separate historical stages of control over the site.

The Second Punic War was principally waged in Italy and Spain, from which Hannibal marched across southern France to invade Italy in 218 BCE. The Romans responded by launching an attempt to conquer Carthaginian Spain. They also sought its mineral wealth. Scipio captured Carthago Nova (Cartagena) in 209 BCE. The historian Polybius later reported that Scipio 'told the working men that for the time being they were public slaves of Rome, but if they showed goodwill and industry in their several crafts he promised them freedom upon the war against Carthage terminating successfully'. The strongest of the prisoners became galley slaves on the same basis.

Scipio pressed on to defeat the Carthaginians at Baecula (208 BCE) and Ilipa (206 BCE). These victories gave the Romans control of the fertile Guadalquivir valley, the major agricultural area in Spain. Captured in 206 BCE, Gadir became Gades.

The knockout blow was delivered by Scipio at Zama in North

Africa in 202 BCE. In the resulting peace settlement, Carthage was forced to cede its Spanish territories to Rome, including its claims to the Balearic Islands, although the Romans only finally subjugated the latter in 123 BCE. Meanwhile, the new gains from Carthage had been organised in 197 BCE as two provinces: Hispania Citerior and Hispania Ulterior.

THE BALEARIC ISLANDS: A DIFFERENT HISTORY

A devolved province of Spain that covers 1 per cent of its land area and in 2016, with 1,107,220 people, had 2.3 per cent of its population. The early history of the islands is unclear but there are legends of Greek origins. The Bronze Age has left a large number of stone monuments, notably on Menorca (Minorca), for example at Naveta d'Es Tudons. Their function is unclear, but it is believed that many were linked to funeral rites. The Museo de Menorca in Maó (Mahón) is of interest for this culture. The Phoenicians ran the islands, and the art they left can be seen in the archae- ological museum of Ibiza and the museum there for the Puig des Molins necropolis, which includes Phoenician funerary chambers and a bust of the goddess Tanit. The Balearics passed, after the fall of the Phoenician colony of Carthage, into the Roman sphere, although the Roman conquest did not occur until 123 BCE. The Romans recruited men from the islands to fight with slings. Conquered by the Vandals in the 460s, and the Byzantines in the 530s, the islands submitted to a Muslim fleet in 707, but were sacked by Vikings in the mid-ninth century. The use of the islands for piracy led the Emirate of Córdoba to take direct control in 902. An independent *ta'ifa* (kingdom) from 1050, the islands were contested by the Almoravids and Almohads in the twelfth century, and an Italian-Catalan crusade of

1113–15 had scant impact. In 1229–35, however, Aragónese forces conquered the islands. In the aftermath, churches were built, for example the cathedrals at Ibiza and Palma and the monastery of Nuestra Señora de Llue on Mallorca. On Mallorca (to the English, Majorca), there is a variety of architectural styles in the capital, Palma, but relatively few Muslim remains.

ROMAN CONQUESTS

The conquests organised in 197 BCE still left much of Spain, more particularly the Meseta, the north and the west, each extensive regions, outside Roman hands. Moreover, these areas were further from the Mediterranean and thus less exposed to Roman forces moved by sea, as Scipio's had been in 209 BCE. There was also a major difference between overthrowing another 'foreign imperial presence', in the shape of Carthage, and subjugating the interior. The former was more vulnerable to attack and more focused on cities, notably ports, that could be besieged. The targets in the remainder of Spain were far more diffuse.

These points help explain the length of time it took the Romans to conquer Spain, but there were more significant issues. In particular, alternative commitments came to the fore, underlining the extent to which it is always necessary to approach a nation's history in a broader context. Having defeated Carthage, Rome was drawn into a series of wars with Macedon that left her in control of Greece, but that absorbed much of her energy through to 148 BCE. There were also other major struggles, including war with the Seleucid king Antiochus in 192–189 BCE, as well as the Third Punic War (149–146 BCE).

Nevertheless, gains were made in this period in Spain, and it was followed, in 139–133 BCE, by the successful conquest of much of Spain, including of the tribes the Romans termed the Lusitani, the Gallaeci and the Vaccaei; although there was firm resistance, for example, in 147–139 BCE by Viriathus, the leader of the Lusitani. (There is a somewhat unimpressive statue of him at Zamora, the flag of that province honours his victories and a 2010–12 television series, *Hispania: La Leyenda*, also focused on him.) Meanwhile, settlements were established by the Romans in areas under control, as at Corduba (Córdoba) in 152 BCE.

THE SIEGE OF NUMANTIA, 134–133 BCE

Numantia was a Celtiberian Iron Age hill fort, controlling a crossing of the River Douru, north of the modern city of Soria in Castile. The Celtiberians of Numantia repelled a Roman siege in 153 BCE and continued to be defiant, defeating a Roman army in 137. Besieged for thirteen months by Scipio Aemilianus in 134–133 BCE, the Numantians refused to surrender despite famine, and most committed suicide. Celebrated in later Spanish culture as an instance of bravery until death, notably in Cervantes's well-received play *El cerco de Numancia* (*c.* 1582 CE, published 1585), which presents the triumphant destiny of Spain as rising out of the ashes of Numantia. In this play, true love is counterpointed with Roman lust, and collective self-sacrifice is seen as heroic. The city was rebuilt by the Romans. The ruins were identified in 1860 and declared a national monument in 1882. Pottery from Numantia can be seen in the Museo Numantino in Soria.

Then, there was a major period, for Rome, of focus on other foes and possibilities, as well as on the exigencies of domestic conflict. The civil wars involved fighting between Romans in Spain as well as Italy, for example the Sertorian War of 80–72 BCE, in which Quintus Sertorius received support from local Spanish tribes. Order in Spain was finally restored by Pompey the Great, only for there to be fresh fighting in the war between him and Julius Caesar. After Pompey was killed in 46 BCE, his sons continued resistance in Spain, raising an army of three legions and taking control of almost all Hispania Ulterior, notably Corduba. Caesar rapidly advanced from Italy in late 46 BCE and after initial successes fought a major battle at Munda, probably near La Lantejuela in Andalusia, crushing his opponents. Corduba then surrendered. The city of Munda was then besieged:

> Shields and javelins taken from among the enemy's weapons were placed to serve as a palisade, dead bodies as a rampart; on top, impaled on sword points, several human heads were ranged in a row all facing the town, the object being not merely to enclose the enemy by a palisade, but to afford him an awe-inspiring spectacle by displaying before him the evidence of valour.

It surrendered.

Aside from the conflicts between Romans, north-west Spain was not brought under full control until 17 BCE. The strength of the resistance frequently impressed Roman commentators. This proved a way to praise their own successes, but was also an accurate description of the situation. In the nineteenth century, this resistance attracted interest from nationalist commentators and artists engaged with the idea of an exemplary pre-Roman national origin. Alongside the strength of the resistance came the many challenges posed by the environment, notably those of operating in the mountains, of the climate and of logistical support.

In the nineteenth century, those seeking an exemplary national pedigree could look back to the resistance to the Romans. It was relatively uncommon to cite this, however, because of a preference for claiming a Roman legacy and for focusing not on the resistance to the Romans, but, instead, on the eventually successful medieval resistance to the Muslims. The latter resistance could be presented as having an exemplary Christian character.

ROMAN SPAIN

By the time of the final defeat of the Cantabrian tribes, Spain was a major part of the Roman economy. The key elements were metals and Andalusian agriculture. The former included gold, tin and copper, and brought great wealth to the imperial treasury. Recent excavations have much expanded our knowledge of Roman production. In 2014, major gold mines from the first century BCE were found in Las Médulas in north-west Spain. It has been suggested that this was the largest mining gold pit of the Roman world, and was one in which hydraulic systems were used to bring high-pressure water to the site for processing. In 2017, archaeologists excavating the city of Munigua in southern Spain found a large mining operation for copper and iron using ventilated underground galleries, so that the miners would be able to go even deeper in pursuit of the deposits. The mines had been in use earlier, notably by the Carthaginians, but the Romans greatly increased production there. Recent excavations have also provided evidence of a large fourth-century CE Roman palace in Córdoba.

Andalusian agriculture specialised in wine and olive oil, with Córdoba famous for the latter. Other significant imports from Spain included *garum*, the fermented fish sauce the Romans used as a flavouring, wool and horses. Remains of the workshops that produced *garum* can be seen in the ruins of Baelo Claudia north-west of Tarifa and in the basement of the Museo Picasso Málaga. The ruins also include the remains of a basilica, a forum and a theatre, while the basement of the Museo Picasso includes remains of the Phoenician fortifications.

The significance of Spanish production to the wider Roman economy meant that Spain's infrastructure became even more important. Roads had been built by the Romans originally in order to exert power and authority, notably to move troops for conquest and counter-insurgency. These roads crisscrossed the peninsula, and their junctions became significant settlements, notably Emerita Augusta (Mérida), where the theatre, amphitheatre and temple of Diana survive. In turn, the cities became crucial to the economy, and in particular to the movement of goods to ports from which goods were exported to Rome, especially Tarraco (Tarragona), Carthage Nova, Sexi (Almunécar), Malaca (Málaga), and Gades, the last the key port for Andalusia. Built in the second century, the Torré de Hércules in Corunna is the oldest still-functioning lighthouse, and the view into the ocean from the windy site is most impressive. Goods such as olive oil, wine and *garum* were exported from Spain not only to Italy, but also elsewhere in the empire, including to Britain.

GADES

The prosperity of the port increased greatly under the Romans. Julius Caesar gave the inhabitants Roman citizenship in 49 BCE and Augustus's census revealed considerable wealth, which essentially stemmed from trade and from the ownership of agricultural land. The Romans, who brought fresh water by means of an aqueduct, maintained the Phoenician temple to Melqart, whom the Romans conflated with Hercules. Somewhat differently, the girls of Gades were exported to Rome where they were prized for their expertise in dancing and singing. The port was destroyed by Visigothic invaders in the fifth century.

Major cities served as provincial capitals. Corduba (Córdoba) for Baetica, the province of Andalusia and southern Extremadura,

Emerita Augusta for Lusitania (Portugal and the western Meseta) and Tarraco for Tarraconensis, the province covering the bulk of the peninsula. Some cities were onetime military bases, notably Legi (León) and Asturica (Astorga). Moreover, a legion headquarters continued to be located in north-west Spain, a testimony to the importance of its gold and silver mines. There was no city on the site of what became Madrid, although the search for an exemplary history ensured that, after it became the capital in 1561, it was provided with supposed descent from a city called Mantua Carpetana, which was a fiction.

Buildings focused on the cities, as with the forum and amphitheatre at Corduba, but were not only seen there. Aqueducts and bridges were key parts of the infrastructure of the Roman world. The aqueducts provided large quantities of water to the cities and that at Segovia, built in the first century CE to bring water from the River Acebeda in the Sierra de Fuenfría, still operates. It has two tiers of arches and is 388 feet long. Near Tarragona, it is possible to see the two-tier aqueduct that supplied Tarraco. In modern-day Córdoba, walkers can cross the Puente Romano, the bridge built across the River Guadalquivir under the Romans. It was subsequently repaired by the Muslims. Also in Córdoba, there is the reconstructed Temple Romano. At Alcántara, the bridge over the Tagus is largely restored, but the dramatic central arch is Roman. The Roman bridges at Mérida survive, although only a few arches of the two aqueducts. At Salamanca, the Puente Romano crosses the River Tormes. At Tarragona, it is possible to visit the remains of the circus, the forum and an impressive amphitheatre.

The cities were the forcing houses of Romanisation; the centres of government and of Roman religious cults; and the locations to which the wealth generated in the countryside was transferred, notably through taxes, rents and expenditure. Landowners tended to live in the cities, where Roman dress and the Latin language were adopted. Romanisation was much weaker in areas that were mountainous and/or remote from cities, and where the economy was more a matter of subsistence and/or pastoral agriculture. It was these areas that particularly attracted the settlement of the 'barbarian' invaders who succeeded Rome.

Thus, there was an important environmental, cultural and geographical tension, with the south and the east looking to Rome to a degree that other areas in Spain only did if those areas focused on mineral production. This tension was to play a role in the Byzantine (Eastern Roman) reconquest of parts of eastern and southern Spain in the sixth century. Thereafter, however, this region was to divide, with southern Spain looking from the thirteenth century to Castile, while the east became part of Aragón. Geography might appear to make such developments inevitable, but, for geography to pass into geopolitics, it needs humans upon which to act, and human agency plays a large part in this process: there is little that is inevitable.

ITÁLICA

One of the best places for Roman remains is at Itálica, about 5 miles (8 kilometres) north-west of Seville. Founded by Scipio in 206 BCE to settle veterans and to control the Gualalquivir valley, and built onto a native Iberian town, it was the birthplace of the Emperors Trajan and Hadrian. There remains an impressive and large amphitheatre able to seat twenty-five thousand people, which shows the size and significance of the city, as well as the role of imperial favour, as this was one of the largest amphitheatres in the empire. Houses whose ruins contain mosaics can also be visited. It remained a city under the Visigoths in the sixth century, but then passed into ruin. Excavations began in the 1820s, but in recent decades have been more significant.

STRAINS

The Roman Empire reached its greatest extent when ruled by the Spaniards, or rather Romans born in Spain, Trajan (r. 98–117 CE) and his protégé, Hadrian (r. 117–38 CE). This rule reflected the contribution of what became Spain to the empire, a contribution also seen in military manpower; and indeed Trajan and Hadrian rose to power because of this. This contribution was also seen in other spheres, for example with writers, notably Lucan and Seneca.

Spain was affected by the more general developments of the empire, ranging from politics to the spread of disease. These developments included the spread of new religions. Mithras was worshipped, notably in Emerita Augusta. Judaism spread. This was as a consequence of the diaspora that followed the suppression of the revolt in Palestine in 132 CE, a diaspora that resulted in Jewish communities in Tarraco, Toletum, Emerita Augusta, Corduba and Gades. Judaism also spread in the new and very different form of Christianity, which was able to spread without ethnic limits.

Persecution provided Christianity with martyrs. Thus, in about 304, St Vincent, a deacon of the church of Zaragoza, and his sisters were martyred under the Emperor Diocletian, as was St Cucufas. Although martyred in Rome in 258, St Lawrence was born in Spain, probably in Valencia.

By c. 300 there were about twenty bishops in Spain and, in 312, Christianity became the official religion of the empire. It diffused rapidly and left a major imprint in the cities of the later empire. Tarraco (Tarragona) became the primatial see of the Spanish church, a position it held until taken by Toledo in the eleventh century.

These cities were also heavily fortified in the late third and fourth centuries in response to attacks from 'barbarians'. At Lugo in Galicia, it is possible to walk along the well-preserved walls, which are in part the original third-century Roman ones. Every year, *Arde Lucus*, a Roman festival, is celebrated at Lugo.

For Roman Spain, 'barbarian' attacks had begun in the 170s,

with raids by Berber tribesmen from north-west Africa. Allowing for the currents, the sea passage from there to Spain was not only short but also relatively easy to make. The situation became much more serious in the 260s. The protection offered by the frontiers, and by the intervening Roman control of Gaul (France), could not stop Germanic war-bands from crossing the Pyrenees and sacking Tarraco.

There was also political, fiscal and economic instability within the empire itself, and Spain briefly became part of a rebel empire, based in Gaul, under Postumus. Aurelian (r. 270–5) reunited the Roman Empire, however, and brought a measure of revival.

To strengthen the administration, Diocletian (r. 284–305) redrew provincial boundaries and introduced a system of joint rule that saw Spain linked with Italy and North Africa. This, however, did not provide lasting stability, and, instead, looked towards the lasting division of the Eastern and Western Empires in 395. Spain was part of the more vulnerable West, and, in 409, was invaded by a Germanic confederacy of Alans, Suevi and Vandals. Roman influence continued but it had been fatally weakened, and, as with England, political and military links with Rome were sundered in the 410s.

THE SUEVI

This was a group of Germanic tribes, earlier defeated by Julius Caesar, some of whom, after the invasion of 409, settled in Galicia. They swore fealty to the Western Emperor Honorius (r. 393–423) and created a sub-Roman kingdom from 410 to 584. The extent of their territories was restricted by the expansionist Visigoths in the 450s, and the Suevi then were affected by division. They converted to Christianity in the fifth century, and merged with both the Visigoths and the local population.

The legacy of Rome, however, was very important. It left Christianity, Latinity, an urban structure and an experience of unity, as well as remains that are not only still impressive, but which also helped define the imagination of Rome's successors. The loss of Latin, towns and Christianity seen in Britain did not happen in Spain, which indicates the depth of Romanisation.

Recent archaeology has helped expand our knowledge of Roman Spain and has provided more sites for tourists as well as more material to consider in museums. Archaeological museums today contain many impressive and interesting Roman remains: that in Seville holds a bronze hermaphrodite from a villa, as well as a sculpture of Mithras slaying the bull; that in Albacete holds dolls of ivory and amber with movable joints; and those in Mérida and Tarragona house striking mosaics. At Ampurias in Catalonia, some of the Roman houses can be seen. Aside from city remains already mentioned, there are also rural sites, such as the Mausoleo de Centecelles near Tarragona, which includes an impressive mosaic-decorated cupola.

CHAPTER THREE

Conquerors, 400–1000

VISIGOTHS

Like other parts of the Western Roman Empire, Spain succumbed to 'barbarian' invaders in the early fifth century. In part, such invasions were not a new process, not least because some of the 'barbarians' arrived as Roman auxiliaries who were hired to help provide military strength and who thereby settled. This was true of the Visigoths who were used by the Romans to oppose invasions of Spain by the Suevi and Alans, who were thereby restricted to western Spain.

The Vandals, en route to North Africa, contributed their share of damage. In some accounts, they provided the basis for the name Andalusia in the shape of Vandalasia, the home of the Vandals. That derivation has been criticised, however, and *Andalus* is traced by some to an Arabic-language version of the name of the Atlantic.

In 454, the Visigoths invaded Spain, driving the Suevi into the north-west. In the late fifth century, the Visigoths came to conquer most of Spain, as well as southern France, but, in 507, they were defeated by the Franks and their presence in France was greatly lessened. This was part of the process by which the Pyrenees eventually came to be a key political boundary.

In the mid-sixth century, benefiting from rebellions within Visigothic Spain, Byzantium (the Eastern Roman Empire) reconquered Cartagena, the southern coast of Spain, and the Balearic Islands as part of a more general process of reconquest that also led to the recapture of much of Italy and part of North Africa. Spania was a province of the Byzantine Empire from 552 until 624. In 1983, excavations in Cartagena revealed major walls from the Byzantine period, and a Byzantine Wall Museum has been opened.

Visigothic Spain was not to succumb readily. Instead, it revived, both territorially and ideologically. Leovigild (r. 569–86) conquered the Cantabrians and deposed the last king of the Suevi, as well as recapturing Córdoba as part of a driving back of the Byzantines. His issue of a law code and of new coinage, and his introduction of new regal styles, were important to the fixing of a new style of monarchy, one probably inspired by Byzantine practice. The Visigoths, moreover, continued Roman administrative structures and also Latin. Reccared I (r. 586–601), in 587, renounced the Arian heresy in favour of Catholicism, and thus helped to unite the Hispano-Roman population with their Visigothic rulers. Arian uprisings against this change were overcome. Aside from the religious element, distinctions in dress and funerary customs between the Visigoths and the Hispano-Romans were ended. The Visigoth reconquest gathered pace from 614 and only the Balearics were not regained.

Slavery was important to the Visigoths, with many of the slaves gained by raiding, and they were even recruited into the army. Slavery was linked to non-membership of the tribe, and there were slave revolts. In 694, Egica (r. 687–702) decreed that the Jews of Spain who refused to convert be consigned to slavery as a punishment for alleged conspiracy, although it is unclear whether this happened in full. The Visigothic period has left a legacy of churches, as with the seventh century Santa Comba de Bande and the Basilica of San Juan Bautista near Palencia, and of gold and silver jewellery.

Under Francisco Franco, the authoritarian, centralising dictator from 1939 to 1975, the Visigoths were much admired by the regime because they established unity in the peninsula after the post-Roman divisions and converted to Catholicism. Franco praised the Visigoths when establishing a museum devoted to them. After Franco's death, they fell decidedly out of fashion.

MUSLIM CONQUEST

The rapid fall of Spain to Muslim invaders in, and after, 711 was one of many dramatic successes by the forces of Islam. Explanations in Christian Spain of its fall were for long religious, providential and moral: 'God testing His People' as well as the 'Coming of Antichrist' were key themes. The major literary work of the period is the *Commentary on the Apocalypse* by the monk Beatus from Liébana in the far north of the Peninsula. There was also a theme of judgement in the fall of Visigothic Spain in a longstanding story of rape, revenge and betrayal, in which a rape by Roderic, the last king, played a central role. This approach related success against the Muslims to morality, an account that, conversely, could serve to explain the success of later monarchs. In practice, Visigothic failure was due to Muslim strengths as well as to Visigoth disadvantages, notably divisions and other military commitments including that against the Basques.

Crossing the Strait of Gibraltar in 711, the Muslims defeated and killed Roderic that year or the next, following up by rapidly taking Córdoba, Toledo, Mérida and Zaragoza. Having overrun most of Spain, the Muslims pressed on to invade France, where the south provided readily accessible targets. Initially successful, they were defeated at Tours in 732 or 733 and driven out of France, losing the major city of Narbonne in 759.

Meanwhile, within Spain, the Cantabrian Mountains had helped make the north difficult for Muslim attackers to access and had provided refuge for the Christians. This refuge served as the basis for a medieval Christian Spain defined by war with the Muslims and based for long in northern Spain, including in the upland regions to the south of the Pyrenees, for example around Jaca, which was the first capital of Aragón. At the same time, the inhospitable lands in northern Spain were of only limited interest to the Muslims. They were defeated there in 722 at Covadonga in Asturias, and a statue of the Virgin Mary, to which prayers had been made, attracted much of the credit. As a result, a monastery and chapel were built later in the century. The nineteenth-century statue of the Christian leader Pelagius is prominently displayed beneath the Cross of Victory. Another sculpture, in bronze, dating from 1891, is in Gijón.

The Christian kingdoms of the north sought to assert continuity with the Visigoths and, through them, with the Romans. Thus, holy relics were brought from Toledo to Asturias, where, in Oviedo, in the Cámara Santa, Alfonso II in the ninth century provided a shrine for the relics. This continuity challenged the idea of any linkage between Visigoth Spain and its Muslim successor. The Christian north was an area in which monasteries were established. Some survive to the present offering an instructive counterpart to Muslim architecture. One of the most impressive monasteries is the Benedictine one of Ripoli in Catalonia, although it is the twelfth-century remains that are striking. So also with the ninth-century monastery of San Juan de la Peña, which eventually became the pantheon of the rulers and nobles of Aragón and Navarre. The mountainside setting is dramatic and meets every requirement for Romantic landscape, as does that of the monastery of Leyre, which was the earlier pantheon.

Horseshoe arches feature prominently in churches built from the ninth century. It has been argued that this form of arch was used in the Visigothic period, but the horseshoe arches from the early tenth century in San Miguel de Escalada, for example, reflect those in the great mosque in Córdoba and may have been constructed by builders from *al-Andalus* (Muslum Spain).

Under Charlemagne in the late eighth and early ninth century, the Franks tried to extend their hegemony to south of the Pyrenees, but they found it difficult to sustain a presence there, not least as a result of the failure of the 778 campaign to end opposition. This failure was important in ensuring that Christian Spain was divided among independent kingdoms. The situation was similar in Muslim Spain, in that distant centres of authority were unable to sustain control. The history of Spain, however, might well have been very different had what became France not been centred on Paris but, instead, in Languedoc, and therefore able to exert more consistent power.

THE DEATH OF ROLAND, 778

The defeat of Charlemagne's rearguard by Basques at Roncevaux Pass in Navarre, as he withdrew following the capture of Pamplona, became a key episode in medieval literature. Charlemagne's biographer, Einhard, recorded: 'That place is so thoroughly covered with thick forest that it is the perfect spot for an ambush . . . the Franks were disadvantaged by the heaviness of their arms and the unevenness of the land.' The eleventh-century epic poem *The Song of Roland* provided a much-embroidered heroic account that affected later views.

Frequent warfare brought devastation to northern Spain. Although there was incessant conflict within, and between, the small Christian principalities, as authority was asserted and power contested, the focus on conflict was that between these principalities and the Muslims. Muslim raiding was for long a major aspect of life in the principalities. It had functional purposes in the quest for booty, notably slaves. There were also, certainly later, ideological goals, particularly the punishment of unbelievers. The determination of men to assert their role and masculinity through military activity was also significant.

There was countervailing raiding by the Christian principalities. This raiding encouraged Muslim fortifications. The most significant in the long term was Madrid. It was founded in about 860 as a castle in the middle of nowhere, in order to help control routes south from the Sierra de Guadarrama.

Throughout this period, however, the weight of activity was on the part of the Muslims, and it was not surprising that the Christians built a line of defensive positions along the River Douro. At the same time, Muslim divisions, notably between the Arabs and the Berbers in the 740s, weakened their impact, as, from the 750s, did rivalry between the key dynasties in the Muslim world: the Abbasids and the Umayyads.

Much of the Christian population in the Muslim areas eventually adapted Muslim culture and language, as a result of which they were known as *Mozarabs*. The extent of early Islamicisation is a matter of controversy, however, and there were relatively few places to worship. The process of Islamicisation appears to have escalated in the tenth century when many of the indigenous population migrated to Córdoba, the thriving, prosperous capital where everyone wanted to be. The wealth of Spain was focused in the south, notably in the valley of the Guadalquivir. This proved the basis for the strength of Córdoba, the capital from 756.

THE MEZQUITA

The most dramatic site in Córdoba, the Great Mosque (Mezquita), was begun in the late eighth century, and was constructed by demolishing or adapting the church of Saint Vincent, itself built on the site of a Roman temple dedicated to the god Janus. The site was chosen for the location and for the enormous width of the walls which provided a natural defence against assault. The original mosque was completed in 786 and subsequently expanded, notably, with a new minaret, by Abd ar-Rahman III in the 930s, and in the 960s and 970s with an expansion in scale and with a new *mihrab* (prayer niche). Later that century, more bays were added to the prayer hall, upsetting its balance. In turn, after a chapel built in 1371, a cathedral was built in the centre of the mosque from 1523. The Mezquita, however, is dominated by its bays of columns stretching to the edges of one's view. Other Muslim remains include the *hammam* (bathhouse) and a water wheel.

In the mid-tenth century, under Abd-ar-Rahman III (r. 912–61) and his impressive successor as caliph, Al-Hakam II (r. 961–76), Córdoba was seen as a major power and received embassies from Baghdad, Byzantium and Otto I, the Holy Roman Emperor. Moreover, the future Pope Sylvester II (r. 999–1003), as the monk Gerbert of Aurillac, during his stay at the monastery of Ripoli, may have visited al-Andalus in the 960s when it was at its intellectual and cultural peak. The transmission of Arabic mathematical knowledge to Christian Europe and the introduction of the abacus and astrolabe are attributed to Gerbert, who was later described as a necromancer and anathemised because of his alleged links with Islam. From the 940s to the 990s, Córdoba had its heyday. This has left much for tourists to see, including the Medina Azahara, a palace and administrative centre west of Córdoba. Built from 936, in part with material from Roman sites but also with North African marble, and finished in 976, it was plundered in 1010 and is now a ruin, part of which awaits excavation.

The term *convivencia* is frequently used by historians to refer to the multi-ethnic, multi-religious, yet supposedly 'tolerant' culture of al-Andalus. The important Jewish presence there greatly contributed to intellectual life. The translation 'schools' in Toledo helped in cultural transmission, while Al-Hakam II, who liked books and supported scientific work, encouraged the translation of books from Latin and Greek into Arabic.

Long History: The Cases of Alicante and Salamanca

Many Spanish cities have a long history, not only back to the Romans, but earlier. These histories reflect the extent to which conquerors built on earlier foundations while agrarian society continued to look to the same centres. The position of many cities as communication nodes was important.

Settlement in the Alicante area has lasted for over seven thousand years, but the first clear settlement on the site of Alicante was built by the Carthaginians in the fourth century BC. Their settlement, Akra Leuka, was followed by Roman Lucentum, which came under Visigothic control, before being conquered by the Muslims who were responsible for the modern name: *Alicante* is Arabic for city of lights. As a reminder of the far-from-fixed nature of political boundaries, Alfonso X of Castile captured the city in 1246, but, in 1298, it passed to the Crown of Aragón, becoming part of the kingdom of Valencia. Having done well in the fifteenth and sixteenth centuries, Alicante was hit by the expulsion of the *Moriscos* in 1609 and then by backing Charles III in the War of the Spanish Succession. It benefited from the economic growth of late nineteenth century Spain. A Republican city in the Civil War, Alicante did not fall to Franco until 1 April 1939, the last city to do so. From the 1960s, the city grew rapidly due to tourism.

Another city with a long history is Salamanca. It was a pre-Roman foundation established by the Vaccaei, or Vettones, that was captured by Hannibal for the Carthaginians in 220 BCE, before falling to the Romans. The city became a major transport hub for them as it had a bridge on the Via de the Plata, a north–south route which ran from Mérida to Astorga. After rule by the Alans and

Visigoths, Salamanca was captured by the Muslims in 712, being resettled by the Christians from the tenth century. University teaching had begun by 1130, although a royal charter did not follow until 1218. The university became a major centre of legal studies. A World Heritage Site from 1988, the old city has two cathedrals as well as important seventeenth-century buildings. It is vibrant and yet also has considerable charm.

CHAPTER FOUR

Two Spains,
1000–1492

Under Al-Mansur (r. 977–1002), almost every Christian capital in Spain was sacked, in a persistent series of attacks, as were religious sites such as the monastery of Santo Domingo de Silos south-east of Burgos. It is also possible that he burnt the library of Córdoba. The liberal, open-minded caliphate of Al-Hakam II, who loved the arts, the science and books, was very much pushed aside. However, after the death of Al-Mansur, the Caliphate of Córdoba disintegrated into civil war and a series of independent kingships or *ta'ifas*. The most important of these was based in Seville, which gradually became pre-eminent in southern Spain, replacing Córdoba. Elsewhere, the *ta'ifas* were weakened by constant strife. They were forced to pay heavy tributes or *parias* to the Christians, and this burden undermined them further as well as providing money for Christian rulers to spend on building and warfare.

The weakness of the *ta'ifas* led to Christian successes and helped explain why Islam did not have the lasting success it had in North Africa and the Middle East. The Christian advance into Spain had already led the (Christian) kingdom of Asturias to move its capital from Oviedo to León in 914, while, after being captured in 920, Nájera became the capital of Navarre.

More dramatically, the advance resulted, after a long siege, in the capture of Toledo in 1085 by Alfonso VI of León and Castile (r. 1065–1109). He was helped by the inadequate leadership of the Muslims in Toledo. The ancient Visigothic capital and the primatial see of the Spanish Church, this was the major position in the Meseta, as Madrid, which fell at the same time, had not yet been developed as a city. In the Reconquista, the legitimacy of the conquerors rested in part on the notion of reconquest. Alfonso referred to himself as 'Emperor of all the Spains', and moved his capital from León to Toldeo.

Defensive considerations were very important to the location, building and future of cities. Alfonso's son-in-law established a frontier town at Ávila, the strong walls of which are an impressive sight to this day and the largest fully illuminated monument in the world. The cathedral there, built in the twelfth century, is fortified. Moreover, towns were relocated and rebuilt as they became less exposed to Muslim attack. Thus, in Sangüesa in Navarre, the people moved down from the more secure hillside to the bridge over the River Aragón.

The Christian kingdoms of northern Spain drew on Visigothic artistic traditions as well as Muslim influences. They were also influenced by wider European developments, notably those in France and Italy. In particular, the Romanesque architectural and decorative style became important in the eleventh century, both in Catalonia and along the routes to Santiago de Compostela, and especially its cathedral. The Old Cathedral in Salamanca, built in the twelfth century, is a good example of the Romanesque, not least with its carvings of imaginary animals. The cloisters at the Catalan Benedictine monastery of Sant Cugat del Vallès contain 144 Romanesque carvings with beautiful carved capitals including those of birds. The later church is transitional Romanesque to Gothic. The beautiful Romanesque cloisters of the monastery of Santo Domingo de Silos also contain fascinating carvings, notably of birds. Moreover, Christian Spain was affected by the spread of monastic orders from elsewhere in Europe.

In order to resist the Christian advance, the Muslims called in the Almoravids, Saharan Berbers who had overrun Morocco in the 1060s. They defeated Alfonso at Sagrajas (1086) and put a temporary end to the Christian offensive. The Almoravids took over most of the Muslim emirates in the early 1090s, Badajoz falling to them in 1094. The Almoravids, however, suffered a reverse when El Cid, a Christian soldier of fortune, captured Valencia in 1094.

EL CID AND HEROISM

A soldier of great ability and ambition, Rodrigo Díaz de Vivar, known later as El Cid, was a Castilian noble who fell out with Alfonso VI of León and Castile and became a mercenary and then a freelancer in his own interest. El Cid comes from the Arabic *sayyid*, or lord, or derived from a form of the Arabic word *asad* (lion), as with King Richard *Coeur de Lion* of England. El Cid fought both Christians and Moors, made much money from *parias* (tributes), and ran Valencia himself from 1094 until his death in 1099, fighting off the Almoravid Berbers. His widow succeeded him, but was forced to surrender Valencia to the Almoravids in 1102.

Subsequently, El Cid was presented as a role model, as in the anonymous twelfth-century Castilian poem *El Cantar del Mio Cid*. In practice, he reflected the opportunities and opportunism of frontier society. The highly successful 1961 film, with Charlton Heston as the protagonist, romanticised him in a story of conflict, betrayal and Sophia Loren. El Cid's body, fitted to an iron frame on his saddle, is posthumously victorious, and El Cid is described as 'the purest knight of all'.

The pattern of entrepreneurs of power could also be seen elsewhere, as in the mountains north-west of Málaga, where the church of Bobastro is what remains of the stronghold of Umar ibn Hafsun (*c.* 850–917), a brigand of indigenous stock who successfully defied the caliphate at Córdoba before converting to Christianity. Bobastro was finally conquered in 927.

At the other end of the Mediterranean, the First Crusade in the late 1090s launched nearly two centuries of conflict in what later became Israel, Palestine, Lebanon and Syria. Meanwhile, drawing for their wider significance and legitimacy in part on this conflict, Spain had its own crusading wars. These were a matter of attacks by both sides. In the early eleventh century, under Yusuf ibn Tashfin (r. c. 1061–1106) and his son Ali ibn Yusuf (r. 1106–43), the Almoravids overran the rest of Muslim Spain (1110–15), recaptured Valencia from the Christians (1102) and defeated Alfonso VI at Uclés in 1108, although they failed to regain Madrid in 1109.

Thereafter, the Christian states regained the initiative and expanded considerably. Under Alfonso VI and Alfonso VII, León was particularly strong. Alfonso VII inherited the united throne of León-Castile-Galicia in 1126. He fought Aragón, Navarre and rebellious nobles. In 1135, Alfonso was crowned Emperor of Spain in the cathedral of León. He introduced the Cistercians to Iberia, and campaigned against the Almoravids from 1138. Campaigning until he died in 1157, he expanded his power southward to the River Tagus and raided well south of there; in 1147, in a major expansion of activity, he captured Almería on the Mediterranean coast.

Alfonso divided his kingdom between his sons, so Castile separated from León in 1157. Due to success in war against Alfonso VII in 1141, Portugal had already become fully independent in 1143. Navarre had broken away from Aragón in 1134, but, in contrast, Aragón and Catalonia united in 1137, and then overran the lower Ebro valley in 1148–9. An independent Portugal, meanwhile, expanded greatly with the capture of Lisbon in 1147, a capture to which English crusaders greatly contributed.

From the 1150s, the Almoravids were replaced in Spain by the Almohads, Shi'ite sectarians who had already conquered Morocco in the 1140s. They lent new energy to Muslim resistance, creating problems for Alfonso VII, although some Muslims preferred to turn to Christian assistance, notably the rulers of the Ta'ifa of Albarracín who sought help from Navarre. The Almohads conquered Almería in 1157, and it was not gained anew by Castile until 1489. Alfonso VIII of Castile (r. 1158–1214) was able to take Cuenca in 1177, but was heavily defeated by the Almohads, under Caliph Ya'qub al-Mansur (r. 1184–99), at Alarcos, near Calatrava, in 1195.

The different periods of Muslim rule were characterised by contrasting emphases in architecture and the decorative arts. Almohad architecture had a simpler style than that of the earlier Córdoban caliphate. Almohad architecture and decoration can be seen in their capital, Seville, notably in the Giralda, which was originally a minaret. There are similar structures in Rabat and Marrakesh.

In the early thirteenth century, however, the Reconquista gathered pace again, recovering the energy that had been shown in the late eleventh century. In 1212, Alfonso VIII of Castile, in command of the united armies of Castile, Aragón, Navarre and Portugal, advanced south from Toledo. Having captured Calatrava, he crushed Caliph Muhammad al-Nasir (r. 1199–1213) at Las Navas de Tolosa on 16 July after a surprise attack. This was to be the crucial and lasting victory of the Reconquista, and was understood at the time as a key success. The victory was explained in terms of divine support.

The exploitation of the victory was helped by the collapse of the Almohad Empire as a result of succession disputes. In contrast, León and Castile, which had been divided since the death of Alfonso VII in 1157, were united in 1230 when Ferdinand III, King of Castile from 1217, inherited León from his father, Alfonso IX of León (r. 1188–1230). Such processes of division and unification were highly significant to the politics of conflict, politics that at least in part helped explain the flow of the warfare. As a result, fortifications were not only built to ensure control from and/or over the Muslims.

Most of southern Spain was overrun by 1275. Division among the Almohads after the death of Yusuf II in 1224 was crucial; as Almohad forces were transferred to Morocco, al-Andalus was divided, and the Castilians were able to find local allies. Alfonso IX defeated the army of al-Andalus and captured Badajoz in 1230. In a key dynamic of success, the energetic Ferdinand III (r. 1217–52), who was to be canonised by the Church in 1671, overran the valley of the Guadalquivir, taking Baeza in 1227, Córdoba in 1236, Huelva in 1238, Murcia in 1243, Cartagena in 1245, Jaén in 1246, and Alicante and Seville in 1248. The Muslims were expelled from Seville.

Ferdinand left some of his conquests under vassal Muslim governors, but his son, Alfonso X (r. 1252–84), conquered them and absorbed them into Castile: Niebla (1262), Murcia (1264) and Alicante (1266). Only the kingdom of Granada was left under the Muslims. While in theory, from 1238, a vassal of Castile, it was in practice independent.

Conquest saw Christianisation in conquered areas, notably with church-building and renaming, although the architectural aesthetics of the Islamic world were also adopted in many respects. In Toledo and Seville, the cathedrals were built on the same foundations as the mosques they replaced. The Muslim legacy was removed or reused, as in Jaén where the large eleventh-century Muslim baths were built over. Moreover, in areas that were already parts of the Christian kingdoms, there was a process of architectural celebration of victory, with churches built or extended. The Gothic style became important from the thirteenth century. The cathedral of León remains a dramatic legacy. At the same time, there were important transitional Romanesque-Gothic works, such as the monastery of Santa María la Real in Aguilar de Campoo in northern Castile.

Alfonso X sponsored official history, written in Castilian, as an aspect of a more general engagement with culture as a means for national identity, as well as a political tool celebrating his victories over the Muslims. A patron of astronomy and science, who produced a major legal compilation, the *Siete Partidas*, Alfonso also tried to make Castilian the official language of law and administration, and had the Old Testament translated. Ferdinand III was a leading patron of the friars, founding many of their houses in Andalusia. At the same time, there was a major linguistic exchange, with hundreds of Arabic words adopted into Castilian, as well as many Arabic works translated.

Meanwhile, James I of Aragón (r. 1213–76), the 'Conqueror', was in his own way as dynamic as Ferdinand III. James had captured Majorca (1229), Menorca (1232), Ibiza (1235) and the kingdom of Valencia (mostly in 1238), subsequently campaigning in Murcia. The Portuguese advanced south to conquer the Algarve. Navarre was, for reasons of geography, unable to take part in this process of expansion. Instead, it looked north, being linked to France until brought into Castile by conquest in 1512.

After the sustained burst of activity, although Tarifa was captured in 1292, the Christian monarchs devoted much of their energies to attempting to resettle the lands they had conquered. Many Muslims had fled from them, or, especially after a large-scale rebellion in 1264, been expelled as a security threat. Others stayed to till the soil. Indeed, many Muslim communities remained, especially in reconquered territory in Aragón. They were known as Mudéjares, received special dispensation, and were legislated for. The fact that many townships had Christian, Muslim and Jewish communities living side by side has led to the application of the term *convivencia*. Alfonso X is credited with policies that facilitated this process.

Some Muslims, however, were forced into slavery. Thus, the Aragónese conquest of Minorca and Ibiza was followed by much of the Muslim population being sold into slavery, which produced both money for their captors and land for settlement. The supply of slaves from lands captured in the Reconquista was supplemented by raiding, especially into North Africa. Moreover,

Catalan merchants imported slaves from North Africa. Barcelona, Valencia, Cartagena, Cádiz and Seville were major slave markets, an aspect of the cityscape that has left no legacy.

Resettlement by Christians as Christian kingdoms expanded southward was part of a longstanding process of growth and development through internal settlement. Migration and colonisation were key elements of policy. They drew on a broader process of population increase and agricultural development, but there were specific political aspects as authority was consolidated. This process included the establishment of towns, including Ávila, Segovia and Salamanca in the 1080s and 1090s. Military bases were designed also to serve as governmental centres and economic nodes. The foundation of military orders, notably those of Santiago, Alcántara and Calatrava in the twelfth century, was part of the process. The first, the Order of Calatrava, was founded in 1158. The military order gained, settled and protected extensive estates. Castles were manned by them, for example Alarcón by that of Santiago.

New monastic orders were also a help to settlement. Thus, in 1144, the Cistercians, in response to an invitation from Alfonso VII, settled in the Soria region between Zaragoza and Madrid. The monastery of Santa María de Huerta that they built from the 1160s is an impressive Gothic work, notably with the imposing refectory. Other major Cistercian sites include Poblet and Santes Creus, both of which can be reached from Barcelona, as well as Cañas in Rioja and Veruela near Tudela. As with the general pattern in Christian western Europe, settlers were attracted by charters of liberties, although militarism was also part of the process, as with the *caballeros villanos* (commoner knights) in Castile.

Resettlement included church building, both the conversion of mosques, as with the Santa María cathedral in Valencia, and new buildings. In Córdoba, Ferdinand III founded fourteen churches including the Iglesia de San Miguel. The nearby Medina Azahara was in part dismantled in the fifteenth century to provide material for the monastery of San Jerónimo. The massive cathedral at Seville was built over the mosque, and Ferdinand III was buried there. Churches that had become mosques were converted back to churches, for example the Christ of the Light church in Toledo.

The process of reconquest has left many commemorative occasions across Spain. Thus, in Alicante province, in Alcoi/Alcoy, a town established in 1258 by James I of Aragón when he built a castle to control a crossing of the River Serpis, there is an annual festival, *Moros y Cristianos*, to represent the Reconquista. The intervention of St George on behalf of the Christians is depicted.

GOVERNMENTAL CHANGE

England was not alone in the early development of parliamentary institutions. They were also seen in some of the Spanish kingdoms in the form of periodic assemblies, in which the monarchs were given advice by their feudatories, and had institutional structure. Known as *cortes*, these assemblies validated taxation and could present grievances and raise matters. The first known *cortes* date from 1188 in León. This development was taken further by the creation, in Aragón and Catalonia, of standing committees to handle matters between sessions.

At the same time, there was legal codification in response to the revival of Roman law, and a related professionalisation of government. The accompanying increase in royal powers and pretensions, however, met with opposition from the nobility, with rebellions in Aragón and Valencia from the 1260s to the 1340s, and in Castile in the 1270s.

The process of settlement had to respond to the environment, to economic possibilities and to the question of scale. Further south, there were large, lightly populated areas, and more Muslims. Large estates were created, mostly to the benefit of the Church and the nobility, with the military orders providing a key bridge. Most Christian peasants remained further north.

Over the long term, from the tenth to the fourteenth centuries, agricultural prosperity was helped by a rising population, which provided markets and workers, as well as by improved technology. The wealthy found it easier to benefit than independent peasant proprietors, many of whom were hit by problems and reduced to subordination.

Increased prosperity also led to the rebuilding and extension of existing religious sites. Thus, the ninth-century monastic church in Ripoli was replaced by a larger work in the eleventh century, and the twelfth-century portal survives. It provides a vivid account of biblical history, notably of the Exodus, the Book of Kings, a Vision of the Apocalypse, and other episodes. A theme is that of struggle, which was appropriate for the Reconquista. In the depiction of the Exodus, Moses is presented as keeping his arms uplifted in order to ensure victory and troops are shown in combat.

The rulers also fought each other, including intervening in civil wars in Castile, Portugal, Navarre and Aragón. Rulers displayed a sort of chess-like sense of power and power-rankings, as when Peter IV of Aragón (r. 1336–87) sought to persuade the King of Portugal to abandon his alliance with the King of Castile by arguing that the latter was reaching for domination over the entire peninsula. This was in the 'War of the Two Peters' (1356–66) with Peter I of Castile, a conflict that led to the Castilian civil war in which Aragón backed Peter I's illegitimate brother, Henry of Trastámara, who defeated and murdered him in 1369, becoming King of Castile (r. 1369–79).

Conflicts were exacerbated by foreign intervention during

the Hundred Years War between England and France. Thus, English archers played a significant part in the battle of Aljubarrota (1385), where the Portuguese defeated a Castilian attempt at conquest. John of Gaunt took a role in the politics of Castile. The third son of Edward III of England, in 1372 he married, as his second wife, Constance of Castile, daughter of Peter I, and assumed the title of King of Castile and Léon in right of his wife. In 1386, he invaded Galicia and received the submission of much of it. Pressing on in 1387 with the backing of Portugal, he failed to engage John of Trastámara, John I of Castile (r. 1379–90), in battle and his campaign became a disease-ridden search for food. John and his wife then renounced the claim to Castile and León in return for money and the marriage of their daughter Catherine to John of Trastámara's son and heir, Henry, later Henry III (r. 1390–1406).

The Marinid Sultanate of Morocco, which had supplanted the Almohads in 1269, began attacking Christian Spain in 1275, and had some successes. In 1340, however, Alfonso XI of Castile (r. 1313–50) decisively defeated the Marinids at the battle of Salado, then building a large monastery at Guadalupe in thanks to the Virgin of Guadalupe to whom he had prayed before the battle. The capture of Algeciras on the Strait of Gibraltar in 1344 prevented further Moroccan intervention.

THE HEART OF ROBERT THE BRUCE

Dying in 1329, Robert the Bruce, King of Scotland, instructed Sir James Douglas to take his heart to the Holy Land and carry it in battle against the enemies of Christ. En route, Douglas took part in Alfonso XI's siege of the Moorish castle of Teba. Accounts vary greatly, but one of the most credible suggests that, to inspire his men, Douglas threw the silver case containing the heart into the battle and charged in to his death. The heart was taken to Scotland to be buried in Melrose Abbey. In the centre of the village of Teba, a block of Scottish granite commemorates the episode.

Meanwhile, in the Atlantic, the Castilians, from 1402, began to colonise the Canary Islands, seizing the native Guanches, whom they regarded as inferiors, as slaves. They also encountered a vigorous resistance, although in 1496 opposition was finally overcome.

The death from plague, the Black Death, of Alfonso XI in 1350 during an unsuccessful siege of Gibraltar encouraged a shelving of the Reconquista and a focus, instead, on domestic issues. The Black Death of 1348–50 itself led to the death of about a third of the population. Land was abandoned, villages deserted and production fell. Social tensions rose markedly as landlords sought to increase their return from the now smaller workforce. The latter sought to protect itself by creating brotherhoods. Sheep-rearing, which required fewer workers, expanded and produced benefits for those involved, principally major landowners.

THE MESTA

The meseta became the setting for the power of the Royal Council of the Mesta, a body, created in Castile in the thirteenth century, to regulate the issues created by the massive expansion in livestock breeding. In particular, sheep were a key way to provide wool, meat and cheese. The number of sheep in Castile rose from maybe half a million in 1300 to possibly five million by 1500. The long-distance movement of sheep created disputes with landholders. It could also be seen as a low-efficiency option for large tracts of land.

Many developments in the period were significant in the long term. These included the foundation of universities, notably Salamanca (1218), Lérida (1300), Valladolid (1346) and Huesca (1354). These produced an educated administrative cadre, as well as Humanists.

The Black Death as well as the related social tensions encouraged religious hostility toward both Mudéjares (Muslims under Christian rule) and, more particularly, Jews. Violent pogroms, as in Toledo in 1355 and Seville in 1391, led to the killing of large numbers, and many Jews were forcibly converted to Christianity, becoming *conversos*. They were an intermediate group located between the majority Old Christians and the hardcore Jewish population. The Inquisition, the rationale for the expulsion of the Jews in 1492, and the longstanding Spanish preoccupation with 'purity' of blood all reflected the response to the *conversos*, as well as the more general hostility to Jews. Politics played a role as alleged favouritism towards the Jews was one of the charges against Peter I of Castile (r. 1350–69). There were also problems for Jews in al-Andalus, including a massacre in Granada in 1066 and more persecution under the Almoravids and Almohads.

Under the Trastámara dynasty from 1369 to 1516, Castile saw considerable instability. In 1418–69 there were divisions within the royal family as well as within the nobility, and an overlap between the two. Many of the impressive castles of the period, for example Alarcón, were the sites of conflict in the period. The castle of Alarcón allegedly contains the bloodstains of a murderous suitor whose body was mixed in with the mortar. The claims to Castile of Isabella, the half-sister of Henry IV (r. 1454–74), were contested by her half-niece, Joanna la Beltraneja (1462–1530), the possibly illegitimate daughter of Henry, who had failed to limit aristocratic power. Aragón had supported the aristocracy, notably the League of Nobles formed in 1460, against Henry. In the War of the Castilian Succession (1474–8),

Isabella, who became ruler in 1474, was backed by Aragón (she was already married to her cousin, Ferdinand, the heir apparent of Aragón) and most of the aristocracy and clergy, and Joanna by Portugal (she was married to Alfonso V) and some of the major aristocracy. The battle of Toro (1476) led to the collapse of Joanna's cause and she renounced her claim. In Seville, the St John of the Kings Monastery was built as a thanksgiving for victory at Toro.

Aragón, meanwhile, looked eastward across the Mediterranean. An empire was created that ultimately encompassed the Balearic Islands, Sicily (1282), Sardinia (1322) and Naples (1435), the last meaning rule over southern Italy. This inheritance drew on the Catalan maritime tradition, which competed with those of Genoa and Venice. In 1380, Peter IV of Aragón (r. 1336–87) remarked to his heir: 'If Sardinia is lost, Majorca, without its food supply from Sicily and Sardinia, will be depopulated and will be lost, and Barcelona will also be depopulated, for Barcelona could not live without Sicily and Sardinia, nor could its merchants trade if the isles were lost.' He was trying to convince his heir to keep up the dynasty's long and hitherto intractable effort to conquer Sardinia, as well as to persuade him to seek a bride among their own relatives in Sicily.

There was no comparable maritime tradition in the later Middle Ages in southern Spain, which was affected by the Reconquista. Nor did Castile greatly support the maritime life of north-western Spain, although long-distance fishing based there was significant. Instead, it was to be Portugal that first took forward the Atlantic potential of the Iberian peninsula.

Meanwhile, the Aragónese inheritance was partitioned in 1458, with Naples passing to Ferrante, the illegitimate son of Alfonso V (Alfonso the Magnanimous) of Aragón. The latter had spent most of his time on Italian power politics. Despite this partition, Aragón remained concerned about these politics, in part in rivalry with France.

In contrast to the Ottoman (Turkish) success in the Balkans in the fifteenth century, the Castilian advance against the Muslims resumed in the late fifteenth century. This advance was closely linked with the dynastic union in 1479 of the ruling houses of Aragón and Castile, in the persons of Ferdinand and Isabella. Their target, the kingdom of Granada, was weakened from 1482 by civil war and exposed by a lack of support from elsewhere in the Islamic world. Polygamy/concubinage, and an absence of primogeniture, helped lead to more than one claimant in a situation that was settled with violence. The kingdom's strongholds were picked off one by one from 1485, the year in which Ronda fell, culminating with Granada itself at the start of 1492. Largely German-manned artillery played a role in the Spanish success. In addition, the size of the invading army was significant, as was the use of economic warfare in the shape of the destruction of crops. Furthermore, Muslim cities could resist bombardment only to fall as a result of hunger, which was the case of Málaga in 1487 and in many respects of Granada itself. Even so, the conquest took nearly a decade.

In January 1492, Ferdinand and Isabella entered their new city. Muslim rights, customs and religious liberty were guaranteed. In 1494, their success led to Ferdinand and Isabella receiving the title 'the Catholic Majesties' from Pope Alexander VI, who was born Rodrigo de Borja in Valencia in 1431, and had been Archbishop of Valencia.

Architectural commissions responded to the new sense of glory, with the development of the Flamboyant Gothic or Perpendicular into what was to be known as the Isabelline style, one of exuberant decoration, in particular in church-building, as in the cathedrals of Astorga, Burgos and Seville, notably the vaulting in the last. The entrance to the National Museum of Polychrome Sculpture in Valladolid, which is housed in the Colegio de San Gregorio, is a monument to the richness of the Isabelline style.

PILGRIMAGE TO SANTIAGO DE COMPOSTELA

In the early ninth century, the alleged tomb of St James the Apostle was discovered at what became Santiago de Compostela. He had supposedly preached in Spain, been killed in Judaea, and then been buried in Spain by his fleeing disciples. This holy site became a location of miracles, and the kings of Asturias and later León actively encouraged the cult. There were legends of Saint James intervening in battle in order to help the Christians against the Moors, notably at Clavijo near Logroño in 844. Foreign pilgrims began to arrive in numbers in the eleventh century, with major pilgrim routes developing from France where much of the pilgrimage takes place. The pilgrimage continued into the sixteenth century and was revived in the late nineteenth century. There are many routes now, including one northward from Portugal. In 2016, over 277,000 pilgrims made the journey to Santiago de Compostela. The cathedral is a largely Romanesque building but includes Gothic work as well as a superb Baroque facade. The nearby monastery of San Martín Pinario is also worth particular attention, but the whole historic part of Santiago is of a piece. Major stops on the route include Eunate, with its fine Romanesque chapel, Puente la Reina, with its old bridge and a Y-shaped cross in the Church of the Crucifix, Los Arcos with the dramatic Baroque interior of its church, and Burgos.

NEW WORLDS

Castile traded from West Africa from 1453, but ceased to trade there in 1479, surrendering its claims to trading rights in Guinea and the Gold Coast to Portugal through the Treaty of Alcáçovas.

This was a reflection of the longstanding Spanish willingness to purchase slaves from others.

At the same time, a new world for Spain was opening up as, in the name of Ferdinand and Isabella, the Genoese-born Christopher Columbus (*c.* 1451–1506) reached the West Indies in 1492. On his return, he was received by Ferdinand and Isabella in Barcelona in 1493. In 1494, by the Treaty of Tordesillas, the Atlantic world was divided between Portuguese and Spanish zones. Africa was awarded to Portugal, and what was then known of the Americas to Spain. Brazil, which was to fall into the Portuguese zone, had not yet been 'discovered'.

CONTESTING THE PAST

In response to the Francoist approach to Spain's past, that emphasised Christian identity and purpose, there has been a positive post-Francoist engagement with al-Andalus. It has been argued that a tolerant coexistence of Christians, Jews and Muslims in medieval Spain produced a Spanish culture that was not simply Christian. The weight placed on this cooperation and legacy is controversial and the degree of tolerance is generally exaggerated. Nevertheless, the thesis about al-Andalus greatly contributes to the importance of medieval Spain within the post-Francoist historical culture and, indeed, in the attempt to create what is presented as a modern integrationist civic politics that is also in line with Spain's past.

The legacy of the Middle Ages remains contentious as well as malleable. There was a widespread, albeit varied, attempt to fashion a more benign past. Addressing both Houses of Parliament at Westminster, on 23 April 1986, King Juan Carlos took a stance very different to that of earlier monarchs when, as a matter of praise, he described 'the ancient Cortes of Lérida as being the first example in Europe where a monarch had to obtain the consent of the citizens represented in that Parliament before he could increase the taxes called for by reason of the constant warfare required by the Reconquest'. In 2004, the Socialist-dominated government of Aragón indicated that it was ready to abandon the heraldic shield of Aragón – which portrayed four severed Muslim heads – as it was seen as insensitive. In turn, the opposition, the conservative People's Party, criticised the proposed step.

CHAPTER FIVE

New World Empire, 1492–1598

THE NEW WORLD

Initial contact between Europe and the Americas in the early-modern period came first from Christopher Columbus's arrival in the West Indies in 1492. His voyages were part of a pattern of Iberian expansion, with, as an important element, non-Iberian navigators and economic interests, notably Italian, taking advantage of the support of the expansionist Crowns of Portugal and Castile. These rulers, in turn, sought to supplement their own resources with those they could recruit to their service. This expansionism was territorial and religious, as well as economic. Drawing on their longstanding ideological crusading role in driving Islam from Iberia, a task apparently achieved with the fall of the last Muslim kingdom, Granada, in 1492, the Crowns of Portugal and Castile had already taken the fight with Islam into North Africa. They also seized the islands of the eastern Atlantic – the Canaries, Madeira, the Azores and the Cape Verde Islands – which served as important stopping-places on the route to the West Indies and South America. Gran Canaria was finally subdued by the Castilians in 1483 and Tenerife in 1496.

In contrast to the Portuguese success in the Indian Ocean, Castile, following Columbus, made the running in the Americas, with, as a result, Portugal restricted there to Brazil, which had been 'discovered' as part of the Portuguese effort to find better winds and currents to push forward the search for a route into the Indian Ocean. Moreover, Portugal did not seek to establish a territorial presence in North America to the north of the Castilian zone, although Portuguese interests were to play a role there, notably in fishing. In the papal division of the New World in 1493, followed by the Treaty of Tordesillas in 1494, North, Central and most of South America were allocated to Castile, or Spain as it can be termed after the union of the inheritances of Castile and Aragón. Vulnerable to invasion, Portugal was not well placed to defy neighbouring Spain in this, while from 1580 to 1640, after a successful invasion, the kings of Spain were also kings of Portugal, in a personal union similar to that of England and Scotland in 1603-1707.

CONTESTING COLUMBUS

Christopher Columbus was a figure of controversy from the outset, and the present fuss over his reputation was as nothing compared with what he had to put up with during his lifetime. The travails of navigation, which included a shipwreck off Portugal in 1476 and mutinous sailors on his voyage to the Bahamas in 1492, were immaterial compared to the brutal politics of the Spanish New World. In his case, they did not lead to murder or execution, but in 1500 he was removed from office and sent back to Spain in chains.

Controversy followed him in death. Dying in Valladolid in 1506, his remains were moved to Seville, then Santo Domingo, then Havana, then back to Seville, being repatriated as an effect of the loss of Spanish control of Cuba to American invaders in the war of 1898. An impressive tomb in Seville cathedral is claimed as his final resting place, except that it is also claimed that the remains sent from Santo Domingo to Havana in 1795 were not the correct ones, and that he rests in the Dominican Republic.

The late nineteenth century was a period of particular memorialisation. Aside from the monument to Columbus in Seville cathedral, a monument originally intended for the gloomier cathedral in Havana, there is the prominent *Mirador de Cólon* (Columbus Monument) opened in 1888 during the Universal Exhibition, at the foot of the Ramblas in the centre of Barcelona, which commemorates Columbus's visit to the city and reception there by Ferdinand and Isabella in 1493. Copies of the monument can be found elsewhere.

At any rate, the cosmopolitan Columbus (in Spanish Cristóbal Colón), born in Genoa around 1451, who took part in Portuguese trading missions before entering the service of Spain, is currently a figure of controversy as part of America's contentious 'culture wars'. In 1992, there was a storm of disagreement over how best to commemorate the anniversary of his crossing the Atlantic in 1492, and, in particular, whether it should be presented as a background to expropriation, slavery and genocide. The controversy has rumbled on since and, in 2017, led to the NYPD providing round-the-clock protection for the impressive monument in Columbus Circle, Manhattan. In Los Angeles County, the Board of Supervisors and the City Council decided to replace Columbus Day with 'Indigenous Peoples' Day', allegedly because Columbus was an oppressor. Baltimore's Columbus monument was vandalised.

Columbus is criticised for enslaving the Native population and for exposing them to diseases that led to a form of genocide. Indeed, the term Holocaust has been used, one of the many uses of a word that should be employed with precision in order to avoid what is in effect Holocaust-diminishment. The debate has been both politicised and become in America an aspect of the contentious nature of a 'melting pot' society, with claims by some that their heritage is being trashed, while others regard the celebration of Columbus Day, which became a national holiday in 1937, as an offensive step. Certainly, there is no fixed or single account of the past. Indeed, the honouring of Columbus in 1937 was in part a rejection by the Democrats of the emphasis, under the Republicans, in the 1920s, on a WASP identity for the United States, an emphasis also seen with the limitation of immigration.

Columbus certainly is capable of bearing multiple interpretations. Much that he stood for appears anachronistic. Whereas for long a mercantilist, and essentially secular, account of the 'Age of Discovery' was offered, one focused on economic advantage, more recently figures such as Henry the Navigator, Columbus and Vasco da Gama have been approached in terms of their beliefs. There has been emphasis on their wish to secure money and allies to further the reconquest of Jerusalem, which they regarded as a crucial preliminary to the Second Coming of Christ. Thus, time, as well as space, was at issue and exploration was a form of theology. In his *Book of Prophecies*, compiled before his fourth voyage to the Caribbean, in 1502, Columbus argued that the end of the world would occur in 155 years, and that his own discoveries had been foretold in the Bible.

The Spanish conquest of the Caribbean was incomplete, with only some of the larger islands, principally Hispaniola, Cuba and Puerto Rico, seeming attractive for seizure and settlement. This left later opportunities on different islands for other European powers, notably France, England and the Dutch, and ensured that the Natives remained dominant in certain islands, such as St Vincent. The Spaniards, however, brought European diseases, particularly smallpox, and the devastating inroads of disease helped ensure that the demographic balance in the West Indies rapidly changed, and also greatly demoralised the Native population. The impact of disease was to be a factor that encouraged the import of slaves from Africa.

Once seized, these islands, especially Cuba, became important bases for Spanish activity. Cuba provided Spain with a springboard for the invasion of Mesoamerica (modern Mexico and Central America). To take advantage of the deep water of the largest natural port in the Caribbean, Spain established Havana in 1519. An earlier attempt, in 1515 at nearby Batabanó, had been abandoned because of infested swampland and the lack of a sheltered harbour.

In 1519, Hernán Cortés landed at Veracruz on the coast of what is now Mexico with about 450 soldiers, 14 small cannon and 16 horses. His overthrow, on behalf of Ferdinand and Isabella's grandson, Charles I (the Holy Roman Emperor Charles V, r. 1519–56), of the Aztec Empire, based in Mesoamerica in what is now central Mexico, was rapidly achieved. Montezuma, the Aztec leader, was fascinated by Cortés and, worried that he might be an envoy from a powerful potentate, was unwilling to act decisively against him, although the account that Montezuma saw him as a god has been questioned. Cortés reached Tenochtitlán, the Aztec capital, without having to fight his way there. In 1520, the situation deteriorated from the Spanish point of view. A massacre of the Aztec nobles in the courtyard of the Great Temple helped lead to an Aztec rising and Cortés had to flee Tenochtitlán, having had Montezuma killed. Against formidable resistance, however, Cortés fought his way back into the city in 1521, crushing resistance.

Weaponry played a role. No American people had firearms or horses. Their societies were reliant on wood and stone, not iron and steel. Slings, wooden clubs and obsidian knives were no match for the weapons of the Spaniards, whose cannon, arquebuses and crossbows all had a greater range and killing power than their rivals' weapons. In hand-to-hand combat, the Spaniards also benefited from the power and flexibility of their single-handed steel swords. Metal weapons were more effective than stone, while metal armour offered more protection than cotton-quilted. The Aztecs probably could not use captured fire-arms because they had no gunpowder and lacked the necessary training.

Spanish firearms, however, were few and slow, and much of their impact was psychological. Aztec wooden clubs, studded with flint or obsidian, proved effective against Spanish horse-men, thanks to the skill of the warriors, while the Maya quickly learned to use stakes to scare Spanish horses. The Spaniards also found it helpful to adopt the native quilted-cotton armour as it was more appropriate for the climate, although they retained their steel helmets, which were useful against slingshots.

In some respects, Spanish conquest was a remarkable step, but it was also part of a wider pattern of territorial change in 1515-30 with the overthrow of the Mamluk Empire in Syria and Egypt by the Ottomans, the Lodi sultanate in northern India by the Mughals, and the kingdom of Hungary by the Ottomans. Each, in its way, was a striking achievement and, together, they serve as a reminder of the possibility of change and, in particular, of the extent to which states that lacked any real grounding comparable to the engaged and mobilised mass publics of the nineteenth and twentieth centuries could readily fall when their rulers and élites were overthrown. This process was eased, and, in part, achieved, by recruiting part of the existing local élite and reconciling it to the new rulers. Thus, many of the Rajputs were swiftly recruited by the Mughals, while the Ottomans rapidly used Mamluk troops and administrators.

The Spanish conquest of much of Central and South America in the early and mid-sixteenth century fits into this pattern. The Spaniards exploited existing divisions within Central Mexico, notably forming an alliance with the Tlaxcaltec, a people sur-rounded by Aztec territory, subordinated to the Aztecs, and resentful. They and other allies provided significant numbers to help in the conquest of Tenochtitlán in 1521. Native support was essential in order to match the massive numerical superiority of the Aztecs, who learned to alter their tactics to counter Western arms, especially firepower. In Mesoamerica, the battle superiority of the Spaniards promised those who allied with them a good chance of victory, but the availability and willingness of many of the Mesoamericans to cooperate against the Aztecs reflected the nature of the Aztec Empire, in particular the absence of a practice and theory of assimilation.

Subsequent Spanish expansion from the Aztec territories owed much again to local support, including frequently in distant lands and against those who were not traditional enemies. In 1524–6, resuming earlier (pre-Spanish) patterns of attempted expansion from central Mexico, Pedro de Alvarado invaded Guatemala with Native allies, overrunning the area only to undermine his success (and that of his allies) by excessive violence and harsh demands for tribute and labour. As a result of continuing opposition, his brother Jorge recruited between five and ten thousand Native warriors for his invasion of Guatemala in 1527, and he only succeeded in 1529 after large-scale butchery of the population. The importance of Native support, which provided fighting power, intelligence and the logistics of porterage as well as obtaining and preparing supplies, was probably greater than that of other factors in Spanish success: of the impact of new diseases, of Spanish military technology and of divisions among the local population.

Subsequently, Viceroy Antonio de Mendoza used ten thousand local allies in the Mixtón War of 1540–2. Moreover, indigenous local soldiers were employed as a defence force, so that in *Nueva Galicia* by the 1590s local *flecheros* (bowmen) were guarding roads and silver mines, receiving fiscal and legal advantages in return.

In South America, Panama, founded in 1519, became the base for Francisco Pizarro's expeditions to Peru in 1524, 1526 and 1531–2. In the last, he rapidly conquered the Inca world, capturing the ruler, Atahualpa, in November 1532, and occupying the capital, Cuzco. Pizarro then faced serious opposition, however, not least in 1536 when Manco Inca brought a degree of cohesion to the resistance. At that point, the Spaniards were not only successful because their fighting quality brought victory in battle. In addition, sufficient local people supported the invaders and their puppet emperor to provide Spain with major battlefield and political advantages. Memory of Inca oppression played a role. Leadership was significant, with the assassination of Manco Inca being important to Spanish success. Nevertheless, the conquest took more than seven years.

In part, this length of time reflected the extent to which the Spaniards sought conquest, not raiding. Military action was followed by the symbolic ownership shown by naming the new landscape. This process was complemented by the arrival of colonists and their crops and livestock, by Christian proselytisation and the destruction of rival religious rituals, and by the introduction of administrative and tenurial structures, for example the town-based patterns of control based on Classical Rome. In addition, the degree of Spanish acceptance of local élites and local material cultures, as well as of local adaptation to the Spaniards, were important factors.

It is possible, alongside the seizure and slaughter, to paint a more benign account of the Spanish conquest and, in particular, to discuss the Christianity of Spanish America as syncretic: drawing on local roots and practices, as well as being European in its origins. This account of a melded sacred space can then serve as a key indicator of a more general pattern of cooperation, as consensus was elicited, and this pattern can then be seen as the basis for the politics of Spanish America. In particular, a causal line can be drawn from syncretism and consensus to stability. This stability can be regarded as a central characteristic of Spanish America, as well as a possible reason why its society proved less dynamic, both then and subsequently, than that of British America.

Yet, such an account ignores both much of the process by which the Spaniards established their presence and also the comparative dimension. In the Americas, there was a typecasting of Native societies as harsh, primitive and uncivilised, and this typecasting encouraged not only total war and cruelty on the part of the conquerors, as in Mexico, but also a determination to extirpate the distinctive features of their society. There was a destruction of Native religious sites and an eradication of practices deemed unacceptable, these practices being discussed by Spanish commentators to demonstrate the superiority of Spanish rule. While Christian worship in Spanish America might contain elements of compromise, there was no compromise about Christianity. The Inquisition became important to the campaign to end Native religion, such as with the burning of idols.

The situation was different to the position across much of Eurasia where there were important confessional tensions, but without conquest by the Ottomans, Mughals and Manchus leading to the ending of other religious practices. Yet the Spaniards and their descendants never outnumbered the indigenous or mixed population. As a result, although the Spaniards could make unremitting war on the pagan deities, as well as use control over Native labour to lessen the position of the indigenous nobility, they left large tracts of land in the hands of cooperative Natives, particularly those who had readily allied themselves with the conquest.

Spanish practice was to be followed by other Europeans. Proselytism was regarded as a product of superiority, a justification for conquest and as a way to secure control. The net outcome was an assault on Native culture far greater than that seen, for example, by conquerors, non-Western and Western, in India, and, as a consequence, a disruption of Native society that contributed, alongside disease, to its breakdown. The result, established from the outset in the New World, was a pattern of conquest that was more total than that generally seen elsewhere. It was a pattern that looked in particular to the Reconquista and can be seen as arising from a belief in Christian manifest destiny. Yet, as a reminder of the continual need to locate Spanish history within broader patterns of European development, the harshness of Spanish rule was strengthened by key aspects of Western history and public culture in the sixteenth century. The assault by a revived Islam in the shape of the Ottoman Empire, an assault that also involved the enslavement of Christians, was particularly relevant to Spanish attitudes. The marked increase in religious violence within Christendom due to the Reformation was also pertinent, particularly the general practice of post-Reformation treatment of the heterodox, not least their dehumanisation by presentation as animals.

Extreme violence extended to the response to other Westerners in the New World, despite, and, in part due to, the extent to which Westerners were outnumbered. Thus, in 1565, a Spanish force slaughtered Huguenots (French Protestants) who had established a presence in Florida. The difficulty of controlling and caring for captives was a factor in prisoner massacres, but the central drive was that of a religious intolerance and self-righteousness, and the deliberate destruction of those held to be threats. This practice was not tempered in the case of fellow Christians with the large-scale enslavement seen between Christians and Muslims in the Mediterranean.

With the Aztecs and Incas, the Spaniards faced the consequences of overthrowing empires, but, elsewhere in North and South America, the context was different as they were opposed by tribes. That remark, however, should not be taken to imply that circumstances were similar in all cases. Instead, there was considerable variety in environment, economic development, social patterns and political organisation. Some tribes were sophisticated, for example the emerald-mining Muisca of the highland interior of Colombia who were conquered following a rapacious Spanish expedition of 1536. Yet, combined with difficult terrain,

Native opposition could pose formidable difficulties. Operating in Venezuela, Panama and Colombia from the 1580s, Bernardo Vargas Machuca recorded both the dangers posed by traditional Native weapons and tactics, such as poison arrows, rocks rolled down from on high, ambushes and pits, as well as Native ability to respond to Spanish capability and limitations, such as profiting from the damaging impact of rain on gunpowder.

To a considerable extent, the scope and nature of the Spanish Empire reflected the strength of local resistance. Where local support was absent, for example in central Chile, the Spaniards faced grave difficulties in the Americas. In Chile, the Spaniards were pushed back from the southern Central Valley in 1598–1604: thereafter, the River Bío Bío was a frontier beyond which the Araucanians enjoyed independence.

In northern Mexico, the Spaniards encountered opposition from the nomadic warriors of the Gran Chichimeca who used their archery to deadly effect in terrain that was often difficult for the Spanish cavalry. The Spaniards, in turn, raised allied Native forces, so that the conflict became another version of the long-standing struggle between nomadic and sedentary peoples. The Spaniards found their opponents difficult to fix, and the conflict took too much of the profit produced by the silver mines of the region, while there was also the challenge posed by the Natives capturing and using Spanish horses in order to win greater mobility. In the event, an abandonment by the Spaniards of their aggressive policies, including slave-raiding, and a switch to a more peaceful process of bribing opponents with gifts, combined with Christian missionary activity, helped lessen tension. Indeed, cultural dominance and the destruction of independent indigenous activity was not the only situation in the Americas, not least because of the significance of the frontier, a 'middle ground' of great depth that was part of the Spanish Empire. This 'middle ground' was not so much a zone or region as, for long, a description of part of the area and practice of Spanish activity.

In northern Mexico, the alteration in Spanish policy provided an opportunity to increase settlements and establish forts, and thus to change the landscape of settlement.

Rumours of bullion encouraged Spanish expeditions north from Mexico into the American interior, such as that of Francisco Vásquez de Coronado into what is now New Mexico, and thence into the Great Plains in 1540. The rumours proved erroneous. There were certainly no benefits to match those found in Mexico. Similarly, there was no follow-up to the expedition of Hernando de Soto who, between 1539 and 1542, brutally pillaged the Lower Mississippi and nearby lands. In 1540, he won a battle with the Choctaw at Mobile (Selma, Alabama), in which his cavalry was able to dominate the open ground without competition. After Soto's death, Luis de Moscoso pressed on in 1542–3 into what is now eastern Texas. The diseases brought by this expedition proved devastating for local people.

The lack of benefit is not the sole reason why Spanish interest in America north of Mexico was limited, but it was important. In 1598, the Spaniards were able to press north to establish a position in what they called New Mexico, but the settlement of Santa Fé was very much to be an outlier, not least because it did not have the Pacific access that had been anticipated. Further south, helped by the malaria that the Spaniards had unwittingly introduced, much of the Yucatán, the centre of Mayan civilisation, was conquered in 1527–41, although the Itzás of the central Petén were not defeated until 1697.

More generally, Spanish colonial policies and practices, including the end of Native religious rituals, affected local society and limited the possibility of post-epidemic population recovery. The resulting problem was compounded by the commercial opportunities created by plantation agriculture and by mining, each of which required large workforces. The obvious solution was to obtain slaves from the Native population outside the span of Spanish territorial control. The Spaniards carried out large-scale slaving in the sixteenth century among Natives in Honduras and Nicaragua; this enslavement proved an aspect of warfare. The benefits gained from the sale of slaves helped to destabilise Native society by encouraging conflict between tribes in order to seize people for slavery, which was a process also seen in West Africa. People were commodified as a result, which proved a central aspect of the way in which the slave trade affected relations between Europeans and Native Americans.

Despite the benefits gained from the slave trade within the Americas, there were also problems for the colonists including the availability and cost of slaves, with Native resistance and flight proving key factors. Moreover, control over Native labour within the area of Spanish control was affected by royal legislation, which sought to address clerical pressure to treat the Natives as subjects ready for Christianisation, rather than as slaves. Indeed, Native slavery was formally abolished in the *Leyes Nuevas* (New Laws) of 1542. However, aside from the rebellion this legislation helped cause among the Spaniards in Peru, the implementation of edicts took time and was frequently ignored by local officials and landowners. Furthermore, systems of tied labour, especially the *encomienda* (land and Native families allocated to colonists), and forced migration, notably the *repartimiento*, under which a part of the male population had to work away from home, represented de facto slavery.

Native slaves remained important in frontier regions distant from the points of arrival of African slaves, such as northern Mexico. Nevertheless, the equations of opportunity and cost were to favour the purchase of slaves in West Africa and their shipment across the Atlantic. Initially, Africans were shipped into Spanish America via Spain, but, from 1518, *asientos* or licences were granted for their direct movement. As it was initially more expensive to supply Spanish America with African slaves than with Native slaves, the Africans were often used as house slaves, a form of high-value slavery that indicated their cost.

By the mid-sixteenth century, the situation had changed and, rather than providing a marginal part of the labour force, Africa was becoming steadily more important as a source of slaves, not least because it was believed that Africans were physically stronger than Natives. African slaves remained more expensive than Native labour, which could be controlled in various ways, including by making service an element of debt repayment, but the number of African slaves transported across the Atlantic increased greatly over the following century.

Spanish culture faced problems in how to assess America and its Native populations. The Reconquista and the Christian mission provided a framework, but not the only one. In addition, Classical literature provided pertinent models, Roman expansion serving as a reference point for its Spanish successor. At the same time, the Spaniards had to respond to a New World that included much not known to Classical (Western) writers, notably different animals and plants, for example avocados. Indeed, Spain played the key role in the Columbian exchange: the introduction into Europe of maize, potatoes and tomatoes, and of horses, pigs and wine to the Americas.

The claim that the New World was the Ophir and Tarsis from where King Solomon had obtained bullion and ivory, and, more specifically that Peru was Ophir, was dismissed, in part on the grounds that there were no elephants in the New World. Some of the arguments of Classical writers were disproved, for example Aristotle's claim that it would be too hot to live in the Tropics. More generally, the lack of Classical sources for the Americas encouraged a reconceptualisation of the nature of authority, with the stress on eyewitness accounts and contemporary experimentation proving important to the process by which America was understood by the Spaniards. Moreover, alongside a destructive contempt for Native cultures, which were seen as heathen and evil, there were attempts to adapt them. Native religious cults were given a place within Christianity.

There were attempts to understand the cultures. Sent to Mexico to act against 'idolatry', the Franciscan Bernardino de Sahagún (c. 1499–1590) came to appreciate Aztec culture and the Nahuatl language, documented many texts and created his own research methodology. The growing complexity of racial classification posed by intermarriage, however, led, as in Spain, to yet more racial categorisation.

There are some architectural references in Spain to the New World. In Ronda, the palace of the Marquis of Salvatierra contains, holding up the pediment, two statues of pairs of bound naked American slaves.

SPAIN AS A GREAT POWER

It was possible for Spain to make spectacular gains over some non-Western opponents, notably the Aztecs and Incas, but fail in the face of other opponents, particularly the Ottoman Turks in the Mediterranean. The key contrast at any one time throughout the early-modern period to that of other contemporary major world powers is that of a unique global range and related ambition on the part of Spain, and with the globe understood in modern terms. The Spanish Empire, especially after Philip II's acquisition of the Portuguese throne in 1580, had an unprecedented range among major global powers and knew it was in this position. That range brought significant economic advantage, as well as the ability to act as a regional force in a number of separate areas, and to a hitherto unique extent. In a very different context, this prefigured the situations of nineteenth-century Britain and the modern USA. Early-modern China as well as the Mughal Empire in India lacked this capability and ambition.

In addition to acting as a regional force in a number of separate areas, Spain also had the option of contemplating more global coordination. The practicality of doing so, however, was gravely limited given the technology of the period (notably for the transmission of messages and the movement of troops) and the resources available. So it was with bold ideas, for example of action against China. These ideas were a product of fantasies by Spanish officers already spending time in the Far East. They were rejected out of hand by Philip II and the government in Madrid, which became capital of Spain in 1561. The Spanish presence in the Philippines, established from 1565, was weak and, by the standards of the modern state, limited. Indeed, there was no reason to think that in normal circumstances Spain would have managed to overthrow the Incas in the 1530s, let alone the more powerful Chinese. In the former case, the aftermath of a devastating civil war was the key context, and this was also true of the Manchu overthrow of Ming China in the 1640s. As with the Spanish overthrow of the Aztecs in 1519–21, local division weakened the response to the outsiders and produced assistance for them. This was not an element that Spanish commentators chose to emphasise. Instead, there was a stress on cultural values, including religious support. The importance of the horse was exaggerated because of the association of cavalry with honour and social status.

Among the major world powers, only the western European ones, and notably Portugal and Spain, had the capacity to act in more than one hemisphere. Whereas the Ottoman Empire sought distant power projection, into the Indian Ocean, it did not match the consistent effort being made by Spain to deploy power at a greater range. Moreover, the Ottomans failed in the Indian Ocean and did not persist in their efforts there. The net effect was a contrast, in terms of distance, between a transoceanic Spanish and an essentially trans-Mediterranean Ottoman Empire. This was a differentiation linked to that between an empire that drew heavily on precious metals and one based more exclusively on land and trade. Spain's commerce with the Americas was controlled from the *Casa de Contratación* (House of Trade) founded in Seville in 1503 and, in response to the river silting up, transferred to Cádiz in 1717.

DOMESTIC POWER

Imperial success helped keep the nobility busy and also provided governmental opportunities for them. Isabella brought stability. At the same time, there were tensions, notably as the monarchs sought to expand their power. This could involve displacing aristocrats from their positions of local control, as when Isabella took Cádiz (1492) and Cartagena (1503) from their noble owners and when she ordered the battlemented towers of the houses of the nobility in Cáceres to be lopped. Castile dominated Spain, with about 80 per cent of its 5.5 million population in 1500.

Ferdinand and Isabella's daughter, Juana (r. 1504–55), the mother of Holy Roman Emperor Charles V (Charles I of Spain), was a crucial figure in the dynastic politics of Renaissance Europe. As a result of her inheritance, the widowed Juana nominally governed Spain, the Americas, Naples and Sicily but, mentally troubled, she could not even govern her domestic servants. Concerns about Juana's mental health were religious: according to prevailing beliefs, a monarch considered unfit to govern must have offended God, while the bond between Juana and her realms meant that the sins of one could affect the other's salvation. The divine will, as revealed in the Queen's apparent madness, thus explained as well as justified Juana's separation from the government. Juana's position facilitated a shift towards a more corporate and familial, and a less individual, idea of royal authority in early Habsburg Spain. Juana inherited Castile on the death of Isabella in 1504, but Ferdinand governed as regent until Charles came of age.

The end of rule from Castile, as it was absorbed into Charles's far-flung empire, caused a political crisis in the late 1510s and early 1520s, one that was not helped by Charles's use of the French language and of non-Spanish advisors, his demands for new taxes and his disruption of existing patronage networks. The rising of the *Comuneros* in Castile (1520–1) and of the socially more radical *Germanías* (brotherhoods) in Valencia (1519–20) and Majorca

(1522–3) were suppressed, crucially with the victory at Villalar over the *Comuneros* in 1521. Their failure to retain aristocratic support was fundamental: at Villalar, their army was largely bereft of the valuable leadership and fighting force of the Castilian nobility, which had been alienated by the growing social radicalism of the movement and won over by Charles's redistribution of royal favours. Juana's refusal to support the *Comuneros* helped Charles to re-establish his authority. The *Comunero* leaders were beheaded in Segovia, a centre of the rebellion. Toledo and Valladolid were other centres.

Thereafter, the situation was far more stable, helped in large part by the devolution of Crown authority and power to local communities and the nobility. Charles abdicated in 1556, handing over Spain to Philip II, not because he was forced to, but because he wished to. In 1591, a rebellion in Aragón was both limited and rapidly suppressed. The army that did so was largely recruited by the Castilian nobility from their estates, which indicated the continued importance of that military resource, as did the force raised by nobles in 1580 to provide supplementary support to the army sent to invade Portugal.

THE GOALS OF EMPIRE

By 1535, the Emperor Charles V (Charles I of Spain) had an empire stretching from newly conquered Peru, where the Inca capital Cuzco had been captured in 1533, to Germany and Austria. His personal goals were important to how this empire operated. As with other dynasties, the concern with rank and *gloire* affected choices and helped resolve conflicting priorities. Dynastic objectives were hereditary ones. For example, if Ferdinand of Aragón had not, in the 1500s, pursued the interests of his forbears in southern Italy, then it would possibly have remained in the French orbit, and this remained a prospect both in the 1520s and the 1640s. This outcome would have compromised the Spanish position with the papacy.

His grandson, Charles, was even more determined to dominate Italy, and succeeded in doing so. Charles's ambitions focused
heavily, but not exclusively, on honour and glory. Bringing together
four inheritances – the Habsburg, Burgundian, Aragónese and
Castilian – was important to this process. Charles's reputation
played a major role in the choices he made, not least in resolv-
ing the conflicting priorities of his various dominions. In this,
Charles followed the emphasis on prestige and rank seen with
his predecessors. With its stress on honour and dynastic responsibility the political culture was scarcely cautious or pacific.
This can be seen in the buildings and churches of the period,
for example the palace of Charles in Granada and the Charles V
rooms in that of Seville.

As protector of the Church against Protestants and Muslims,
and its propagator in the New World, Charles presented the new
global role for the Spanish monarchy that had been begun under
his grandparents and that can be seen in the Sala de Audiencias in
the Alcázar in Seville, where a *retablo* by Alejo Fernández shows
the Virgin of the Navigation spreading her protective mantle over
the conquistadors, their vessels and Charles. In 1556, having abdicated, Charles retired to the monastery of Yuste where he lived
until his death in 1558. The grandiloquent Latin inscription above
the entrance to the royal mausoleum in the Escorial palace built
near Madrid by his son, Philip II (r. 1556–98), was to refer to him
as 'the most exalted of all Caesars'. With trans-oceanic power,
manifest destiny and universalism became more significant. At
the same time, Philip's policies in his later years have been seen
both in terms of messianic imperialism and, more convincingly,
with reference to the idea of traditional dynasticism.

The trans-oceanic was not the sum total of Spain's maritime
power. Despite the constraints posed by the need to maintain
naval capability, constraints that Philip did not adequately appreciate, there was also the ability to sustain significant fleets both
in Atlantic and in Mediterranean waters. The range of maritime

environments and tasks required was considerable. Thus, under Philip, Spain deployed fleets in the Azores and the eastern Mediterranean, the Tagus, the English Channel and the North Sea, as well as more distant waters. This deployment was of a different order to other Western powers in the late sixteenth century. The distinctive aspect of the Spanish mobilisation of resources was both its depth and its extraordinary wide reach, and on land and at sea. As a result, Spain was a major military power in many geographical contexts, but also had uniquely heavy costs and numerous opponents.

SPAIN AS A MEDITERRANEAN POWER

The struggle with the Ottomans became the end product of what had been the long Spanish theme of conflict with Islam, a theme that was integral to Spanish history, identity and ideology at this point. This was a topic that Franco was to echo and transform into a conflict with modernity, notably 'alien' Communism.

Success against Granada in 1492 for what was seen as the new 'Chosen People' was followed by the stepping up of conquest in North Africa, as the Mediterranean was not seen as a barrier. At the outset of the sixteenth century, the Ottomans were not yet established in the western Mediterranean, as they were to be on the coasts of what are now Algeria and Tunisia. Instead, the Spanish military machine had been well-honed by the long war for Granada, while Spain's opponents in North Africa were weak and divided. The town of Melilla was gained in 1497, Mers-al-Kébir in 1505, Oran in 1509, and Bougie, Tripoli and the Peñón d'Argel position dominated Algiers in 1510.

The situation for Spain in the Mediterranean deteriorated in the 1520s as Charles I of Spain focused much (though far from all) his attention on his role as the Emperor Charles V, beginning a longstanding problem for Spain under Habsburg rule. Charles devoted more resources to war with Francis I of France, notably in Italy, than to competing with the Islamic powers, and this was particularly clear on land. This was the decade of Charles's crushing defeat of Francis at Pavia (1525), as well as of more decisive success in 1529, decisive in that it led to a longer peace. The character of a dynastic model of power, however, was that, alongside the issues of family interest and personal will, there was also the deployment of the collective power of the dominions ruled. In this, as in other cases, it is unclear how best to define 'Spain' and how the composite monarchy can best be considered, a point that has resonances in later discussion of Spanish nationhood. For example, does the ability to gain military commitments from Naples and Sicily, and still more to draw upon resources from client-allies, notably Genoa, Tuscany and the Order of Malta, constitute 'Spanish' power and throw light on Spanish identity?

Although it is possible to focus on his personal prioritisation, Charles was also deploying collective power, both against France and the Ottomans. Thus, Spain, which at this point is difficult to define, was devoting resources and military power in the 1520s and 1530s not only against France, but also to war with the Ottomans, both in the Mediterranean and in holding the Hungarian frontier. Moreover, in fighting Francis over Italy, Charles was fulfilling the goal of Ferdinand of Aragón, as well as of his other grandfather, the Emperor Maximilian I.

In turn, the Ottoman Empire became far more important as a Mediterranean power. The rapid and totally successful Ottoman conquest of Egypt in 1517 was particularly significant. It greatly strengthened the Ottomans as a naval power and also ensured that they were able to ground their Mediterranean position on strong economic underpinnings, especially the agriculture and commerce of Egypt. This grounding proved significant for Ottoman power projection further west in North Africa and, as a consequence of the replacement of the local Islamic regimes by direct Ottoman influence, the Spaniards were pushed onto the back foot and came to fight a defensive, reactive struggle to retain footholds and influence, and to protect maritime links between Spain and Italy. The Spanish presence in North Africa was far weaker than that of the Ottomans, and required large infusions of support. The Barbary 'pirates' of North Africa raided Spain's coasts, notably the southern coast. As a result, there was much fortification, for example under Charles I and Philip II, in Gibraltar. In Almería, when the cathedral was built in 1524 to replace the mosque, it was fortified.

The Ottoman capture of Tunis from Mulay Hasan, its pro-Spanish ruler, in 1534 led to a response from Charles in 1535. Charles's concern with his reputation helped lead him to risk his own person, which made it easier to elicit aristocratic participation in the campaigning. Large numbers of Spanish nobles took part. Launched with eighty-two war galleys and over thirty thousand troops, this expedition was in large part paid for with Inca gold from South America, which repaid loans from Genoese bankers. The ability to move money represented an important aspect of the Spanish military system. Mounted in ferociously hot conditions, this expedition displayed amphibious capability as well as success in fighting on land. Although defended by a large Ottoman garrison, the fortress of La Goletta at the entrance to the Bay of Tunis was successfully besieged. A week later, nearby Tunis was captured. Following a pattern similar to that of the retention of Native aristocracy in the Americas, notably in Mesoamerica, Charles installed a pro-Spanish Muslim ruler in Tunis, while Spanish troops remained at La Goletta. His success was recorded in the 1554 Flemish tapestries displayed in the Gothic-style Salones de Carlos V in the palace in Seville.

VALLADOLID

Located in northern Spain (Old Castile) at the confluence of two rivers, Valladolid was a small pre-Roman and Roman settlement that became important as a centre of Castilian power and a commercial and manufacturing city as well. Ferdinand of Aragón and Isabella of Castile married there in 1469 and made it the Court residence in place of Burgos, a position Valladolid lost in 1561 to Madrid under Philip II, although it briefly regained it in 1601–6 in part as a reaction against Philip's reign. The loss of political power meant a decline that limited growth and left it with many architectural gems including the Plaza Mayor (main square) and the unfinished cathedral. Valladolid was the centre of Spanish Renaissance sculpture, and the works of Alonso Berruguete and Juan de Juni can be seen there.

RELIGIOUS ORTHODOXY

The conquest of Granada was rapidly followed by religious persecution, in large part because religious orthodoxy was regarded as crucial to political loyalty and to the authority of the Crown. The Jews in 1492, in both Aragón and Castile, were ordered to convert to Christianity or leave. Only three synagogues survived the Jewish expulsion, two in Toledo and one in Córdoba, and that only because they were transformed into churches. Jewish graveyards were destroyed and built over. Former Jewish quarters that can be visited include the Judería in Córdoba, the Barrio Santa Cruz in Seville, and the quarter in Cáceres.

The Muslims in Castile (though not Aragón) were given the same choice in 1502, but the conditions for leaving the kingdom made exile very difficult. Aragón and Valencia followed in 1526. The status of Mudéjares, Muslims living in Spain, thus came to an end. Conversion was imposed by force in Granada in the 1500s. There was also cultural control. A huge bonfire of Arabic books was held in Granada in 1501. Mosques were destroyed and/or rebuilt as churches. That at Ronda became a church in which the minaret was converted into a belfry. The church also retains a horseshoe arch from the mosque. In

Teruel, long a centre of Mudéjar art, the mosque was closed in 1502.

Other ethnic and religious minority groups also faced persecution. Roma were consigned as forced labour to the mercury mine at Almadén as well as to the galleys. Mercury was used in the production of silver.

Conversion was not enough. Purity-of-blood laws were passed in order to ban Jewish conversos from particular honours and positions. Conflict with Ottomans was matched by a harsh attitude towards Moriscos (ostensibly converted Muslims) within Spain. In 1568–71, in response to prohibitions of their language and traditional dress, the Moriscos in Granada rebelled, unsuccessfully seeking help from the Ottomans, only to be brutally repressed. Large numbers were slaughtered, in part by troops raised by the Spanish nobility.

This mobilisation of society reflected the imposition of an ideological norm of authoritarian Catholicism. In rural Spain, there was an important drive to implement the reforms laid down by the Council of Trent (1545–63). This drive was pushed by the Inquisition, the Holy Office, in the 1560s and 1570s, although the rate at which, and extent to which, the reforms were implemented varied. Those with different views were treated harshly. Lucrecia de León, a young woman of modest background born in 1568, was, from a teenager, a prophetic dreamer who was seen by her supporters as a divinely inspired seer. Her dreams criticised the government of Philip II. In three dreams in 1588, she saw a seven-headed dragon – the seven deadly sins – breathing fire across Spain. Philip ordered the Inquisition to arrest her on charges of heresy and sedition, and she was tortured and confined in a convent. The Inquisition was primarily designed to ensure orthodoxy among Christians.

In the lands of the Crown of Aragón in the late sixteenth and early seventeenth century, the frequent *autos-da-fe* (burnings) organised at the behest of the Inquisition were popular because those punished were mostly outsiders. In the kingdom of Valencia, the Inquisition's attempts to repress the worst excesses of erroneous doctrine were seen as laudable, and it continued in the eighteenth century to demonstrate an impressive capacity to attract fresh recruits. At the same time, religious tension contributed to a debilitating sense of uncertainty and crisis.

At the international level, Spain backed the cause of Catholic interests, notably in France, the British Isles and the Holy Roman Empire. The founder of the Society of Jesus, or Jesuits, Ignatius de Loyola, was a Spaniard. The sanctified setting of his birthplace can be visited in Guipúzcoa.

THE BURDENS OF EMPIRE

There was nothing on the global scale to match Spanish imperial success. The scale of Spanish activity, and the many problems and burdens to which this gave rise, helps explain a continued and, in part, increasing reliance on military outsourcing, and a dependence on private resources and capital, in order to sustain military activity. Spain was better able than her enemies to sustain the new challenge of large-scale and protracted warfare because Spain had the advantages of New World silver, credit facilities and the capacity to mobilise resources as a composite monarchy, and to use 'soft influence' in order to draw in the resources of other states. These advantages and strengths outweighed the inefficiencies of early-modern Spain.

Beginning in the mid-1570s, Spain turned from conflict with the Ottomans in order to take the leading role in the French Wars of Religion (1562–98) within western Europe. Spain's reconquest of much of the Low Countries, where Philip II was faced by the Dutch Revolt, initially successful intervention in the Wars of Religion, ability to thwart the English attacks on Portugal and the Spanish New World, and continuing dominance of Italy, all suggested that it too was approaching an apex of unprecedented power. Thus, it is mistaken to place Spain on a terminal trajectory by the 1590s.

OPERATIC MISDIRECTION: *DON CARLOS*

Based on Friedrich Schiller's play *Don Karlos, Infant von Spanien* (1787), Giuseppe Verdi's opera *Don Carlo* (1867) is not noted for its verity. Unstable, possibly due to inbreeding, but notably after he accidentally fell down a flight of stairs in 1562, Prince Carlos (1545–68), Philip's heir, was arrested by Philip in 1568 when he prepared to flee the Court, and he died soon after.

In order to hit at Philip, stories were soon woven around Carlos, presenting him as a crypto-Protestant supporter of Dutch liberty, who was having an affair with his young stepmother, Elizabeth of Valois, and was poisoned, for all of which there is no evidence. In the opera, Carlo pledges himself to the cause of liberty and leads a group of Flemish deputies to Philip, only for the king to reject their pleas for freedom. The opera depicts a public burning of heretics in Madrid with a celestial voice welcoming their souls into Heaven. The Grand Inquisitor presses for the killing of Carlo. Philip is presented as an adulterer, while the ghost of Charles V backs Carlo.

At the same time, the costs of war were unprecedented and led to serious crises of indebtedness. Defaults entailed the transfer of burdens onto bankers and meant a compulsory rescheduling of debt. The wars were highly disruptive for government finances, the fiscal system and trade.

Moreover, Spain under Philip found it difficult to move from outputs, in the shape of military achievements, to outcomes, in the form of political settlement. Compromise in the Low Countries, the British Isles and France was difficult for Philip, who saw his religious orthodoxy as simultaneously a providential, dynastic, political and personal necessity.

A common Catholicism, in contrast, helped with Philip's takeover of Portugal. He used both widespread bribery and a successful invasion by land and sea in 1580, having reviewed the army near Badajoz before it invaded Portugal. This process was aided by the willingness to maintain distinct institutions and separate practices and privileges. The son of a Portuguese princess, Philip II became Philip I of Portugal in the absence, after the death in 1578 of King Sebastian while on a foolish invasion of Morocco, of a good rival candidate. An English-backed candidate lacked traction. Although Iberia, divided among four rulers in 1470, was united under one in 1580, no new state of Spain and Portugal was created. This was not simply a prudential choice on the part of Philip, but also a reflection of the deep sense of legitimism that affected both rulers and élites. Philip went on to conquer the Azores in 1582–3, but his navy failed against England in 1588. Although the defeat of the Spanish Armada was regarded as a providential intervention, the English were unable, in attacks in Portugal and the Caribbean, to inflict decisive blows on the Spanish imperial system.

Nevertheless, much damage was inflicted. Most prominently, a large Anglo-Dutch combined operation, involving about six thousand troops, achieved surprise when it attacked Cádiz in 1596. The Spanish fleet there was supported by the guns of the city, but the ably commanded Anglo-Dutch force fought its way into the defended anchorage and conducted a successful opposed landing followed by the storming of the city, which lacked adequate defences. The competence of the English naval gunners was important. The expectation of reward from the city and the merchant fleet were powerful motivating factors for the soldiers and sailors of the combined forces.

El Escorial

A must-go site for any historical tour of Spain, El Escorial is the term used for a royal site about 30 miles (48 kilometres) north-west of Madrid, close to the town of El Escorial. The site, officially called the *Monasterio de San Lorenzo*, a UNESCO World Heritage Site, was at once a royal palace and a monastery, a combination that reflected the requirements of Philip II. He chose Juan Bautista de Toledo as architect-royal to design the site as a declaration of Spain's role as the defender of Christendom. After the architect's death in 1567, Juan de Herrera took charge. The site was also to be a royal mausoleum. The cornerstone was laid in 1563 and the building finished in 1584.

There has been a number of explanations of the gridiron floor plan, including honouring St Lawrence who was roasted to death on a grill, and being based on descriptions of the Temple of Solomon who was a figure of great interest to Philip.

Built mostly of grey granite, and scarcely a work of charm, El Escorial, nevertheless, is very impressive as well as including many artistic masterpieces. The library is particularly notable. More to the taste of Philip's time, the monastery has one of the largest collections of relics, about 7500 in total. Philip died in El Escorial in 1598.

The financial burden was met from a number of directions, including bullion-production, taxation and borrowing. The Americas were crucial to the first, notably the establishment of the great silver-producing centre of Potosí in modern Bolivia in 1545. Mexico was also a major centre of silver production. Taxation pressed hard in Spain and Spanish Italy, notably Naples.

An international credit system proved crucial to the operation of the Spanish system. Spain could realise the potential wealth of silver mines and taxation by turning to German and Italian bankers, notably those in Augsburg and Genoa. Indeed, the integration of a series of regional economies was important to the success of the empire. The bankers, however, were affected by the bankruptcies, or suspensions of payments on debt, of 1557 and 1596. These were, in effect, compulsory renegotiations of loans. At the same time, the sale of *juros* (debt securities) widened those with a commitment to the stability of the Spanish governmental system.

Although agriculture and mining were major sources of wealth, finance and credit were linked to trade, and the latter two were particularly important to rulers seeking cash with which to pay their soldiers and contractors. The Spanish economy did not benefit greatly from the inflow of bullion, however, as it served to finance activity elsewhere, rather than in Spain itself. Spanish industry did not develop the export of finished products. Instead, bullion joined wool as a raw material export. Moreover, the transfer of taxes to foreign bankers lessened the control over taxation and the benefit from it enjoyed within Spain.

LOOKING TO THE PAST

The past was extensively used by institutions and others to advance positions, not least through the continuation of the medieval practice of producing false chronicles, whose authors appear to have regarded themselves as writing what they believed should be in the historical record. For example, the fictional chronicles of Julián Pérez, which came to attention in the 1590s, apparently demonstrated the Christian steadfastness of the *Mozarabs* (Christians under Muslim rule) of Toledo, and also gave that city a higher profile in Spanish history. The *Lead Books of Sacromonte*, texts inscribed on pieces of lead discovered in caves near Granada in 1595–1606, were another forgery that served present purposes, in this case apparently demonstrating the viability of Christian–Muslim coexistence in Philip II's Spain. The need, in sixteenth-century Spain, to confront the emphasis on being 'true Christians' may well have encouraged the forgeries that justified the particular positions of the *Mozarabs* and the *Moriscos*.

And so also more recently. The Franco regime looked back to the Reconquista and the reigns of Ferdinand and Isabella. The devout Catholicism, territorial expansionism and racialism of these monarchs apparently served as a suitable model for Franco. The sixteenth century appeared a Golden Age. In 1949, Franco had the monastery of Yuste, where Charles V had lived in retirement, restored. It had been burnt to the ground during the Peninsular War. Tourists can now visit the monastery including Charles's apartments. Herrera's architecture served as a model for Franco. This hankering back to past greatness, however, had a longer provenance, being used as a comparison by those who focused on Spain's abject failure in the war of 1898 with the United States.

THE FACTS OF LIFE

Much of life remained grim, and as far from the values of the Renaissance as that of the Middle Ages had been from the ideas of chivalry. The situation was common to Europe as a whole, indeed to much of the world, rather than specifically Spanish; but that should not mean such details are excluded from a book on Spain because it is important to an understanding of life there in the past. Sanitation and diet were major problems for the bulk of the population. Housing conditions, in particular the habit of sharing beds, were conducive to a high incidence of respiratory infections. This was a consequence of the lack of privacy that was produced by the limited nature of the housing stock.

In Renaissance Spain, louse infestation was related to crowding, inadequate bathing facilities and the continual wearing of the same clothes. Cleanliness was associated with wearing clean shirts and linen, rather than washing, but both were only possible for a minority. Whatever their wealth, humans had few defences against a whole range of the natural world, from lice, bedbugs and fleas to tapeworms.

The habit of washing in clean water was perforce limited, while the proximity to humans of animals and dunghills was unhelpful. Like the rest of Europe, Spain was a society that conserved, rather than disposed of, its excrement. Animal and human waste were gathered for the purpose of manure, a crucial replenishment of soil fertility; but this manure was a health-hazard, notably through contamination of the water supply. Effluent from undrained privies and animal pens flowed across streets and, on and beneath the surface, into houses through generally porous walls. Typhus was one result.

Alongside the availability, in those towns from Roman times, of public fountains and public taps in streets, clean drinking water was an issue across much of Spain, especially in coastal regions and lowland areas without deep wells. River water was often muddy, while pump water could be affected by sewage. As elsewhere in Europe, this situation accounted for the importance of fermented drinks.

As elsewhere, and reminding us anew that a history of Spain is in part a history of Europe, poor nutrition also contributed to the spread of infectious diseases by lowering resistance. Furthermore, malnutrition limited sexual desire and activity, hindered successful pregnancy, and, if chronic, delayed sexual maturity and produced sterility in women. Problems of food shortage and cost ensured that the bulk of the population lacked a balanced diet, even when they had enough food. Diet was a particular problem for the urban poor, who found fruit and vegetables, let alone meat and fish, expensive, and who were also frequently ill-clad. The peasantry consumed little meat or fish.

Disease was not only affected by nutrition. Harsh weather, notably, but not only, in the winter, could weaken resistance. It was exacerbated by shortages of firewood and by the damp, cold, cramped and insanitary nature of much accommodation.

The persistence of disease ensured that weaker members of the community remained especially vulnerable. The real killer of babies was puerperal fever, the cause of which was not understood until the nineteenth century. Politico-social factors, however, were also significant in famine and disease. Subsistence crises were not simply the result of demand exceeding the amount of food available, but also had their roots in the markedly unequal distribution of resources in Spain and in the limitations of governmental action, however much the latter was alleviated by religious charity.

The situation at the level of the individual was of a hostile and unpredictable environment, of forces that could be neither prevented nor propitiated, and of the efforts of years swept away in an instant. The line between independence and calamity, between being poor and falling into pauperdom, could be crossed easily, fast and frequently. Most individuals had few assets, a situation that continued in Spain until the second half of the twentieth century.

Renaissance art did not capture the grim working conditions of the age. For example, fishing was dangerous, while many places of craft work and industrial employment, including those involved in the production of works of art, craft and architecture, were damp, poorly ventilated, badly lit or dangerous. Exposure to hazardous substances, such as lead and mercury, was a serious problem, while construction work was very dangerous. Millers worked in dusty and noisy circumstances, frequently suffered from lice and often developed asthma, hernias and chronic back problems. The notions of health and safety at work were barely understood, and the issues involved were generally not grasped.

Agriculture was highly vulnerable to the weather and to disease. There were few improved crop strains, and rainy winters produced diseased and swollen crops, while late frosts attacked wheat and other crops. The absence of pesticides and the difficulties in protecting crops and stored foods were serious issues. Mice and rats posed major problems. Animal health, moreover, was a serious issue. The primitive nature of veterinary science was a problem, and the usual response was the slaughter of animals and the prohibition of their movement. The facts of life were frequently deadly.

At the same time, it is necessary to note the diversity of Spanish life, an element that continues today. People adapted to the possibilities of the environment, as with the major patterns of transhumance across much of Spain, or those who gathered annually to fish tuna using the many almadrabas on the beaches located between Tarifa and Cádiz.

CULTURE

Spanish greatness in the sixteenth century, the *Siglo de Oro* (Golden Century), had a variety of cultural consequences. There was influence from abroad, notably in borrowing aspects of the Renaissance, but also an emphasis on indigenous styles, such as a simplified Gothic, seen, for example, in the well-ordered mass of Segovia cathedral, and also the development of a Hispanicised Renaissance style. The latter was known as plateresque, due to it being similar to the delicacy of silverwork (silver is *plata* in Spanish). Seen under Charles V, with some fine examples in Salamanca, notably the Patio de la Escuelas (Schools' Square), this style was counterpointed by a more austere, Italianate Renaissance style, as in the palace of Charles V in Granada. Juan de Herrera at the El Escorial took forward Spanish Classicism.

The Mudéjar style continued to be important. This style describes the use of Muslim decorative influences, and much of it was carried out by unconverted Muslims ruled by Christians but working in terms of Almohad or Nasrid styles, or more generally drawing on Arab stylistic ideas, such as geometric patterns and the use of *azulejo*, which developed in Seville in the thirteenth century. These painted glazed ceramic tiles were originally intended to imitate Roman mosaics. Mudéjar style (a term devised in 1859) essentially involved using Muslim decorative means to enhance structures built in varying architectural styles and over a long period. It can be found clearly in the wooden *artesenado* ceilings tourists still see in monasteries and palaces across Spain, along with the *azulejo* tile work of the kind appearing in Seville's Casa de Pilatos, a Renaissance palace that has little in common with its counterparts in Italy.

The sequence of styles and the time that projects took led to major buildings often being an amalgam of styles, as in Badajoz, where the cathedral has important Gothic and Romanesque work.

Spain benefited from being a mecca for foreign artisans and artists, such as El Greco (Doménikos Theotokópoulos, 1541–1614), who lived in Toledo from 1577 until his death, and from providing opportunities for foreign styles. Italian painters, and those such as El Greco who worked in Italy, influenced the evolution of Spanish work, notably the development of Mannerism and its ability to express spiritual feeling. El Greco made great use of colour and shape in producing a distinctive style. He was also interested in architecture and sculpture, and his altarpiece can be seen in the church of the monastery of Santo Domingo el Antiguo in Toledo. The city also contains the El Greco House and Museum, where there is a view of Toledo, portraits of contemporaries and others of the saints. The cathedral includes major examples of his work, notably *El Expolio*, with Jesus stripped of his clothes. His *St Andrew and St Francis* is in the Prado.

The sixteenth century also saw a major development in devotional music, notably with the works of Victoria (1548–1611). Lyric poetry, picaresque novels and drama all became prominent, the last notably with the playwright Lope de Vega (1562–1635), whose work includes *Fuenteovejuna* (written 1612–14, published 1619), a play in which Ferdinand and Isabella pardon villagers who have killed a cruel and rapacious commander of the Order of Calatrava. This was based on events in a Castilian village in 1476.

Religious influences were relatively apparent, as with the works of the mystic St Teresa of Ávila (1515–82). A Carmelite nun, whose major shrine is the Convent of the Annunciation at Alba de Tormes, where she died, Teresa's works include *El Castillo Interior* (*The Interior Castle*), a guide for spiritual development ending with mystical union with God, as well as an autobiography and the *Camino de Perfección* (Way of Perfection).

DESCRIBING SPAIN: ENGLISH PLAYS

Not a household name, Thomas Kyd (1558–94) is best-known for his highly influential play *The Spanish Tragedy*, which was printed in 1592 and reprinted in London in 1594, 1599, 1602, 1610, 1615 (twice), 1618, 1623 (twice) and 1633. This play, a major hit on the London stage in 1593 and 1597, greatly influenced the presentation of Spain in England. It was staged again in 1601 and 1602 and produced in German and Dutch adaptations. A revenge tragedy about the frustrated and ultimately murderous quest for justice, the play features a Portuguese rebellion against Spain and the injustices of the Spanish royal family, which include murder and multiple treachery by the king's nephew, Lorenzo. *The Spanish Tragedy* includes a play within a play that serves as a model for William Shakespeare's *Hamlet* and leads to five deaths. The work gave force to hostile views of the Spanish

Court as a place of inherent deceit and frequent murder. There is reference to the Spanish Armada.

Shakespeare offered far more on France than Spain, but there were occasional references to the latter. In *Love's Labour's Lost*, probably written in 1594 or 1595 while England and Spain were at war, Don Armado is a pompous braggard of a suitor. Ferdinand, King of Navarre, describes him as:

> a refined traveller of Spain;
> A man in all the world's new fashion planted,
> That hath a mint of phrases in his brain;
> One whom the music of his own vain tongue
> Doth ravish like enchanting harmony;
> A man of complements, whom right and wrong
> Have chose as umpire of their mutiny;
> this child of fancy.

In *The Comedy of Errors*, Dromio of Syracuse cruelly itemises Nell the 'kitchen-wench' in terms of countries, with Spain 'hot in her breath' and the jewels from the Indies 'whole armadoes of caracks to be ballast at her nose'.

CHAPTER SIX

Seventeenth-century Crises, 1598–1700

Don Quixote tilting at a windmill has been frequently employed by historians as an image of an unrealistic Spain foolishly taking on too much in a quest for glory. The well-known, much-reproduced, instructive and seductive image serves a widespread narrative of decline, if not collapse. The great world empire of 1598 is seen as defeated by France, England and the Dutch over the following century. Moreover, in what is widely presented by historians as a 'mid-seventeenth-century crisis', Philip IV (r. 1621–65) faced rebellions, notably in Portugal and Catalonia in 1640. The first eventually left Portugal independent, while Catalonia was only reconquered after major efforts. Thereafter, Spain is shaded by Louis XIV's France, and its economy, society and culture are presented as unable to confront the issues of power and modernisation.

OF THE GOOD FORTUNE WHICH THE VALIANT DON QUIXOTE HAD IN THE TERRIBLE AND UNDREAMT-OF ADVENTURE OF THE WINDMILLS, WITH OTHER OCCURRENCES WORTHY TO BE FITLY RECORDED

At this point they came in sight of thirty or forty windmills that there are on the plain, and as soon as Don Quixote saw them he said to his squire, 'Fortune is arranging matters for us better than we could have shaped our desires ourselves, for look there, friend Sancho Panza, where thirty or more monstrous giants present themselves, all of whom I mean to engage in battle and slay, and with whose spoils we shall begin to make our fortunes; for this is righteous warfare, and it is God's good service to sweep so evil a breed from off the face of the earth.'

'What giants?' said Sancho Panza.

'Those thou seest there,' answered his master, 'with the long arms, and some have them nearly two leagues long.'

'Look, your worship,' said Sancho; 'what we see there are not giants but windmills, and what seem to be their arms are the sails that turned by the wind make the mill-stone go.'

'It is easy to see,' replied Don Quixote, 'that thou art not used to this business of adventures; those are giants; and if thou art afraid, away with thee out of this and betake thyself to prayer while I engage them in fierce and unequal combat.'

(Miguel de Cervantes, published 1615)

Don Quixote is the protagonist in a novel, that by the much-travelled Miguel de Cervantes (c. 1547–1616), published in two volumes, in 1605 and 1615. This is the most important work in Spanish literature. Like Cervantes, who was captured by Barbary pirates in 1575 and imprisoned in Spain in 1597 for discrepancies in his accounts as a tax collector, Spain did face serious problems. However, so did other states, societies and authors. If, for example, the last major plague epidemic in Spain ended in 1685, for France the year was 1720 and for Italy 1743. If Spain had a mid-seventeenth-century crisis, so also did Britain and France, in each of which there were bitter civil wars. In Spain, the first newspaper appeared in 1618 but, in 1627, a law imposing the need for government permission was introduced. The same trend of control, however, could be seen elsewhere.

SOCIETY

The focus in discussing Spain's crisis tends to be on politics; which is why it is instructive to begin with social arrangements. This was a sphere in which there was, in practice, much continuity, both during the seventeenth century and during the centuries on either side. Society was very much stratified, with the weight of the past particularly present in status and privilege, but also in property, notably landed property, and power. Social control by the élite was a fact, not an issue, in politics. Heredity and stability were regarded as intertwined, and snobbery was inherent, clearly so in relation to rank, status and lineage. The rate of social change was rigidly governed by a variety of devices, including marital strategies, inheritance practices and government patronage.

There were tensions within society but it would be misleading to suggest either that there was widespread criticism of the existence of a hereditary hierarchical society or that tensions were only apparent between, as distinct from within, social groups. The peasantry and the nobility, far from being uniform, were generally legally defined groups characterised by internal differences. Nobles vied with one another for local political power and social eminence, a process matched by that of peasants within their own communities.

Power and wealth within Spain were concentrated in the hands of a relatively small number of families. The hierarchical nature, both of society and of the dominant political system; the predominantly agrarian nature of the economy; the generally slow rate of change in social and economic affairs or, at least, of structural change; the unwillingness of monarchs and of the noble-dominated government to challenge fundamentally the interests of the nobility, or to govern without its cooperation; and the inegalitarian assumptions of the period, all combined to ensure that the concentration of power and wealth remained reasonably constant. There was considerable social stability, not least because most wealth was inherited or acquired by marriage. Entails to maintain estates intact were available. Most land lost by individual noble families was not lost from the nobility but generally, by marriage or sale, transferred to other nobles or to those who were ennobled. These factors were generally true in Europe.

Most Spanish nobles, including the fictional Don Quixote, were poor *hidalgos* (noblemen). They lacked power and wealth, although, in comparison with the bulk of the population, they could be fairly placed in those categories. Those who enjoyed power and wealth tended to be nobles not only by birth but also by inherited family position. Government sought the consent of the powerful nobles, not so much through constitutional necessity but because of its reliance on nobles as the effective administration in the community, and also because cooperation was seen as desirable as well as essential, a source of legitimacy as much as of implementation. Successful government initiatives were generally those that the nobility was willing to support, acquiesce in or at least not actively seek to thwart. The co-option of members of old noble houses, the ennoblement of non-noble officials and the promotion in the aristocracy of low-ranking members who held important offices helped to sustain the noble dominance of central government. The council system of government caused delay, but also permitted aristocratic representation, which included non-violent opposition by nobles. In addition, the nobles' dominance of local government was both a practical response by the Crown to the real power of the nobility in the localities and in accordance with cultural values and ideological norms.

The response of the nobility, both as a whole and of individual nobles, was influenced by a mixture of precedent, privilege, self-interest, the interplay of traditional and novel views, and the political context. Distinctive noble status was defined by the past: the individual past of noble birth and family status, and the collective past of grants of privileges in return for services.

The nobility was articulated by patronage relationships and

kinship. These linked the Court nobility, with its social eminence and favoured access to the monarchy, to the poor provincial nobility. With the exception of the greater aristocracy, most nobles were provincial in every sense of the word. Noble dominance of local government was important both governmentally and politically, and took two forms: control over the relevant posts, and the allocation to the nobles of many responsibilities that might otherwise have fallen into the public sphere. There was also competition for patronage, and this could lead to serious feuds, as in Aragón in the 1570s and 1580s between the Count of Chinchón, a leading minister, and the Duke of Villahermosa, the most prominent noble. This struggle encompassed rivalry at Court and fighting in the localities.

The nobility pressed hard on the peasantry, who suffered many burdens. At the same time, there were also what could be termed the middling orders, middle class or bourgeoisie. In rural society, the middling order was composed of the agents of landlords and, where they existed, tenant farmers. There was a widespread aspiration among them to rise in landed society.

Towns
The middling order was a key element in the urban population. The vast majority of towns did not enjoy any marked growth. Many were economically and demographically dormant market centres. Nevertheless, they helped to form the commercial and fiscal infrastructure that sustained more dramatic and substantial cases of growth.

Yet, towns also competed, which reduced their collective political strength. Rivals for economic and other benefits, towns sought a cooperative partnership with government. Locations of administration, both state and religious, towns were centres of production, trade and consumption. They were in a symbiotic, but also difficult, relationship with their rural hinterlands. They were markets for their products, but also often harsh would-be controllers of the relationship, not least in the provision of loans. There were also disputes over the allocation of tax obligations.

Yet it would be a mistake to present town and countryside simply as rivals. Nor should these clashes be necessarily regarded as town–country antagonisms. There were important links. Peasants flocked to towns, not only to market, but also to attend fairs or religious ceremonies.

Towns shared in the inegalitarian and hierarchical nature of Spanish society. The smallest group of townspeople were the wealthy and prominent, their power expressed in, and deriving from, their ability to organise others, generally economically and often politically. Their strength extended into the rural hinterland, where they would enjoy influence as a result of their power as a source of credit, tend to own estates and, if merchants, control rural industry. Within the towns, this group might be employers or landowners but, more commonly, would enjoy political power as a result of social status and control over the institutions of urban government. Some members of the group would possess noble rank, though the importance of that varied greatly. Most derived their income from trade, official and particularly judicial positions, and the profits from wealth invested in land or in interest-paying loans.

The largest urban group was the poor. They lacked political weight and often were not citizens of the town in any legal sense. Their poverty stemmed from the precarious nature of much employment in even the most prosperous of towns and the absence of any effective system of social welfare. Most lacked the skills that commanded a decent wage and many had only seasonal or episodic employment. A large number were immigrants from the countryside. As a result of their poverty, the poor were very vulnerable to changes in the price of food and generally lived in inadequate housing. Those who were fit tended to be treated harshly.

In between these two groups, although not separated rigidly

from them in economic terms, was a third one enjoying a more settled income than the poor. Many in this group were artisans, their economic interests and social cohesion often expressed through guilds or other fraternities of workmen. The consistent pattern of tight intermarriage within socio-economic groups (endogamy) made entry into the élite of merchants and magistracy difficult. Artisans were generally far more socially integrated than day labourers, servants and paupers, not least due to membership of guilds and fraternities. Municipal government and military orders excluded artisans: in Galicia tanners could not hold public office, obtain membership in a guild or religious confraternity, or aspire to the priesthood. As citizenship was generally rightful membership of an urban community, such exclusions were highly significant.

POLITICS

This was a fearful society in which ideas of racial purity and religious conformity were enforced, not least with strict codes based on 'purity of blood'. Moriscos, who formed much of the labour force in Valencia, were expelled in 1609. Such ethnic and religious tensions drew on long-held animosities. These could be linked to more specific factionalism. For example, in 1474 conversos (converted Jews) and the Cristiano Viejo (Old Christian) majority fought in the streets of Córdoba, a conflict that was related to those between urban and aristocratic factions. In 1609, the Moriscos were seen as a potential fifth column who might help the Ottomans and the Barbary States of North Africa. In 1680, the Natives in New Mexico rebelled against Spanish oppression, led by a victim of Spanish attempts to suppress Native religion. Some Moriscos who were regarded as useful were not expelled, but by 1614 most had been. Their plight was terrible, as contemporary sources make clear, including a graphic painting, *The Expulsion of the Moors*, by Vicente Carducho.

The expulsion of the Moriscos was one of the major events

of the reign of Philip III (r. 1598–1621). This was at once a period of great difficulty, notably the plague of 1599, and also of Spain as a great power, one that leaves a splendid visual legacy in the equestrian statue of the king in the Plaza Mayor in Madrid. The account of Spanish decline finds much of fault in this reign of Philip, not least with poor governance. Philip III lacked the diligence of Philip II and chose to turn to a *valido* (favourite). That itself would not have been a key problem but he relied on a *valido* who was not up to the task, in this case the Duke of Lerma, who was displaced in 1618 by his son, the Duke of Uceda.

For Philip IV (r. 1621–65) the key minister was the Count Duke of Olivares. He was more talented than Lerma or Uceda, but was not ultimately able to reconcile an intractable and costly war with discontent within Spain. Spain was largely successful in the 1620s, but could not sustain this situation.

The burden of war had relaxed slightly after a twelve-year truce was negotiated in 1609 with the Dutch. There were local struggles but full-scale conflict was avoided, for example in 1614 in the Jülich-Cleves dispute. Full-scale war, however, resumed in 1621 and Spain was then involved in continuous conflict until 1668. Thus, there was a pressure not only on the finances, but also on administration and political structures and systems. In practice, Spanish bureaucracy showed remarkable agility, dedication and inventiveness. Private contractors and public officials worked fruitfully together. In the case of keeping fleets supplied, forest legislation sought to conserve timber stocks, efforts were made to provide sailors and soldiers with nutritious food and good medical care, and severe discipline was enforced on erring fleet commanders and bureaucrats alike.

Nevertheless, finances provide a key problem, one focused on by the *arbitras* (arbitrators), politicians and others who produced writings arguing for change. Among their targets were the devaluation of the currency by manipulation, and its inflationary consequences. Minting large quantities of copper coins (*vellón*) from 1603 destabilised not only the finances, but also the economy as a whole. Beginning a full-scale war in 1635, one that lasted until 1659, neither France nor Spain was able to impose a crippling defeat on the other. France survived a Spanish invasion in 1636, although Spanish troops advanced as far as Corbie.

The fiscal burdens of war posed growing political problems. Spain had the largest empire in western Europe, but its financial, political and military system also proved unequal to the strains of the war. The attempt in 1624 to introduce a Union of Arms, in which the parts of Spain raised troops in accord to their population and size, was rejected by Catalonia, and, in 1627, there was a governmental bankruptcy. In 1637, attempts to raise taxes in Portugal led to a rebellion there. A crisis caused by the burdens of war-support and by attempts to share the cost caused the Catalan rising in 1640. There was another successful rebellion in Portugal that year, as well as a conspiracy in Andalusia in 1641, which may have been an attempt to secede and to make the Duke of Medina Sidonia the king, or an attempt to overthrow Olivares. In 1648, there was a similar conspiracy in Aragón. In contrast, France faced rebellion, the Fronde, in the centre of power from 1648 until 1652. Each side sought to exploit the rebellions in the other, France sending forces into Catalonia and using the opportunity of the rebellion there to conquer the in-between province of Roussillon, its capital, Perpignan, falling in 1642. The crisis and the related sense of malaise helped lead to Philip IV parting with Olivares in 1643: the count-duke had been very reluctant to leave office. He was replaced by his nephew, Don Luis de Haro, Marquis of Carpio, who was chief minister until his death in 1661.

The Fronde proved useful to Spain in permitting the reconquest of Catalonia. Barcelona fell in 1652 after a fourteen-month Spanish siege had reduced the population, already weakened by the plague, to starvation. By the Peace of the Pyrenees (1659), signed in the aftermath of the Spanish defeat in the battle of the Dunes near Dunkirk (1658), France gained Roussillon and

Artois, as well as the marriage of Philip IV's daughter to the young Louis XIV. This step gave Louis a stake in the Spanish succession. The two powers fought again in 1667–8, 1673–8, 1683–4 and 1689–1697. Spain lost significant possessions from the Burgundian inheritance, notably Franche-Comté, which the French conquered in 1674 and were ceded in 1678. In the 1697 peace, however, Louis returned Barcelona, which he had captured earlier that year.

The Spaniards had less success against Portugal, which successfully won independence in a war of 1640–68. The Portuguese had benefited from the Spanish focus on the Catalans in 1640–52. In 1657–9, and again in the 1660s, as both sides deployed larger forces, Spain failed to reconquer Portugal. Until the late 1650s, the war was essentially a small-scale matter of raids and plundering. In 1657–9, Spain, still fighting France with her new English ally, lacked sufficient soldiers. Although various systems for raising troops were employed, the government relied on a contract one, whereby individuals formed units in return for payment. Successive political and military crises, with the rise in Spanish commitments and heavy losses of men, strained the system. The cost of raising troops by contract rose rapidly, and it became more difficult to field sufficient forces. France backed Portugal.

In 1663, Philip IV, now at peace with all bar Portugal, concentrated his forces, stiffened by all who could be recruited, including criminals, against Portugal, only to face defeat at Ameixial where the Portuguese were backed by English troops sent by Charles II, who had married a Portuguese princess. Two years later, defeat at Villaviciosa ended the hope of reconquering Portugal.

War was a major burden for Spain, not least as it had to prepare to resist invasions. During the personal union of Portugal and Spain (1580–1640), there had been no need to consider the fortresses along the frontier and by 1640 most were totally dilapidated. By 1710, however, after more than thirty years of work,

Ciudad Rodrigo was one of the best-fortified towns in Spain. Separately, in 1688, the French envoy was impressed by the strength and modernity of the citadel at Pamplona. Moreover, there were no rebellions in the latter decades of the century to match those in mid-century. In addition, whereas the *cortes* of Castile in the first half of the century had made frequent complaints, it was effectively dissolved in 1665 and therefore not in a position to focus discontent.

EXPLORING THE EMPIRE

The interior of the New World represented a formidable challenge to Western understanding. Franciscans and Jesuits were especially active in exploration. Manuel Biedma explored north-eastern Peru, including the valley of the Ucayali, between 1658 and 1686, while Antonio de Monteverde explored the valley of the Orinoco in 1663.

The establishment of missions on the coast of Lower California led to the search for a land route from Mexico around the head of the Gulf of California in the 1690s and 1700s. Later, the creation of settlements on the Upper Californian coast, notably San Diego in 1761, Monterey in 1770 and San Francisco in 1776, was followed by a more ambitious search for overland routes.

WARS FOR RELIGION

State and Church remained closely linked, with the tradition of conquest for Christ strong, and difficulties experienced in converting natives leading to a harsh attitude that also justified imperial expansion. When Nojpetén, the capital of the Maya people known as Itzás, was stormed in 1697, Martín de Ursúa, the interim governor of Yucatán, ordered his men to plant the flag with the royal arms of Spain and religious standards among the Itzá temples 'in which the majesty of God had been offended by idolatries'. Ursúa thanked God for his victory and then joined soldiers and Franciscans in destroying a large number of 'idols'. If gold or silver, such idols were melted down. This was religious war against opponents presented as guilty of human sacrifice, cannibalism and killing priests. Five years earlier, when Santa Fé was regained by the Spaniards after the Pueblo rebellion of 1680, there had also been a reimposition of Catholic control. Franciscan priests absolved Natives of the apostasy and baptised those born after 1680, with the governor serving as godfather for the children of the prominent. In the first clash for control of Lower California, the battle for Loreto Conchó of 1697, a well-armed Spanish missionary party fought off a Native attack.

On the other side of the Pacific, Spain, deploying troops, established a mission on Guam in 1668. The island chain was renamed the Marianas to signify the role of religion. Further south in the Pacific, Spanish missionaries from the Philippines reached the Palau Islands in 1710, but a hostile response cut short the opening.

Religious conflict was also a key element in Spain's policy in Europe, notably until the late 1630s when Catholic France pushed aside Protestant powers to become Spain's leading opponent. In contrast, in the 1600s and 1620s, the Dutch and English had been the major opponents.

Religion was important to the private life and public image of the monarchy. A strong Catholic devotion was seen in both, with participation in religious education, ritual and patronage key aspects of royalty's role. Ferdinand, one of Philip III's sons, although never ordained a priest, became Cardinal-Archbishop of Toledo (Primate of Spain), as well as Governor of Catalonia, Governor of the Spanish Netherlands (Belgium) and commander of the Spanish troops in the dramatic victory over the Swedes at Nördlingen in 1634. Philip IV founded seventeen convents and monasteries in Madrid, following the seventeen under Philip II and the fourteen under Philip III.

CULTURE

The seventeenth century saw a shift from the Classicism of the Herreran style, which was the basis of much early-seventeenth-century work, for example the nave of Valencia cathedral, to a more ornate Italianate Baroque that became significant in the later decades as with the towers on the Jesuit College of Salamanca. The Spanish Baroque style is named Churrigueresque after José de Churriguera (1665–1725) and his brothers, who were responsible for important work in the early eighteenth century, such as the Plaza Mayor in Salamanca. In painting, there was a transition in the seventeenth century from Mannerism to a more naturalistic approach and style. The latter was also seen in sculpture.

SEVENTEENTH-CENTURY ARTISTS

Born in Seville with Portuguese New Christian parentage, Diego Velázquez (1599–1660) was formally trained and in 1617, at the end of his apprenticeship, examined and given a licence to work as an independent painter, a profession governed by guild rules. Much of his early work was on religious topics, as in his *Immaculate Conception*, *St John the Evangelist* and *Christ in the House of Martha and Mary*, all of about 1618, and all held in the National Gallery in London. At this stage, Velázquez also produced *bodegones* or genre paintings that showed life in that period, for example *The Old Woman Frying Eggs* and *The Waterseller of Seville*. *The Triumph of Bacchus* (1628) is a variant of this.

Appointed *Pintor del Rey* (the Royal Painter) in 1623, Velázquez came to focus on portraits, notably of Philip IV and of his family. Some of his works were for the Palacio del Buen Retiro, others for the transformation of the Alcázar palace. Paintings contributed strongly to an image of monarchy. The future Charles I of England was very impressed, on his visit to Spain in 1623 in pursuit of his unsuccessful plan for a marriage with the daughter of Philip IV, by this image of Spanish monarchy.

Victory was celebrated in Velázquez's *Surrender of Breda* (1635), which recorded a successful siege of a major Dutch-held position in 1625. Visits to Italy, where he painted a superb portrait of Pope Innocent X in 1650, helped in the maturing of Velázquez's style, seen in particular in the use of light, and in *Las Meninas* (1656: Prado), a famous Court scene in which the figures are very carefully staged.

Boy Delousing Himself is not the subject of the most impressive works of many painters, but the *c.* 1645 painting on that topic by Bartolomé Esteban Murillo (1618–82) captures his soft use of light and his sympathy towards children. The youngest son of a Seville barber-surgeon, Murillo engaged in a range of genres, including portraits and religious works, and also offered realist treatments of life as in *Two Boys Eating Fruit* (*c.* 1650). Many of his religious works can be seen in the Prado, including the *Immaculate Conception of the Escorial* (*c.* 1660–5). Others can be viewed in situ, for example the *Vision of St Anthony of Padua* in Seville cathedral. Murillo died several months after falling from the scaffolding around the main altar of the Capuchin Church in Cádiz on which he was working.

A clear testimony of the impact of religious concerns was provided by the paintings of Francisco de Zurbarán (1598–1664), the Extremadura-born and Seville-trained painter who worked for churches and monasteries. His powerfully depicted religious figures balanced between the shadows and the light, this world and that of God. Those painted for the monastery of San Pablo El Real in Seville partly survive in the church of María Magdalena there, and the Seville museum holds his masterly *Apotheosis of St Thomas Aquinas*. The paintings for the monastery of San José of La Mercel Calzada in Seville can be seen in a number of galleries including the Prado and the Real Academia de Bellas Artes de San Fernando in Madrid. The full range of religious themes were covered. Called to Madrid in 1634–5, Zurbarán painted for the Buen Retiro palace, producing battle paintings and mythological scenes, including *The Defence of Cádiz against the English* and the *Labours of Hercules*, both of which can be seen in the Prado.

Religious history was a theme in the painting for the high altar at the monastery of Jerez de la Frontera, which was built on the site of a battle in 1370 where Spanish troops were saved from a night ambush by a miraculous light that revealed the Moors. The painting, which depicted the battle, can be seen in the Metropolitan Museum in New York. The paintings of fifteenth-century monastic life for the monastery at Guadalupe can still be seen in the original setting. In the 1640s, with Spain in crisis, Zurbarán worked on commissions for Spanish American patrons, then focusing anew on religious works for Spanish monasteries in the 1650s and early 1660s. He retained to the close his ability to interplay form, light and texture.

SPANISH AMERICA

Spain remained the leading power in the New World, with transatlantic maritime routes crucial both to Spain and to its colonies. At the same time, Spain faced challenges. The English colony established at Jamestown in the Chesapeake on the eastern coast of North America in 1607 was regarded as an invasion of Spanish rights and led to protests. Although the defences at Jamestown were prepared to resist Spanish attack, it did not come: Virginia was too distant from the centres of Spanish power, the closest of which was at St Augustine on the Atlantic Coast of Florida. Nevertheless, England, France and the Netherlands also established colonies in the Caribbean and on the Guiana coast of South America. In 1655, England captured Jamaica, although hopes of conquering Cuba and Hispaniola proved widely over-optimistic.

Spain was obliged to adopt increasingly sophisticated and expensive measures in order to defend its colonies. These included fortifications, such as that at St Augustine in Florida, as well as the strengthening of convoy systems to protect trade. Paradoxically, Spain came to benefit from being a part of alliance systems, notably those in the 1670s and 1690s directed against France. As a result, the Dutch and English then focused their energies on attacking France, which lacked the strength to focus on Spanish America. Instead, in the 1670s, the French fleet concentrated on an unsuccessful attempt to support a rebellion in Sicily against Spanish rule. In contrast, alliances with Spain in the eighteenth century meant vulnerability to attack from Britain.

CHAPTER SEVEN

Eighteenth-century Revival, 1700–92

ON THE GRAND TOUR IN SPAIN WITH THOMAS PELHAM

Full of youthful enthusiasm, the well-connected Thomas Pelham (1756–1826), later Second Earl of Chichester, visited Spain in 1775–6, shortly before Britain and Spain went to war in 1779 as the War of American Independence broadened out, with Spain coming in as the ally of France. Pelham stayed for many months in Madrid, where he benefited from the hospitality of a relative, the ambassador, Thomas, Second Earl of Grantham. From Madrid, Pelham went on a trip to Andalusia and thence, via Granada, Alicante, Valencia and Barcelona, to France. This was a most unusual tour for anyone, let alone a Briton, one that benefited from Grantham's connections, notably in arranging accommodation where there was none available for the public, and Pelham described the tour in letters to his parents. He decided to 'see the south of Spain, which is not only a very interesting tour from its having been the scene of so many transactions in the Roman History and consequently retaining many curious antiquities but likewise as being the most fruitful and commercial part of modern Spain'. It was necessary to prepare carefully for the journey:

> My bed is repairing, and a boiler is making that may hang under my chaise to boil my dinner, for there are as many precautions to be taken for travelling in this country as if I were going into Arabia: my journey from Lisbon has taught me all the *desagremens* and how many of them are only imaginary ones for after two or three days travelling

you fancy your boiled chicken or rabbit better than all the
. . . ragouts from a French kitchen.

Setting off for Córdoba in late September 1776, Pelham took a
lot of food because he was concerned about what he might find en
route, and a Spanish edition of *Don Quixote*, the latter designed
to aid his language skills:

the inns we stop at being the same as those in which he
met with so many adventures: the room I am writing in is
worthy of one of his castles – no window, a hole in the wall
that admits light in the day and is stopped up with a board
at night, an indifferent door, a large pillar in the middle
of the room that supports the roof, and round which our
servants are to lay down our armour and set up our beds,
and the walls naked except where some pedlar has left a
few shabby prints.

Pelham found Andalusia 'most delightful', but was delayed
at Cádiz by the heavy rainfall which swelled the rivers, making
them difficult to cross by ferry: as elsewhere in Europe, there
were few bridges. The same cause held him up at Lorca, while he
was unimpressed by the quality of the roads near Gibraltar and
Cartagena. Pelham's phlegmatic character enabled him to bear
the difficulties of Spanish travel:

it is really beyond all description but I make it a rule to
go into a Pasada without asking any questions, have no
wants, and as little intercourse with my landlord as possible who is never satisfied, with what you give him and
will cheat whenever he has an opportunity: we buy our
own provisions and that for our beasts [horses], all which,
excepting game, are as dear and by no means as good
as in England. After all this, I can assure you with great

truth that I never felt the least annoy or uneasiness, for the want of conveniences in the inns makes one more active in providing them for oneself, and when found they give double pleasure from their rarity: I would never recommend a Spanish journey to a lady, but it is by no means a bad beginning for a young traveller.

WAR AND POLITICS

Across the eighteenth century as a whole, much of government and administration was a product of war or of the drive to do better in conflict. The century had begun with Spain the subject of a bitter and civil war, the War of the Spanish Succession from 1700 to 1715 between Bourbon and Habsburg claimants to the throne. This conflict has been overshadowed by later civil wars, particularly (but not only) those of 1808–13, 1833–40 and, most prominently, 1936–9. Nevertheless, the War of the Spanish Succession was highly significant in terms of the damage caused and the political changes resulting, and especially so during the early eighteenth century.

The attempt to avoid war over the Spanish succession collapsed on the twin obstacles of Charles II's will and Austrian determination. When Charles II (r. 1665–1700), the last Habsburg king of Spain, died childless, he left the whole of the Spanish monarchy to Louis XIV's younger grandson, Philip, Duke of Anjou, who became Philip V (r. 1700–46), with the proviso that, if he rejected the bequest and sought to partition the inheritance, it was then to be offered to his rival, the Archduke Charles, younger son of the Holy Roman Emperor, Leopold I. The will was designed to elicit French support for the maintenance of the empire rather than a compromise that would partition it. Unwilling to lose the prize to the Austrians, Louis accepted the will for his grandson, even though he knew it would cause war.

Hostilities in the War of the Spanish Succession were begun by Leopold in 1701, and a marked deterioration in relations with

France led Britain and the Dutch to rally to Leopold's side in 1702. The war involved an Anglo-Dutch-backed Austrian effort to establish Archduke Charles as Charles III, which failed totally within Spain itself. British dominance of the seas gave Charles, supported by the Mediterranean provinces, a chance. Thanks to British support, amphibious forces captured Gibraltar in 1704, Barcelona in 1705, and Alicante, Majorca and Ibiza in 1706. Madrid was occupied briefly in 1706 and 1710.

Castile, however, remained loyal to Philip, while Louis sent troops to his aid. Despite his reliance on French troops, Philip's cause became identified with national independence. The French defeated the outnumbered pro-Charles force and their allies at Almansa (1707), forcing Charles back to Catalonia, although it was not possible for Philip to exploit this in order to end the war in Spain. In 1710, Charles defeated Philip at Almenara and Zaragoza, before occupying Madrid, but few Castilians rallied to him and his communications became hazardous. As a result, he withdrew from Madrid and, at Brihuega, part of his retreating force, under the command of James, Lord Stanhope, was attacked and forced to surrender by a much larger Franco-Spanish force under the Duc de Vendôme. Charles had now lost Castile. Catalonia, Charles's principal foothold in Spain, could not be protected effectively from Castile, as had been earlier demonstrated in 1648–52.

Local opinion was not the only factor in determining success. The course of the conflict was itself important and, in that, the allies lost a number of major battles, in large part due to French intervention. Partly thanks to the ability of James FitzJames, Duke of Berwick, illegitimate son of James II and Arabella Churchill (sister of John, First Duke of Marlborough), the French benefited from a level of generalship higher than that they displayed elsewhere. Berwick was especially effective in manoeuvre and had a fine grasp of logistics. Furthermore, admittedly in more difficult logistical and political contexts, none of the British generals were as able as Marlborough. Charles's Catalan supporters continued to resist, but they were defeated in a series of sieges: Girona fell in 1711 and Barcelona in 1714. The latter city was defended with popular fervour against overwhelming Franco-Spanish attack. A worker-militia manned the walls and resisted several assaults successfully. Popular enthusiasm was sustained by religious commitment, including the use of sacred relics. Majorca was captured in 1715 once the cover of British naval protection was removed.

In 1711, with allied Spanish troops mutinying for lack of pay, and his own forces short of cannon and powder, John, Second Duke of Argyll wrote from Barcelona:

> having with greater difficulty than can be expressed found credit to keep the troops from starving in their quarters all this while, which for my part I do not see how we shall be able to do any longer, for the not paying the bills that were drawn from hence the last year, has entirely destroyed her Majesty's credit in this place; but though the troops could be supplied in quarters, that will not now do the business, for the enemy is already in motion . . . so that if we remain in quarters, we shall be destroyed *en detaille*, and to get together is not in nature till we have money, for the whole body of troops that were here last year are without all manner of necessarys, having both officers and soldiers lost all their tents, baggage and equipage at the battle of Villaviociosa (1710), besides that the contractors for the mules to draw the artillery and ammunition and carry the bread will by no means be persuaded to serve any more till we have money to pay.

Logistics and finance were more serious problems in Spain than in the Low Countries where the British also operated. This was not only because of the relative poverty and shortage of food in Spain, and its poor roads, but also because the British ally in the Low Countries (the Dutch) was far better able to support its own forces and to pay a portion of the cost of financing allied troops. Such problems underlined the Duke of Wellington's achievement a century later. He was more successful in maintaining cohesion among the allies, supplying the army and winning battles.

The conflict in Spain during the War of the Spanish Succession was often harsh. Guerrillas played a considerable role, and the response was often brutal. The French killed the survivors when the Valencian town of Xàtiva fell in 1707 and left no building standing except the church. The town was renamed San Felipe. As a result, the portrait of Philip V hangs upside down in the local museum of L'Almodí.

Philip's success in the war enabled him to limit regional privileges. In 1707, the political privileges of Aragón and Valencia were abolished, Castilian law was introduced, and high courts were established on the Castilian model. In 1707 Castilian taxes were introduced into Aragón and by 1713 the province was beginning to make an appreciable contribution to Spanish financial needs. In 1715, a high court was founded in Majorca when Philip conquered it from Charles, and in 1718 Majorcan civil law was abolished. In 1716, under the *Nueva Planta* (New Plan), it was forbidden to employ the Catalan language in the administration and courts of Catalonia. Catalan usages and forms were abolished, and Castilian law and practices introduced. Philip V suppressed the six traditional Catalan universities, creating a new pro-Bourbon one, at Cervera in 1717. A large citadel was built in Barcelona in 1715–18. On the French model, Philip also introduced *intendants* (agents of the central government based in the regions) to serve as a new link between central and local government. The central government was transformed from one based on conciliar administration to specialist departments run by secretaries of state.

Yet, these regulations were not enforced in a fashion likely to produce standardisation, and provincial particularism was not destroyed. It was decided in 1711 and 1716 that Aragónese and Valencian civil cases were not to be judged by Castilian law unless the Crown intervened. The *Nueva Planta* stated that Catalan law was to be preserved for matters dealing with the family, property and the individual. Civil and mercantile law remained exclusively Catalan and, until the early nineteenth century, Catalan criminal law remained important. In Navarre and the Basque region, the local laws and courts were preserved because these regions had backed Philip. Moreover, generally, local élites were able to determine the illegitimacy of some central governmental schemes. Thus, opposition in southern Spain frustrated the agrarian reforms of Philip V's son, Charles III.

Government itself could be heavily factional. For example, Pedro, Count of Aranda, President of the Council of Castile from 1766 to 1773, was regarded as the head of what was called the Aragónese Party, a group of prominent individuals who were hostile to what were seen as overly autocratic tendencies within the government. Disturbances in Madrid, the Esquilache Riots, had led to the fall of Leopoldo, Marquis of Esquilache, the previous chief minister, in 1766. Directed against measures to change the traditional garb of Spaniards by replacing long capes with short ones, and affected by a background of rising food prices, these disturbances were in part coordinated by disaffected members of the élite. Aranda restored order. Francisco Goya, an eyewitness, soon after painted a dramatic version of the riots.

Philip V devoted much of his energy to war, fighting each of Austria, Savoy-Piedmont, Britain and France for at least part of 1717–20: Austria in 1733–5, Britain from 1739 and Austria from 1741. His forces invaded Sardinia in 1717 and Sicily in 1718, achieving initial success. In 1719, however, this warfare led to an invasion of Spain, with the French seizing Fuenterrabía and San Sebastián and the British taking Vigo. In contrast, the main Spanish invasion attempt on Britain that year was thwarted by the weather, and a smaller force that landed in Scotland was beaten.

In 1729, a French diplomat reported from Spain that Philip always had a 'passion' for war. Philip's key objective was that of regaining Sardinia, Sicily, Naples, the Milanese, Gibraltar and Belgium, the territories lost in the partition of the Spanish Empire that had brought the War of the Spanish Succession to a close in 1713–14, and, to that end, he re-created the army and navy. Spending on the fleet rose by 800 per cent between 1713 and 1748. The strains of expenditure, however, helped lead to government bankruptcies in 1726 and 1739.

The army benefited from the high tempo of campaigning during the War of the Spanish Succession, and from cooperation at that time with the French army. Moreover, the new Bourbon dynasty, combined with the War of the Spanish Succession, provided both need and opportunity to remake patronage networks in the army and to rethink best practice. The percentage of infantry rose, while in 1734 Philip ordered the establishment of a twenty-three-thousand-strong militia in Castile to free regular troops for service in Italy where Naples was conquered from Austria that year. This militia did not cover Aragón or Navarre. There was also a new and more effective administrative structure for both army and navy. The latter was rebuilt and organised into three departments, based on Cádiz, Cartagena and Ferrol.

Philip's eldest son, Ferdinand VI (r. 1746–59), was more pacific, helping bring about an agreement that kept the peace in Italy from 1752. By then, his half-brother Charles was ruler of Naples and Sicily, and another half-brother, Philip, was Duke of Parma. The emphasis thereafter was no longer on Spain as an Italian power. Instead, the navy was built up as an Atlantic force. Moreover, attempts were made to reform state finances and colonial policy.

Ferdinand's half-brother Charles succeeded him as Charles III (r. 1759–88), and was more bellicose, fighting Britain in 1762–3 and 1779–83. As with earlier conflicts, the wars caused strains and revealed weaknesses. In 1762, British expeditions captured

Havana and Manila. Both were handed back under the subsequent peace treaty of 1763, although Spain lost Florida to Britain. Moreover, the loss of Havana was a major blow to Spanish prestige. It led Charles III to make major efforts to strengthen the security of the empire.

In 1762, British intervention also blocked a French-backed Spanish invasion of Portugal. Initially, Spanish success in overrunning weak and poorly defended Portuguese fortresses, such as Miranda, Bragança and Chaves, led to urgent requests for British troops. After being delayed by contrary winds in the Channel, these troops helped to turn the tide, although the Spanish failure to exploit their early successes by a march on Oporto was also crucial. In the last significant action in the campaign, the British stormed the entrenched Spanish camp, inflicting heavy casualties. Facing the onset of the winter rains, the imminence of peace and the strength of the British presence, the Spaniards and French retreated.

In 1779–83, allied to France and the American revolutionaries in the War of American Independence, Spain reconquered West Florida, with a notably successful siege of Pensacola in 1781. However, a long siege of Gibraltar was unsuccessful, hopes of regaining Jamaica proved abortive, and preparation for a joint invasion of southern England with France in 1779 was thwarted by delay, disease and the British navy. The British navy was able to relieve Gibraltar on three occasions, permitting the fortress to resist the siege. Well-fortified and ably defended, Gibraltar saw off attack. Minorca, however, surrendered in 1782 to a vastly greater Franco-Spanish force after a long siege without relief had let scurvy ravage the garrison. In Central America, the Spaniards captured St Georges Cay, the principal port of the British loggers in Belize, in 1779. A British expedition in 1780–1 to Nicaragua was abandoned after heavy losses to yellow fever. In 1782, a Spanish force took Nassau, the capital of New Providence, the major island in the Bahamas, although the British regained it in

1783. In the peace of 1783, Spain kept West Florida and regained East Florida.

Large-scale Spanish attempts to capture Algiers, mounted in 1775 and 1784, failed badly. Generally forgotten, they serve, however, as a reminder of the significance of religious struggle. Although it was to be France that conquered Algeria from 1830, there is a link from the Reconquista to the struggle in the sixteenth to eighteenth centuries to dominate the western Mediterranean, and then on to expansionism in Morocco from the mid-nineteenth century. The values of the army can in particular be located in this context.

The 1775 attack on Algiers involved twenty-one thousand troops, a fleet of forty-four warships and three hundred and fifty transports. Having been delayed by bad weather, the poorly planned landings were characterised by great confusion. The Spaniards were pinned down on the beaches by heavy fire from Algerine coastal artillery while their own cannons were delayed by the coastal sand. By mid-afternoon, the Spaniards had suffered two thousand four hundred casualties for no gain. Re-embarkation was ordered, but this led to complete panic, with the loss of nine cannon and possibly three thousand prisoners. In 1784, a line of Algerine warships prevented the Spaniards from coming ashore. Algiers was able to send privateers to attack the shores of the northern Mediterranean. In contrast, in 1792, the Spaniards evacuated Oran, their last base in what, with French conquest from 1830, became Algeria.

SOCIAL AND CULTURAL CONTEXTS

After the War of the Spanish Succession, there was recovery and growth, indeed more rapidly than in the 1940s after the Spanish Civil War. Most clearly, this was growth in population. At the same time, in this as in much else in Spanish history, it was variety that was to the fore. Thus, while population growth accelerated after 1770, most of the eighteenth-century increase occurred in peripheral and coastal provinces, such as Valencia, rather than in the poorer agricultural central regions of the Meseta, which continued to yield only a limited surplus of food.

Disease was a major issue. Furthermore, the range of diseases increased. In 1730, a Spanish squadron from the West Indies brought to Cádiz the first European cases of yellow fever. Yet, there was also progress. From 1771, the Basque Society of Friends of the Country campaigned in favour of inoculation against smallpox. Disease, moreover, did not prevent the population from rising in the eighteenth century, although it was hit in the 1790s. In addition, in years of European-wide subsistence crises linked to disease and harvest difficulties, notably 1740–2 and 1816, Spain was able to avoid serious mortality peaks.

At the same time, the general rise in population forced younger sons and poorer sharecroppers to abandon their hopes of acquiring independent peasant status. As in southern Italy, the general rise in population led to an increase in the number of day labourers, who were the most economically vulnerable section of the workforce, and notably an increase in Catalonia, Majorca and southern Spain. Growing rural pauperisation was another consequence of the rise in population. The rise led, as in southern Italy, to a greater concentration on the production of cereals, especially wheat, at a time when, in general, insufficient attention was devoted to the raising of animals, the principal source of manure. As a result, agricultural productivity was hit further. The problems of population growth were widespread: in the towns, unemployment and begging became more serious problems as people migrated from rural poverty. Visitors to Spanish cities frequently commented on the number of beggars. This particularly offended northern Europeans.

The harshness of life extended to a sense of conflict with other beasts, both real, notably wolves, and imaginary. The Prado holds a vivid painting of *Andromeda and the Monster* by Juan Antonio de Frías y Escalante (1630–70). Near Zaragoza in

1718, there were reports of an ox-sized beast with a head like a wolf, a long tail and three pointed horns. Witches and other diabolical agents were also part of a hostile world that was particularly threatening in the dark, and that can be seen in Goya's spectral later works.

Belief in God, indeed, was an important aspect of the search for stability in an essentially unstable and threatening world. Manuals of piety, religious tracts and sermons that stressed the transitory nature of life on Earth and the spiritual dangers facing the rich were very popular and frequently reprinted. Reliquaries, prayers, processions and bell-ringing were all part of the attempt to win divine support.

The hostile environment was understood in terms of retribution, with the possibility of gaining remission by good actions, either in terms of religious service or by satisfying the demands of the occult and spirit world. The world of God and the world of the Devil were in conflict, as described in the fifth century in St Augustine's *City of God*, whose triumphs were the subject of paintings by Claudio Coello (1642–93) and Miguel Meléndez (1679–1734) that are held at the Prado. This conflict very much encouraged the active church-building and religious observance of the period.

Despite the confidence of some in the possibility of human progress, the majority of the population lived in a precarious fashion, fearful of the future and possessing only limited aspirations. This popular conservatism was to play a major part in hindering government plans for change, and could also ensure that national politics appeared very marginal. Instead, for most, politics was really the world of the local community.

AGRICULTURE

Agriculture was the most significant part of the economy, and the harvest the key factor in individual and collective fortunes. Low productivity was a major problem, one that put pressure on living standards. Internal colonisation was a response: the extension of the cultivated area, whether achieved through the digging of irrigation ditches, the clearing of trees or the removal of stones, was essentially the product of labour-intensive methods and helped lead to higher production, though not to greater productivity per farmed hectare.

In contrast, Catalonia was an area of particular agricultural improvement. Tenurial practice was a key element as much useful land there was owned by the cultivators, and they benefited directly from raised productivity. Thus, continuity among the farming population, in the shape of the inheritance of family farms, encouraged agricultural improvement in Catalonia, a situation that contrasted with the position in the large estates that covered much of Spain. In Catalonia, as in England and the Low Countries, the spread of fodder crops, such as clover, coleseed and turnips, helped to eliminate fallow and to increase the capacity of the rural economy to rear more animals. They were sources of crucial manure and of valuable capital, for, as had been the case for centuries, animals were the most significant 'cash crop' in the economy. The spread of convertible or 'up and down' husbandry, in which land alternated between pasture and arable, resulted in increased yields when the land was cultivated and improved grass at other times. Catalonia also produced wine and brandy.

In a country where economic reform proved far easier to propose than to implement, however, it was not surprising that much agriculture remained traditional. This was notably so as the sheep of the Mesta set off in the autumn on their march from their open summer grazing lands in central Spain to the lowlands. This was the largest animal migration of animals in Europe and one that had perplexed Don Quixote. Moreover, much agriculture remained at a subsistence level, the diffusion of agrarian improvements was limited, and areas of potential demand and supply were often poorly integrated. There were multiple structural problems. For example, there was generally a lack of adequate animal stock, which meant gruelling human labour. Weak animals pulled poorly constructed ploughs, producing an inadequate seedbed. Weeds had to be pulled out by hand. As agricultural production failed to keep pace with demand, food prices increased and malnutrition became widespread. These were scarcely the themes of agricultural scenes in paintings such as the harvesting attractively depicted in *Allegory of Summer* by Mariano Salvador Maella (1739–1819) held in the Prado in Madrid. Fishing also involved much hard manual work. At the same time, the important whaling and cod industries on the Biscayan coast help to explain the prosperity of ports such as Bilbao.

INDUSTRY

The market for craftsmen's services and for industrial goods was limited by the money spent on food. Moreover, most industry was not mechanised to any significant extent. Products were generally for a local market, and the capacity for innovation was limited. Industrial units were usually very small, with scant specialisation, either in machinery or in labour. There was a general disinclination to innovate. Spain was far from matching England in using steam power, and did not follow the attempts in that direction found, for example, in France. Spain lacked good coal sources, which limited the use of steam power.

Spanish industry was hampered by a weak domestic market, inadequate capital, poor communications, backward techniques and active foreign competition, for example from French exporters of cotton cloth to Spain and to the Spanish Empire. The government acted largely only in order to limit foreign products. Thus, in 1719, it was decreed that only Spanish cloth should be used for military uniforms, while, in 1757, the import of Genoese paper and silk products was prohibited. A depression in the silk-stocking industry in Nîmes in southern France in 1786 was blamed on a Spanish import ban. Free trade was scarcely to the fore. Gerónimo de Uztáriz, the author of *The Theory and Practice of Commerce and Maritime Affairs* (Madrid, 1724), was an admirer of Louis XIV's Minister of the Marine, Jean-Baptiste Colbert, who had supported state activity, and he emphasised the need to use the government's power in order to help Spain catch up in the race for economic growth. He saw overseas trade as the key to development.

Moreover, Pedro Rodríguez, Count of Campomanes (1723–1802), a lawyer and economist born in Asturias, actively pressed for state support for industrial activity in the 1770s, and was President of the Council of Castile from 1783 to 1791. He backed the Economic Societies of Friends of the Country.

Although many of Campomanes's schemes failed, the last decades of the century witnessed the spread of the putting-out system with some industrial processes carried out in workmen's cottages, as well as the emergence of new types of industrial production relying upon wage labourers. As yet, however, technological transformation was selective, change slow, and there was no Industrial Revolution, whether based on steam power, factories or other factors. Yet Catalan calicos, known as indianas, found an important market in the New World. Moreover, Spain played a pioneering role in producing cigarettes and had impressive state tobacco factories, notably that in Seville, which can now be walked through as it is part of the university.

INFRASTRUCTURE

So too with transport. There was both limited development and a sporadic emphasis on change. Poor communications greatly magnified the impact of distance and imposed serious burdens on the economy. Indeed, concern about the situation led to plans for improvement. Philip V (r. 1700–46) began a star of wagon roads radiating from Madrid to the various coasts of Spain. These roads were designed to foster political centralisation as well as to bring economic benefits. The linkage of politics and economics was a frequent feature of policy, and one very much seen today.

Philip's policies helped encourage a degree of market integration, a process that had already begun in the late seventeenth century.

In order to increase industrial activity in central Spain, the government of Charles III (r. 1759–88) planned a series of canals to link this region to the sea, and thus to overcome the centrifugal effects of geography upon the economy. The canal of Aragón, built in the 1780s alongside the River Ebro, brought activity to the upper Ebro valley. On balance, however, communications remained poor and acted as an economic drag, and certainly so as compared to the situation in France and Britain. Spain was more similar to southern Italy.

The financial infrastructure was also weak. The government's project of 1749 to establish a general bank that could deal in letters of exchange with all of Europe ran into problems, as the merchants were willing to borrow money from it but not to provide money in return for its letters of exchange. This exacerbated the general problem of the export of Spanish coinage. A negative trade balance with France led to French towns like Toulouse becoming important centres for dealing in Spanish coin. More positively, Tomás López de Vargas Machuca, Geographer of the Royal Domain from 1770, transformed the mapping of Spain.

NOBILITY

Spain remained a society dominated by the aristocracy, although the majority of the nobility continued to be poor. Measures taken to restrict their numbers led to a fall in the size of the nobility: from 722,000 in 1768 to 400,000 (4 per cent of the population) in 1797. In 1773, poor *hidalgos* were ordered to take up manual work. This did not, however, entail any attack upon the existence of the nobility. With the exception of Ferdinand VI (r. 1746–59), the kings were prepared to grant a significant number of promotions to the senior ranks of the aristocracy, but at the same time very few new *hidalgos* were created. The Asturian writer and official Gaspar Melchor de Jovellanos (1744–1811), author of the

Report on the Agrarian Law (1795), pressed for agrarian reform, notably the splitting up of large estates, and the secularisation of Church holdings, and hoped that the nobility would become a bureaucratic élite. The last was also the goal of Peter the Great in Russia.

The Spanish nobles, however, saw no reason why they should change their destined role. Noble privileges remained strong. Seigneurial justice was not abolished, as it was in Portugal in 1790. Yet, the burden of feudalism was uneven. Whereas feudal conditions for serfs were particularly bad in Valencia, they were quite progressive in some other areas.

Towns

In contrast, there could be attacks on the powers and privileges of towns. After the successful siege of Barcelona, Philip V confiscated all the revenues of the city and limited its privileges, an issue that is recalled to the present by Catalan separatists. More generally for Spanish towns, his success in the War of the Spanish Succession led to the diminution of municipal autonomy by the nomination of a *corregidor*, an official representing royal authority. In 1766, the government reacted firmly when the élite of Lorca, which controlled many municipal offices and was opposed to the royal reforms being implemented by the governor, took advantage of, and exacerbated, popular concern over the price of grain in order to drive out the governor and seize power.

Towns could be a major problem for the countryside as they pursued their efforts at economic control over their hinterlands. In 1761, the Jesuit Pedro de Calatayud attacked the merchants of Bilbao for exploiting the small rural sheep-owners in the purchase of wool for export and for forcing them into usurious contracts. Indeed, he criticised merchants in general.

There was considerable resistance across society to governmental attempts to introduce change. In 1783, Charles III issued an edict declaring artisans fit for municipal office and their trades 'honest and honourable'. This alteration of the traditional hierarchy of honour had little effect and municipal governments remained dominated by landowners. That of the town of Horche resisted royal orders to elect manufacturers to office from 1781 to 1794.

There was less urban disorder in the eighteenth century than in the sixteenth, seventeenth, nineteenth or twentieth. Nevertheless, bread riots in Madrid in 1766 were exploited by courtiers keen to overthrow reforming ministers.

Social Issues

The rising population exacerbated social problems. Workhouses to confine beggars and vagabonds proliferated after 1750. They were paid for out of endowed revenues held by religious confraternities and by 1798 had been founded in twenty-five towns. There were never enough workhouses, however, and most lacked the financial resources necessary to implement projects for helping the poor.

Charles III was keen on solutions. In 1775, with the ad hoc *leva* (military draft), he instituted compulsory military service for men between seventeen and twenty-six who lived in idleness: those caught sleeping in the streets, young men admonished by their parents for idleness and artisans who abandoned their work. There were regional exemptions from conscription in Catalonia and the Basque provinces, however, where local militia operated instead. At the same time, other decrees were issued against gypsies, itinerant salesmen and all who lacked visible means of support. In 1774, Charles ordered the creation of schools in Galicia and Asturias to teach the population how to make linen at home. In 1786, a general decree stipulated the establishment of spinning schools in all the towns and villages of the kingdom. There was not as yet a real engagement with labour-saving machinery.

RELIGION

Religious identity remained crucial. Following the capture of Oran in 1732, the British envoy reported: 'there is scarce a Spaniard who does not think himself half way to his salvation by the merits of this conquest' from the Muslims.

The Inquisition was directed against Protestants, alleged Jews and crypto-Muslims. In Granada in the 1720s, 250 people were sentenced by the Inquisition for the last. Nevertheless, Philip V did not assist the Inquisition in its financial difficulties, and the institution appeared increasingly redundant from the mid-century.

The Church remained a powerful presence. In Castile, it owned about one-seventh of the grazing and farmland, and the rise in agricultural prices and rents helped to keep clerical wealth buoyant. There was little in the way of the growing toleration and de-Christianisation perceived in France. Spain followed Portugal and France, however, and in 1767 expelled the Jesuits, who were accused of responsibility for rioting in Madrid the previous year.

There was a long tradition of clerics in senior government posts. Nine of the twelve presidents of the Council of Castile in 1700–51 were clerics, while both Aragón and Catalonia had clerical viceroys in the 1700s. Nevertheless, governmental control over the Church increased. The concordat (agreement) of 1753 with Pope Benedict XIV gave Ferdinand VI more control over the Church. Charles III subjected the regular (monastic) clergy to his authority, creating Spanish congregations, as for the Carthusians in 1783. Attempts were made to reduce the number of friars. Monks and friars were particularly important in Spain because of the archaic nature of the parochial structure and the number of parishes that lacked incumbents.

There was talk of secularised education and, in 1766, Campomanes proposed a general reform of the universities. In combination with reforms within the university, a new plan of studies was issued for Salamanca in 1771 and the government came to intervene directly in many issues of internal governance.

Although the Council of Trent (1545–63) had required every bishop to establish a seminary, the situation in Spain was inadequate. Under reforms ordered by Charles III in 1766, however, new ones were founded and existing ones improved, and, whereas there were twenty-eight seminaries in 1747, there were another eighteen fifty years later.

In 1765, the Swedish envoy, Count Gustaf Philip Creutz, observed, 'The Pyrenees in particular are the barriers to the enlightened world. Since I have been here [1763] it has seemed to me that the people are ten centuries behind.' This jaundiced view scarcely did credit to the efforts of Charles III. Moreover, the succeeding decades were to see a growth in secular intellectual activity associated with officials such as Campomanes and Jovellanos. Nevertheless, Spain lacked the sophisticated reading public and density of unofficial cultural institutions seen in France. Moreover, the Spanish Church was far more hostile to new ideas than many French and German clerics. Some of the leading Spanish preachers attacked these ideas bitterly.

The Church had much influence in cultural matters. The Inquisition sought actively to prevent the circulation of corrupting works, especially French books. Moreover, the clergy was able to restrict the spread of theatre outside Madrid, plays being banned in Granada in 1706 and Seville in 1731, and has been blamed for mid-century restrictions, which included actresses being forbidden to wear trousers.

The Church was also a major patron of the arts. The admission piece by Francisco Goya (1746–1828) for the Real Academia de Bellas Artes de San Fernando was *Christ Crucified* (1780). It is now held in the Prado, and is an impressive work, although, as an instructive instance of modern preferences, it does not engage the interest shown for his non-religious works. Religious themes were more generally significant. For example, religious literature remained important for Spanish presses. Campomanes sought to use the press to diffuse new writings, particularly advances in economics, science and technology, but these never enjoyed a wide circulation, the general reading public at all social levels preferring to read almanacs.

FRANCISCO DE GOYA (1746–1828)

Goya was a highly active painter, whose styles and subjects changed greatly from the late Rococo of the 1760s to the Romanticism of the early nineteenth century, and then on to the dark side of his later paintings. The son of a master gilder, Goya was educated in Zaragoza and worked, from 1774 until 1792, in Madrid painting large oil canvasses for tapestries for the royal palaces. From the 1780s, Goya was successful as a portrait painter and in 1786 was appointed *Pintor del Rey* (painter of the king). His range widened from the mid-1790s, with social commentary and caricatures becoming more common, alongside scenes of witchcraft and madness. At the same time, religious projects continued, as did portraits. In 1814, in part in order to justify his position during the French occupation, Goya painted two great works on the rising of May 1808, both now held in the Prado. His eighty-two *Disasters of War* prints (1810– 20) were a product of the Peninsular War. He left Spain in 1824 in response to the suppression of constitutionalism the previous year and died in Bordeaux. A painter of great energy and innovation, many of Goya's works can readily be seen in the Prado, although there are others elsewhere, as in the Fine Arts Museum in Santander. The path from being an Old Master to a forbear of Modernism makes him particularly interesting.

Scientific advances were resisted. Diego de Torres Villarroel (1694–1770), Professor of Mathematics at Salamanca from 1726, was criticised in 1770 by Campomanes for 'believing that his duties had been fulfilled in writing almanacs and prognostications'. He had done so since 1719 and was interested in magic and the supernatural, and a defender of the value of astrology. Torres applied his mathematical and astronomical knowledge to his almanacs, but he also used them to refute the teaching of other sciences, denying the value of modern medicine in favour of the traditional theory of humans being composed of the four humours.

In contrast, Gaspar Casal (1679–1759), a doctor, introduced into Spain the modern, empirical, symptomatic concept of illness. He used this method to describe the symptoms of pellagra and to differentiate it from scabies and leprosy. Moreover, founded in Madrid in 1734, the Academy of Medicine sought to study medicine and surgery from observation and experience. Charles III founded a Royal Botanical Garden in Madrid. He also sent scientific expeditions to Spanish America from 1777 in order to discover plants with medicinal and economic properties. This was part of a sustained Spanish effort to understand and use the natural products of its empire.

Culture

Baroque themes remained very important, and notably in the early decades of the century. The Andalusian Baroque left many buildings with undulating facades. Baroque facades, with their wreathed columns, can also be seen elsewhere, for example the Santa María church in Valencia. Italian architects played a prominent role, as with Felipe Juvara's Neoclassical royal palace in Madrid, which replaced the Habsburg one that burned down in 1734. Gardens, such as that at the Palace of La Granja, also designed for Philip V, also showed Baroque influences.

In the second half of the century, as elsewhere in Europe,

the Neoclassical style became more significant, with works by Ventura Rodríguez, notably the facade of Pamplona cathedral, and by Juan de Villanueva, and a marked Italian influence in painting. Again, as elsewhere in Europe, international styles were presented in distinctive national fashions.

SPANISH AMERICA

Frequent wars in the eighteenth century failed to bring Spain much benefit, but Spain retained most of its empire, and indeed profited from its consolidation. The empire brought economic gains. Cacao, tobacco, cotton, coffee, sugar and indigo were exported from Venezuela, hides from the Plate (Plata) estuary, tobacco, sugar and hides from Cuba, and sugar, dyestuffs, cacao and, in particular, silver from Mexico, where the mines had very harsh working conditions. In 1717, Cádiz was established as the monopoly port for all trade to and from the New World.

In addition, trading networks within Latin America developed, notably of food and textiles, which encouraged economic specialisation. This development, however, challenged the dominance of exports to Spain. The dynamism of the Latin American economy had an impact on social structures, not least on the rise of regional élites that were to play a major role in winning independence.

At the same time, as in Spain, and elsewhere in the world, there were powerful barriers to economic development. These included the limited disposable income of the bulk of the population, the nature of environmental obstacles, not least barriers to easy communications, and an inherent conservatism that interacted with a limited traction within society for reform. Rivers were generally without bridges, and their fords and ferries were vulnerable to spring spate.

From the sixteenth century, the arrival of European migrants and of African slaves, combined with the impact of disease on the Native population, had caused a fall in the relative size of the latter. In central Mexico, the Native percentage in 1646 was 87.2, while Spaniards, whether born in Mexico or immigrants, amounted to 8 per cent, *mestizos* (mixed race) 1.1 and *pardos* (wholly or partly black) 3.7. Compared to the 1560s, this represented a rise in the percentage of every category, especially the *mestizos*, bar the Natives. This trend continued, so that in the mid-1740s the respective percentages were 74 and then about 9 each. As for the whole of Mexico, the population in 1810 has been estimated at about 6,121,000: 3,676,000 Natives, 1,107,000 Spaniards, 704,000 *mestizos* and 634,000 *pardos*. For Spanish America as a whole in 1800, there are estimates of a total population of 16.9 million: 7.5 million Natives, 6.1 million *mestizos* or *pardos*, and 3.3 million Spaniards. Such figures are open to qualification, not simply in terms of counting numbers but also of categorisation, as it is important to give due weight to the extent and impact of mixed unions. Thus, many listed as Spaniards contained some Native blood. The same was true of the *pardos*.

As with Spain, notably in *c.* 1000–1609, the ethnic composition of the colonial population varied greatly, and this was important in creating the character and culture of specific colonies and possessions. For example, there was a higher percentage of Spaniards in central Mexico and Peru than in Central America or New Granada (modern Colombia and Ecuador). The dynamic nature of this ethnic composition could have an impact on social structures and attitudes. Appearance helped to determine responses to those of mixed blood, a category that increased, and in some colonies greatly so. Individuals who looked European were more likely to receive favourable treatment than those who looked African or Native. This has been referred to as a pigmentocracy, and there were terms for the products of particular unions – for example, a *castizo* was the child of a Spaniard and a *mestiza* (Spaniard and Native).

The longstanding clash between *peninsulares* (Natives of Spain) and *creoles* (Spaniards born in America) was exacerbated by Charles III's reforms, which were largely intended to increase central control, security and revenue. These reforms generally ignored *creole* aspirations, both economic and political, and senior officials were mostly *peninsulares*. Administrative reorganisation led to the creation of new territorial units. The viceroyalties of New Granada and the Río de la Plata were established in 1739 and 1776 respectively, and based in Bogotá and Buenos Aires. The first increased control over north-western South America, which could not be effectively governed from the distant centres of Mexico City and Lima. The second was a reflection of the growing economic importance of the River Plate/Plata region, which, from 1778, was allowed to trade directly with Spain, and also a response to Portuguese expansionism from Brazil. Portugal and Spain were engaged in episodic but longstanding conflict in the region as a result.

Although the Latin American Wars of Independence were largely due to the Napoleonic subjugation of Spain in 1808, separatist feeling was already developing in eighteenth-century Spanish America. This was not the case, however, with the Philippines. Spanish settlement there was far less, a contrast that owed much to climate, the absence of bullion and an imperial focus, instead, on the Americas.

SAILING THE PACIFIC

Spanish exploration in the Pacific revived in the late eighteenth century after over a hundred years of limited activity. The Spaniards were worried about British and Russian activity on the north-west coast of North America and the earlier policy of attempting to restrict information could no longer suffice. In 1790, in the Nootka Sound Crisis, Britain and Spain came close to war over the Spanish attempt to enforce claims to a monopoly of trade on this coast. France initially backed Spain but, affected by the developing crisis of the French Revolution, pulled back, which led Spain to reach a settlement with Britain. Exploration also reflected the determination of Charles III to develop his empire. The surveying voyage of Bruno de Hezeta in 1775 led to the sighting of the mouth of the Columbia River, but an attempt in the 1790s to establish a settlement there and to penetrate upriver was thwarted by the difficulty of the river channel and the hostile attitude of the Natives. Other expeditions in the early 1790s showed that there was no navigable north-west passage from the Atlantic to the Pacific to the north of America.

The more wide-ranging voyages of Alejandro Malaspina in 1782–4 and 1790–3 across, and around, the Pacific reflected the energy of the Spanish exploration that was cut short by the French Revolutionary Wars. He died in 1810, his expeditions largely forgotten. Also in the 1770s, there had been extensive exploration of what is now Arizona, Colorado and Utah by Spanish friars.

CHAPTER EIGHT

Revolutionary Crises, 1793–1824

When Charles III died in 1788 to be succeeded by his son, Charles IV (r. 1788–1808), there was no suggestion that the next four decades were to see a scale of transformation for Spain not matched since the 710s.

The Bourbon order and the unchallenged place of the Church were to be swept aside by war, which very much defined Spanish history anew. Yet again, Spain was to become the victim of invasion. This was not as it had first appeared. In 1793, Spain had joined a powerful coalition of most of Europe against Revolutionary France. This coalition, however, did not go well, either for Spain or for any of its allies. Spain initially invaded Roussillon, winning a series of victories, although failing to capture Perpignan. In turn, in 1794, the French drove the Spaniards from Roussillon and invaded Catalonia, winning the battle of the Black Mountain. The French pushed on to besiege Roses, which fell in 1795. In the western Pyrenees, the French were also successful from 1794, capturing San Sebastián (1794) and Bilbao (1795). Food was seized by the French and factories destroyed. The Spanish government was worried that the Basque region might transfer its allegiance to France in return for respect for its traditional laws and Catholic faith. Negotiations with the French on this basis were indeed held in 1794. Spain obtained terms by the Peace of Basle (1795), and then joined France against Britain via the Treaty of San Ildefonso (1796).

This, however, exposed Spain and its empire to the strength of the British navy. In 1797, the Spanish fleet was defeated at the battle of Cape Saint Vincent, a battle in which Nelson distinguished himself, while Trinidad was lost to a British attack. The blockade of transatlantic trade hit government finances hard, leading to increased debt and borrowing. Peace with Britain in 1802 led to Trinidad being ceded to Britain, and was all too brief. It was followed by the resumption in 1804 of the disastrous war, and, in particular, defeat of a Franco-Spanish fleet at Trafalgar (1805), although in 1807 a British attack on Buenos Aires was routed.

Within Spain, poor harvests, notably in 1803–4, led to higher food prices, as well as malnutrition and rioting. In 1807, Spain joined France in successfully invading Britain's ally Portugal. Rifts within the royal family – played out in public and through publications – between Charles IV and his son Ferdinand, who enjoyed much support among the higher nobility and the Church, culminated in 1808 in the 'Tumult of Aranjuez', a coup at Court that replaced the unpopular Charles and his loathed first minister Manuel Godoy, with Ferdinand, who became Ferdinand VII. Napoleon, however, obliged both Charles and Ferdinand to meet him at Bayonne where, under pressure, they had to abdicate in favour of himself. He made his brother, Joseph Bonaparte, Joseph I of Spain (r. 1808–13). The response was rebellion in the name of Ferdinand, notably in Madrid, and what is now known as the War of Independence began.

This rebellion drew on a range of beliefs and tendencies, from liberalism to conservatism, but there was a common sense of rejection of French sway. Indeed, Spanish national identity was in large part to be defined in response to France. The juntas that took power in the provinces directed popular anger at the French, which provided a way to lessen political and social tension. This made it easier to recruit support, and especially so when not too much needed to be done.

The insurgents against France were neither bandits questing for booty nor patriots simply fighting for Crown, Church and country, although both elements played an important role.

Instead, as in Navarre, they were also landowning peasants fighting to protect both their interests and a society that did so. The abolition of Navarre's privileges by the French under Napoleon, their efforts to reform society and their rapacity all aroused great hostility, which was very much forced upon Spain by the French occupiers. At the same time, as so often, the geographical texture of Spanish politics was more finely grained. In northern Navarre, there were more landowning peasants, but in the south of the province there were more day labourers and less harmonious social relations as well as more criticism of the Church. This ensured that opposition to Napoleon in Navarre was stronger in the north.

Moreover, the chronological dimension was significant. Criticism of the war effort grew when the conflict came to involve effort and became difficult. Many did not wish to fight, and desertion rose markedly. This provided a basis for banditry and guerrilla activity. Indeed, the turmoil of the period, a turmoil that included a partial breaking down of political and social structures, was more to the fore than a struggle simply against France. On the other hand, by reflecting and exacerbating a breakdown of governance, this turmoil ensured that the new order was to be constrained by the need to enforce its presence. This was difficult, while control proved elusive.

Initially, the French were defeated on 16–19 July 1808 at Bailén, with nearly eighteen thousand troops surrendering to Spanish forces that had converged on the exposed and badly commanded French army in Andalusia. This was the first defeat of a Napoleonic army in the field. The French forces in Spain then retreated to the Ebro.

In November, however, Napoleon arrived with a large force, and the French regained Madrid, while, in December, the siege of the French garrison in Barcelona was raised. The Supreme Central and Governing Junta, the head of the government rejecting French rule, retreated first to Seville and then to Cádiz, where it could be supported by British warships. The British force in Spain retreated to Corunna from where it was evacuated.

SIR JOHN MOORE: HEROIC FAILURE

The Biscayan port that is most familiar today is Santander, the destination of ferries from Portsmouth and Plymouth in Britain. After that, it is Bilbao with its famous art gallery. In the nineteenth century, in contrast, it was Corunna, the scene of an epic withdrawal in 1809.

The previous autumn, the British army in Portugal under Sir John Moore was instructed to provide support to Spain's government, which was newly at war with France. Moore entered Spain on 11 November and reached Salamanca two days later. An absence of promised Spanish support led Moore to order a retreat, only for an urgent request for help to lead him rashly to decide to press on in order to strike at French lines of communication. A French cavalry force was defeated at Sahagún, but news of French strength encouraged Moore to decide to retreat. With Napoleon in Madrid, the French threat to his communications with Portugal led Moore to fall back towards the port of Corunna, in difficult wintery conditions and in the face of overwhelming French strength. Discipline collapsed in the leading divisions as the army retreated, but the well-trained rear maintained order and held off the pursuing French.

Napoleon abandoned the chase on 1 January 1809 and entrusted the pursuit to Marshal Nicolas Jean de Dieu Soult who caught up with the British at the embarkation port of Corunna. The British fought the French off on 16 January. Soult's army was little larger and the nature of the terrain limited his use of his cavalry. Moore stood on the defensive, anticipated Soult's moves, and handled his reserves ably in order to block them. The army was successfully evacuated the following day, but Moore had been killed in the battle, his death making him a hero. Charles Wolfe's poem on his burial, beginning 'Not a drum was heard', was a classic of the nineteenth-century anthology and school-room. Moore's tomb can be visited in Corunna.

Poorly armed, supplied and trained, Spanish armies and irregulars were repeatedly defeated by the French, notably at Ocaña in November 1809. This battle arose from a Spanish attempt to advance on Madrid. The smaller French force was under Marshal Soult although it was nominally led by King Joseph. The French won the cavalry action and benefited from superior artillery. The Spanish infantry then collapsed. The French had two thousand casualties, the Spaniards eighteen thousand, including fourteen thousand prisoners. The French were then able to invade Andalusia, a situation helped by their victory soon after at Alba de Tormes. Wellington felt badly let down by these defeats of Spanish forces. The French conquered Andalusia (except for Cádiz) in 1810, Extremadura in 1811, and Catalonia and Valencia in 1811–12. Much damage was inflicted. In 1812, the great Benedictine monastery at Montserrat in Catalonia was sacked.

Nevertheless, the burden on the French – in terms of garrisons and casualties – of operating against Spanish forces was considerable: the French casualties in Spain exceeded those from most of Napoleon's campaigns. The Spaniards were generally unsuccessful in formal conflict, and British generals could be critical of their organisation, but their regular and guerrilla operations denied the French control over the countryside and, in particular, greatly harmed their communications and logistics. Spanish amphibious attacks were a particular feature of their operations against French forces in 1810 and 1811. On a number of occasions, substantial expeditions were dispatched to various spots on the coast of Andalusia and then moved inland in order to attack the French. Thanks to Spanish resistance, the French were unable to concentrate their superior forces against Wellington. They would have been able to do so once they had knocked out the Spaniards, which would have been a distinct possibility but for Napoleon's invasion of Russia in 1812.

Wellington's Anglo-Portuguese forces in 1809–11 successfully defended Portugal from French attack, before invading Spain. In 1812, he finally took the two key Spanish border fortresses of Ciudad Rodrigo and Badajoz, each formidable positions, moving on to invade northern Spain, defeating the French at Salamanca, and occupying Madrid. British amphibious forces raided the Biscay coast. Nevertheless, Wellington then had to retire in the face of the concentration against him of larger French forces in the autumn of 1812.

THE BATTLE OF SALAMANCA, 1812

The best-preserved major Spanish battlefield is that among the hills around Arapiles, south of Salamanca, both because of ease of access and because the battlefield is relatively unchanged. The most helpful book for following the battle is Rory Muir's *Salamanca, 1812* (2001). Having captured Ciudad Rodrigo and Badajoz earlier in the year, Wellington invaded northern Spain with an Anglo-Portuguese-Spanish force, defeating the French in the battle of Salamanca on 22 July. Marshal Auguste Marmont's strung-out disposition allowed Wellington to defeat the French divisions in detail, i.e. separately. Noting that the French were overextended, Wellington rapidly and effectively switched from defence to attack and ably combined his infantry and cavalry in the destruction of the three French divisions, one ridden down by a British cavalry charge. The 52,000-strong allied army suffered 5,173 casualties, all bar six British or Portuguese: a Spanish division that was positioned to block French escape routes did not really see conflict. The French suffered 13,000 casualties, including 7,000 captured. Private William Wheeler of the 51st Regiment left a record of the difficulty of the conditions on the battlefield:

> Our support being required on the right of the line we now moved on in double quick time. This raised such a dust that together with the heat of the day we were almost suffocated. The want of water now began to be severely felt, those who had some in their canteens were as bad off as those that had none, for what with the heat of the sun and the shaking it got it was completely spoiled. Those who drank of it immediately threw it up. As we proceeded the fire increased. We were wet with sweat . . . and so great was the quantity of dust that settled on our faces and clothes that we scarce knew each other. In fact we more resembled an army of [chimney] sweeps or dustmen than any one thing I can conceive. Almost fagged to death we arrived at our position on the right of our line; in our front was a hill on which was posted the enemy's line. They welcomed us opening [up with] about 16 guns and several howitzers.

The battle led the French to abandon Andalusia.

In 1813, although a British amphibious force abandoned the siege of Tarragona on the advance of a French army, Wellington invaded Spain again, and Joseph Bonaparte fled Madrid in order to block any British advance on France. Joseph's army was weakened by the detachment of substantial forces to deal with guerrillas in Navarre and the Basque Country. With an Anglo-Portuguese-Spanish army, Wellington won a crushing victory at Vitoria (21 June), which is commemorated by a large monument in the city centre. The French had eight thousand casualties and all their artillery was captured or destroyed, while their baggage was seized, which yielded loot that included important paintings in Joseph's possession. Wellington pressed on to capture San Sebastián and Pamplona. Apart from a few fortresses, French rule in Spain was at an end. Joseph abdicated and returned to France. After the Napoleonic Wars he lived mostly in the United States from 1817 to 1832 before returning to Europe, dying in Florence in 1844.

While the conflict had continued, there was political change. Joseph sought to act as an Enlightened ruler, notably by abolishing monasticism and the Inquisition, but his cause was compromised by its dependence on the unpopular French army, while his prominent Freemasonry also angered Spanish opinion. In contrast, from 1810, Cádiz became the meeting place of the *cortes*, which was designed to represent the sovereignty of all Spaniards including those in the colonies. In 1812, the *cortes* promulgated a constitution that greatly restricted royal power, putting the citizenry first. In addition, seigneurial rights were to be abolished and there was to be free primary education.

This episode both constitutes the background to one of the great might-have-beens of Spanish history and is important to the developmental notion that the war saw the growth of a constitutionalism focused on a Spanish nation rather than provincial liberties. Moreover, this constitutionalism provided the background for judging the subsequent restored Bourbon system. At the same time, such an account underplays the role of the Church in opposing the allegedly godless, secular supporters of Joseph. Similarly, religion was important across Europe to the opposition to France.

Once war swept the French from Spain, the Treaty of Valençay between France and Ferdinand VII in December 1813 led to the restoration of the latter until his death in 1833. He had no wish to be a British-style constitutional monarch and, in 1814, rejected the *cortes* and its constitution. Liberals were purged and those who had served Joseph treated as outlaws. Like Charles IV, Ferdinand relied on the higher nobility and the Church.

EXPERIENCING FRENCH RULE

French rule was brutal, costly and destructive. Goya's canvases in the Prado are the most vivid reminder, but they are scarcely alone. The destruction and despoliation of churches are readily apparent in several in Seville and elsewhere, as in the monastery of Santa María de las Cuevas in Seville. Several paintings by Murillo in the chapel at the Hospital de la Caridad in Seville were looted by the French, but seven remain. In Barcelona, the French garrison maintained order in 1808 by shooting all suspects and confiscating the properties of the wealthy and the Church. Money was drained out of the local economy by seizures and forced contributions, and the black market thrived. Córdoba was stormed and plundered that year. The hard-fought 1808–9 French siege of Zaragoza led to the deaths of thousands of civilians. In Granada, the Alhambra was damaged by the French in 1812. More generally, Spain's economy, society, culture and politics were all put under great pressure; and lawlessness and corruption escalated. Risk and unpredictability made life unsettled, and thus challenged the acceptability as well as legitimacy of French rule.

SPANISH AMERICA

This rejection of constitutionalism by Ferdinand helped cause the breakdown of Spanish rule in Spanish America. Earlier, in response to the French takeover of Spain in 1808, there had been autonomy in Spanish America as, in 1809 and 1810, local juntas seized power in the name of Ferdinand VII, underlining, in response to Joseph I, the contractual nature of royal authority and popular support. This also enabled the local élites to enjoy the authority they sought. The societies over which they wished to preside were changing, demographically, economically and politically, and this made the past a more problematic reference point.

Once returned to control in Spain, Ferdinand sought to reimpose it in Spanish America, sending an army in 1815. This attempt was initially successful. Royal authority was restored and the autonomy movements suppressed, although not in the distant Plate (Plata) estuary.

Ferdinand's cause, however, faced many difficulties. The royalists in Latin America were badly divided, and their divisions interacted with contradictions within Spain's incoherent policies. Civil and military authorities clashed frequently, as did metropolitan and provincial administrations. Thus, in New Granada (now Colombia), the viceroy and the commander-in-chief were bitter rivals. Furthermore, financial shortages forced the royalist army to rely on the seizure of local supplies and on forced loans, which proved a heavy burden on the population and antagonised them from Spanish rule. The royalist forces sent from Spain were also hit hard by disease, especially yellow fever and dysentery, and were forced to recruit locally, leading to fresh political problems. New Granada had largely welcomed the royal army from Spain in 1815, but by 1819 there was widespread support for an independent Colombia.

Moreover, Spain did not possess any technological advantages akin to those enjoyed by the conquistadores in the early sixteenth century. The insurgents, for their part, were partly supplied by arms dealers in the United States. Spanish governments sent relatively few weapons to their troops in the Americas. Most of the weapons used by the royalists were acquired locally. If anything, the insurgents had a slight advantage in weaponry.

Nevertheless, the course of the conflict was not foreordained. As in other wars of liberation, the colonial power enjoyed more success than is frequently appreciated. This was true both of the degree of local support for the Spaniards and of conflict in the field. Victories at Huaqui (1811) and Sipe-Sipe (1815) led to Spanish reconquests of Upper Peru (Bolivia), and that of Rancagua (1814) led to the reconquest of Chile. In 1806 and 1812, the Spaniards suppressed rebellions in Venezuela led by Francisco de Miranda. The Spaniards were helped by the limited support enjoyed by the revolutionaries and by their lack of funds. Although there was revolutionary enthusiasm among the rebel officers, the same was not true of the bulk of the peasant conscripts, who were poorly paid, supplied and armed, as well as inadequately trained.

The conflict swayed back and forth. Simón Bolívar, who had fought under Miranda, escaped to New Granada, raised a volunteer force and invaded Venezuela in 1813. He won a number of battles, but the Venezuelan republic lacked widespread support, and its forces were short of funds and arms. Having fled to Jamaica, Bolívar returned again to Venezuela, but his expedition, mounted in 1816 from Haiti, where French colonial rule had ended in 1803–4, failed to win support and was abandoned. Another expedition was defeated in 1818.

The Spaniards, however, suffered from weaknesses in Spain and from the willingness of independence forces to travel great distances in order to affect the struggle elsewhere. Taking place over a far larger area (Mexico to Chile) than the War of American Independence, and lacking the military and political coherence of the latter (for there was no equivalent to the Continental Congress or the Continental Army), any description of the Latin American Wars of Independence risks becoming a confused account with rapid changes of fortune. Major mountain chains and the problems posed by disease, such as yellow fever on the eastern coast of Mexico, accentuated the difficulties of operations. As in the War of American Independence, there was no automatic success for the revolutionary forces, and they were not inherently better at combat than their opponents. Instead, both sides adapted to the issues and problems of conflict across a vast area in which it was difficult to fix success or, indeed, to arrange logistical support. These problems helped ensure the significance of local and regional dimensions. The result, as in Mexico, could be the fragmentation of the insurgency. The same was true of the Spanish army whose units engaged in counter-insurgency operations with little central supervision, while their commanders tried to build up local power bases. Logistical needs helped compromise the popularity of both sides, while the expropriation and looting involved in obtaining supplies inflicted much damage on society.

Meanwhile, the royalists were also badly hit by shifts in policy within Spain, shifts which alienated support in Latin America and indeed culminated in a civil war in Spain in 1823. At the same time, fighting ability and command skills, especially those of José de San Martín in Chile in 1817–18 and of Simón Bolívar in the more intractable struggle in northern South America and the Andean chain in 1813–25, were important in wearing down the resistance of the increasingly isolated royalist forces.

The international dimension was crucial. Indeed, rather than treating these independence struggles simply as a failure of European power, it is more accurate to regard them as an aspect of a shift in power within the West, namely the major expansion of Britain's informal empire. There had long been British interest in the commercial penetration of Latin America and in supporting its independence from Spain. British volunteers and diplomatic and naval support were important in the Wars of Independence, not least in dissuading possible French intervention on behalf of Spain. Once independent, the Latin American powers which, while colonies, had been excluded by the colonial powers from direct trade with Britain, developed close trading relations and became prime areas for British investment.

The ethnic dimension helped complicate the Latin American Wars of Independence. Largely supported by *mestizos* (mixed race people), the insurgencies were seen as a threat to *criollos*, who feared a race war, and this perception encouraged the *criollo* élites of Cuba, Mexico and Peru to side with Spain. As a result, the royalists were able to use local militias against the rebels. In turn, Bolívar executed prominent *mestizo* leaders, allegedly for advocating race war, but also to retain control of the struggle.

The royalists could win repeated successes, not least from using light cavalry columns. A new generation of active royalist officers from Spain, who had gained experience in insurgency conflict against the French, arrived in Latin America in the mid-1810s and helped the royalists devise new counter-insurgency techniques. In the Papantla region, near Veracruz in Mexico, which had rebelled in 1812, the royal reconquest of the towns by 1818 did not end the insurgency. Instead, it developed into a guerrilla war, with royalist garrisons in the towns unable to control rural hinterlands. In the summer of 1820, a change of approach under a new royalist commander, José Rincón, altered the tempo of the war. Whereas previously the rainy season had served as a break in campaigning, providing the rebels with an opportunity to recover, Rincón planned no such break. In a campaign against the rebel stronghold of Coyusquihui, he circled the area with forts and kept campaigning, which hit the rebels. However, the royalists were badly affected by disease. Both sides agreed to a settlement that year.

Despite royalist successes, notably in Venezuela in 1806, 1812, 1816 and 1818, in Bolivia in 1811 and 1815, in Chile in 1814 and in Mexico in 1815, it proved most difficult to bring the struggle to a close. Insurgents withdrew to more isolated regions from which resistance continued. The royalists failed to devise an effective strategy for reconciliation, and their emphasis on repression, including, in Venezuela, the forcible relocation of civilians into camps, proved counter-productive. Such relocation was also to be seen in Cuba in the 1890s. In Latin America, the ability of revolutionary commanders to exploit the failure of reconciliation and to persist in the face of adversity was crucial. Ultimately, the royalists were defeated in battle in Peru, a bastion of royalism, in

1824, that of Ayacucho on 9 December proving decisive. Antonio José de Sucre, with 5,780 troops, defeated the Viceroy, José de la Serna, and his 9,300 troops by repelling attacks before using his reserves of infantry and cavalry to break through and encircle part of the opposing force. The loss of many of the senior royalist commanders, including the captured Viceroy, in this battle left the royalists leaderless.

The situation was different in Mexico, where an insurrection in 1810 had been hit hard in 1811–12 and 1815, while the guerrilla war had nearly ended by 1820. The royalist effort, however, was weakened by the liberal constitutional revolution in Spain in 1820, rather as the British effort in North America was undermined by the change in the government in 1782. Viewed as an unwelcome development by *criollo* conservatives and by those who wielded power in Mexico, this revolution led to a declaration of independence. In 1821, Augustín de Iturbide, the leading general, searching for a solution based on consensus, agreed with the rebels on a declaration of independence that proved widely acceptable. Under great pressure elsewhere, Spain accepted the situation that year.

Spain had proved unable to control the dynamic of events. Alongside persistent resistance within Spanish America, Spain repeatedly suffered from the willingness of Britain, the leading naval power, to provide assistance to the rebels, notably in the form of trade and recognition. By the end of 1825, Spanish control of the mainland was at an end. The empire was reduced to islands: the Canaries, Cuba, Puerto Rico, the Philippines, the Marianas, the Caroline Islands and the island-like enclaves of Spanish Morocco.

THE CRISIS OF THE 1820S IN SPAIN

In Spain itself, the overhang of the French Revolutionary and Napoleonic Wars was exacerbated by the political, economic and fiscal crises linked to the loss of Spanish America. Ideological division was accompanied by conspiracies. Attempted coups by liberal military figures were defeated in Galicia in 1815 and Catalonia in 1817. A liberal revolution in 1820, however, in which the royal palace was surrounded, obliged Ferdinand VII in 1821 to accept the 1812 constitution. The conservatives rejected this and turned to violence, unsuccessfully mounting a coup in 1822, as well as encouraging a large-scale French military intervention in 1823.

In 1823, the opposing liberal Spanish army, short of supplies and unpaid, was affected by extensive desertion and retreated. Prefiguring the Civil War of 1936–9, the liberals were divided, while their anticlerical measures helped stir up popular antipathy, notably among the peasantry. Moreover, the liberal regime had become very unpopular in rural areas through its imposition of a cash economy, especially when it replaced tithes with cash payments that had to be calculated. Providing an opportunity for increasing financial demands on the peasantry, this measure contributed to the rapid collapse of the regime in 1823.

Although handicapped by poor logistics, the French needed to do little fighting. There was some resistance, notably in Catalonia where there were echoes of the Napoleonic Wars: Catalonia was conquered by IV Corps under Bon Adrien Jeannot de Moncey, who had been made a marshal by Napoleon. At the city of Barcelona, which was blockaded for several months, he found himself in conflict with Francisco Espoz y Mina, who had been a successful guerrilla leader in the Peninsular War, defeating French units in 1812. Francisco Ballesteros, who commanded the liberal resistance in Navarre and Aragón, had played a major role in operations against the French in Andalusia in 1810–1812.

The main French drive was on the capital, Madrid, which the army entered on 23 May, and then, via Córdoba, on Cádiz, to which the liberal *cortes* had fled. The city had been unsuccessfully besieged by the French during the Peninsular War, in part due to the role of the British navy. Now, in contrast, it was besieged by land and also blockaded by sea, and surrendered on 1 October. There was fighting elsewhere, but the French were successful and the opposing generals capitulated: Pablo Morillo in Galicia on 10 July and Ballesteros in Andalusia on 21 August.

In the aftermath of Ferdinand's return to absolute power, liberals were executed, imprisoned, purged or, like Ballesteros and Morillo, fled into exile. This, however, did not end the disorder. In 1827, the 'Revolt of the Aggrieved' in the Catalan mountains was directed against those who were seen as Ferdinand's evil advisers. Support came from purged officers, but the uprising was swiftly suppressed. Yet again, Catalonia served as the basis for opposition to Castile.

Exploring Spain

Attracted by the landscape, British travellers became more frequent. There was a shift toward a Romantic sensibility. In 1784, the new feeling made northern Spain attractive to Henry Read: 'the journey proved more agreeable than I expected. The country and mountains in Biscay are very romantic and the variety of views must ever be pleasing to a traveller.' Two years later, Joseph Townsend (1739–1816), a doctor as well as a vicar, rode on horseback from León to Oviedo, 'through the wildest and most romantic country which can be imagined, rendered tremendous by the rocks, and beautiful by the wood and water'. He went on to publish *A Journey through Spain in the years 1786 and 1787* (1791), which attracted armchair travellers.

Another traveller, Thomas Hardy (not the novelist), looked ahead in 1786 to another reason for tourism, writing from Málaga that poor health had led him 'to elope from one of our northern winters and to seek for summer on the shores of the Mediterranean . . . The climate of this southern coast is certainly the finest in Europe and I am surprised that it is never thought of for the invalids who are sent to shiver in the South of France or in Lisbon.' As a result of the British and French military commitments to Spain from 1808, it became far more familiar to outsiders and of greater interest to them.

EXPLAINING SPAIN

Joseph Blanco White (1775–1841), born José Blanco y Crespo, a Spaniard of Irish ancestry, was a Roman Catholic priest who went to England on entering the priesthood. Editing *El Español* (1810–14), a Spanish monthly published in London that supported the independence of Spanish America, he wrote *Letters from Spain* (1822), some of which had previously been published in the *New Monthly Magazine*. This work contributed to the negative portrayal of Spain. The preface referred to 'Spanish bigotry' and 'the canker which, fostered by religion, feeds on the root of her political improvements'. More positively, in the book there was guidance to public manners. For example:

> The custom of sleeping after dinner, called *siesta*, is universal in summer, especially in Andalusia, where the intensiveness of the heat produces languor and drowsiness. In winter, taking a walk, just after rising from table, is very prevalent. Many gentlemen, previously to their afternoon walk, resort to the coffee-houses, which now begin to be in fashion.
>
> Almost every considerable town of Spain is provided with a public walk, where the better classes assemble in the afternoon ...
>
> Breakfast is not a regular family meal. It generally consists of chocolate, and buttered toast, or muffins, called *molletes*. Irish salt-butter is very much in use; as the heat of the climate does not allow the luxuries of the dairy, except in the mountainous tracts of the north.

CHAPTER NINE

Division and Development, 1825–98

To most outsiders, Spanish history in the nineteenth century is particularly obscure and apparently inconsequential, and more especially so between the mid-1820s and 1898. The Carlist Wars are complex, the political narrative lacks consequence and the general account is one of failure, more especially failure to match the economic growth, social transformation, political development and international consequence of many other European states. That, however, is less than the complete picture. Nor is it one that captures the significance of the period for what came after. Indeed, alongside continuities with earlier years, notably with the ideological divisions of liberals and conservatives, 1825–98 had significant relevance to what was to follow. The reach of the nineteenth century certainly extended to the Civil War of 1936–9 and into the Franco years (1939–75).

Socio-Economic Change

Political strife was contextualised by socio-economic change. Although Spain scarcely saw the extent or rate of economic development and social change witnessed by France, let alone Britain and Germany, that which did occur was significant. First, there were far more Spanish people, and that despite food shortages, disease and large-scale emigration. The population rose from about 11 million in 1830 to 23.5 million by 1930. This was due to changes along the age-profile. While rates of infant mortality fell, average life expectancy rose. As a result, alongside more young people, the average Spaniard was older.

Feeding this population was a major challenge, not least

because of the longstanding problems of poor soil and drought, the lack of countervailing investment and the competition coming from the fresher soils of the New World, the wheat exports of which were eased by railways, steamships and investment. The high tariffs on wheat imports introduced in 1891 benefited landowners but hit urban consumers, which was why such tariffs were opposed in Britain. Landownership was concentrated in the hands of traditional landowners, with their well-nigh feudal control, and those of upwardly mobile bourgeoisie. In contrast, agricultural day labourers did much of the work and received little of the benefit. Indeed, they suffered from higher food prices.

INDUSTRIAL REVOLUTION, BELATEDLY

Industrial change was more transformative, although it was overshadowed by the continued dominance of the economy by agriculture. Key areas of change included textiles, metallurgy, mineral production and railways. Steam-powered textile manufacturing was used in Catalonia to ensure significant growth from the 1830s, and that growth produced employment, capital available for investment, and an important industrial world of both labour and capital. So also with metallurgy in the Basque provinces, notably Vizcaya. Iron there was the basis of steel and shipbuilding. Elsewhere in Spain, there was a major growth in mineral production, particularly of copper, mercury and zinc. Foreign capital played an important role, as it also did in railway construction that developed rapidly after the Railway Act of 1855. Railways were a symbol and reality of integration and convergence. Major stations were dramatic buildings, as in Madrid. Railways encouraged a more joined-up economy.

Industrial output, foreign trade and real per capita income all rose. At the same time, the figures did not compare well with Britain, France and Germany. In part this was due to a shortage of investment capital, in part to a relatively depressed domestic market and in part, probably, to the costs imposed by domestic political instability. This instability was not solely a consequence of economic growth, but the growth played a role, not least by exacerbating contrasts between the centre, where growth was limited and emigration significant, and the more dynamic periphery. Catalonia was the region with most factories. In Madrid, the emphasis was on workshops. Resources were also highly significant, notably a relative lack of coal. In 1905, Spanish coal production was 3,202,000 tons compared to 21,775,280 in Belgium and 236,128,936 in Britain.

The social changes linked to economic growth, more specifically industrialisation, had political consequences. Trade union consciousness grew. Migration from the countryside encouraged urbanisation, notably in Madrid. However, the lack of adequate housing meant that shanty settlements developed. Nevertheless, in 1900, only 21 per cent of the population lived in towns with over twenty thousand people, a percentage well below France and, even more, Britain. As a result, bourgeois political culture was weaker in Spain than in the other two states.

POLITICAL STRIFE

A reaction against economic, social and political change helped fire up the Carlists, the conservative faction so called because they supported the claims of Carlos, the second son of Charles IV and formerly the heir presumptive, after the death of Carlos's brother Ferdinand VII in 1833. Their strongholds were the rural areas of the north, and the cultural dynamic was provided by a committed Catholicism. In contrast, Ferdinand VII's widow, María Cristina, the regent for their infant daughter and heir, Isabella II (r. 1833–68), turned to the *Moderados* (Moderates), liberal élitists who were willing, in the Royal Statute of 1834, to shelve aspects of the 1812 constitution, including universal male suffrage and the unrestricted authority of the *cortes*. The Inquisition was suppressed. In 1833, on the model of the French departments, and in order to end the old kingdoms, Spain was divided into provinces. In practice, each medieval kingdom was subdivided into provinces, each around the city from which it took its name.

This was constitutional liberalism, but not enough to satisfy the *Progresistas* (Progressives). Based on the middle class, they pushed through the sale of ecclesiastical landed property in 1836, although most was bought not by small landowners but, as with the sale of common land, by the already wealthy. This sale, which followed the *Desamortización* (Disentailment) law, led to the dissolution of most monasteries, a measure in line with the intentions of Joseph I (Joseph Bonaparte), and created major opportunities for new building in the cities. Land 'reform', however, was largely unwanted in rural areas because it threatened the existing de facto use of land. The constitution of 1837 extended the right to vote slightly, but there was no significant reform movement.

THE FIRST CARLIST WAR

The most sustained conflict in this period occurred in Spain, one again that is largely ignored in standard works on military history, which is a mistake because of what the war indicated about the nature of campaigning in civil wars. In the First Carlist War of 1833–40, Don Carlos, 'Carlos V', resisted the bequest of the Spanish throne to his young niece, Isabel II, by her father and his brother Ferdinand VII. Opposition to a female monarch was combined with hostility to the constitutional reform supported by Isabel's supporters and, more generally, to liberalism. Dynastism was impacted in specific social and regional circumstances. Carlism, like Miguelism in Portugal, was a conservative movement that drew on peasant anger against liberal government, and thus reflected tensions that looked back not only to the Napoleonic period but also to opposition to the Enlightenment reforms of the late-eighteenth century.

As the government and (unlike in 1936) the army stayed loyal to Isabel, Carlos had to create his own forces. Initial success owed much to Tomás de Zumalacárregui (1788–1835), who became commander of the Carlist forces in the Basque–Navarre region. He was a Basque veteran of the struggle against Napoleon, which indeed served as an important model for the Carlists who emphasised provincial liberties. Zumalacárregui brought coherence to Carlist operations, always a necessity in insurrectionary struggles, and created a successful guerrilla army that made full use of the difficult terrain in order to seize the initiative. This army overran much of the mountainous north, the centre of Carlist support, where regular troops were few, but was less successful when it left the mountains and sought to capture cities, although Córdoba was briefly occupied in 1836. The cities, including Bilbao and Pamplona in the north, were dominated by the liberals. There were the usual legacy fortresses dotted around large towns and key roads, which saw action whenever they found themselves in the path of Carlist invasions. Otherwise, the main fortification effort was in the Basque–Navarre–Rioja region along the River Ebro where, from 1834 onwards, the Cristinos (as the supporters of Isabel and her mother María Cristina were known) constructed a series of blockhouses in a manner similar to the French in Aragón during the Peninsular War. The Carlists responded in kind, and soon there were front lines etched by forts across wooded hillsides. Bilbao was besieged twice by the Carlists, in 1835 and 1836, while, as part of their defence, the Cristinos fortified outlying buildings on the hillsides.

Isabel benefited from the international context, another key element in insurrectionary struggles, although one

that tends to be underrated by those convinced, often mis-
leadingly so, of the value of guerrilla strategy and tactics.
She was supported by Britain, France and, once Miguel
was defeated, Portugal. Although the war in the 1830s did
not match the Spanish Civil War of 1936–9 in which each
side was armed by rival powers, solid international backing for Isabel proved vital. That support, combined with
the weakness of the Carlists when they sought to embark
on conventional warfare, led to their eventual defeat.
Zumalacárregui died in an unsuccessful siege of Bilbao in
1835, and the advance of the Carlists under Don Carlos on
Madrid in 1837 failed to topple the regime.

The battles of the war, such as Laveaga Pass (1835),
Descarga (1835), Mendigorría (1835), Hernani (1836),
Majaceite (1836), Luchana (1836), Chiva (1837), Villar de los
Navarros (1837), Aranzueque (1837) and Morella (1838),
are scarcely known, which distorts the general account of
warfare in this period. In practice, they, and the related military operations, throw light on factors crucial to success
in this, as well as other, periods. In battle, morale, experience, surprise, terrain and numbers were crucial, and all
were as important as effective tactics, if not more so. The
campaigns of the war did not leave much room for complicated operational planning nor for sophisticated tactics
by complex formations. At Laveaga Pass and Descarga,
larger government forces were surprised and routed by the
Carlists. Surprise was also important in the Carlist defeat
at Aranzueque, the end of their operations in central Spain
in 1837. Mendigorría, in contrast, was a pitched battle that
arose from the determination of Zumalacárregui's successor, Vicente González Moreno, to inflict a decisive defeat
on the government forces, but he chose his position badly
and the Carlists, unused to resting on the defensive, had
to withdraw under the pressure of government attacks.

The Carlist losses, about two thousand men, were a major blow, as, earlier, was the end of Zumalacárregui's string of victories.

Yet, government forces also faced serious problems, not least a shortage of pay and supplies. As with other civil wars, strategy, morale and generalship were shot through with political considerations. For example, internal Carlist divisions weakened the movement and helped lead to the end of the First Carlist War. In 1839, Rafael Maroto, the Carlist commander-in-chief, arrested and shot five generals from a rival faction before negotiating the Convention of Vergara with the government's commander, General Baldomero Espartero. Those Carlists who rejected this agreement and fought on in Aragón and Catalonia under Ramón Cabrera were defeated and fled to France in 1840, although Cabrera returned to lead Carlist guerrillas in another war in 1846–9 that was restricted to Catalonia.

Rivalry between Moderates and Progressives was complicated by the increasing role of generals who benefited in prestige from their victory over the Carlists. The war helped in the politicisation of the army and the militarisation of politics. Generals adopted the policy of *pronunciamientos* (declarations) in which they announced their demands. In 1836, Arthur Middleton, a perceptive American diplomat, commented: 'The capital is undoubtedly at the mercy of any of the generals who can dispose of a division of 4 to 5,000 men. So that the question seems now only to be who shall exercise the dictatorship.' General Baldomero Espartero (1793–1879), a veteran of the war against France from 1809 and subsequently, in 1815–26, of the conflict in Spanish America, was responsible for Progressive control from 1840. He had gained valuable prestige from defeating the Carlists at Luchana in 1836, and became regent in 1841, thwarting an attempted coup that year.

Espartero, in turn, was defeated and overthrown in 1843 by the conservative General Ramón Narváez, a veteran of the Carlist War, under whom the Moderates regained power after defeating loyal forces at Torrejón de Ardoz outside Madrid. Washington Irving, the American Ambassador from 1842 to 1846, wrote in May 1844: 'I am wearied and at times heartsick of the wretched politics of this country . . . political adventurers in Spain . . . the dark side of human nature.'

The Moderates reduced the suffrage, created a national police force, the Civil Guard, in 1844, suppressed opposition in Cuba and, by the constitution of 1845, increased Crown prerogatives and the powers of central government. On the pattern of the enlightened ministers of Charles III, the Moderates also sought to use reform in order to modernise Spain. Many of the themes, notably educational reform, were not new, but a uniform system of taxation was an important innovation.

ENDING SLAVERY

There was not much of an Abolitionist movement in Spain in the late eighteenth and early nineteenth centuries, and even the liberal *cortes* twice rejected Abolitionist measures, in 1811 and 1813. In 1814, Spain rejected British pressure to limit the slave trade, and while it responded in 1817, it did little to enforce the treaty. A genuine Abolitionist movement did not spring up in Spain until the 1830s. In Cuba, slavery remained important to the sugar monoculture of much of the economy, which depended on the American investment market and technology. Slavery in peninsular Spain was abolished in 1837, in Puerto Rico in 1873 and in Cuba in 1886. The liberal governments that dominated Spain from 1874 took the key steps, as they also introduced universal male suffrage in Spain in 1890. John, First Earl Russell, the

> British Foreign Secretary, presented the situation in 1862
> in terms of classic British liberal criticism: 'Persecution for
> religion and the slave trade are both odious to Britons, and
> both dear to Spaniards. So much the worse for them.'

In 1854, instability and military opposition led to the overthrow of the Moderates, and the return of Espartero and the
Progressives. The newly established Democrats, who wanted
far more radical change, including votes for all men as well
as agrarian reform, got nowhere. However, demands for more
change, exacerbated by rising food prices, led to the overthrow
of Espartero in 1856 in response to a *pronunciamiento*, or declaration, backed by force, for a change of government by General
Leopoldo O'Donnell, who was of Irish descent.

SPAIN AS A POWER

The early introduction of steam power in the Spanish navy
in the 1840s was due to the need for fast troop transport
and amphibious warfare in support of counter-insurgency
and anti-piracy expeditions. Steamers got preference over
other types of ship because the army was interested in the
strategic mobility that they provided. In 1849, Spain sent
nine thousand troops to help, alongside the French, restore
papal power in Rome. Under General Leopoldo O'Donnell
(1809–67), who ran Spain in 1856, 1858–63 and 1864–6,
Spain, despite its large state debt, was involved from 1859
in a series of imperial episodes that were intended to
ensure public support and that reflected the wish to act as
a great power, as well as a sense that the country should
still have a role in Latin America. O'Donnell was an inter-
ventionist with a strong penchant for dramatic gestures on

the international stage. Spain participated in French-led interventions in Vietnam and Mexico and, on its own, in response to French expansionism in Algeria, in a campaign in Morocco in 1859–60 that led to the capture of Tetuan and Ifni in 1860, and in the resumption of control of Santo Domingo (now the Dominican Republic) in 1861. Yet, Río Muni in West Africa, occupied in 1843, and Ifni did not serve as the basis for additional expansion. Moreover, American pressure in 1866 helped lead Spain to end naval hostilities with Peru and Chile, while it also abandoned its attempt to control the Dominican Republic, which, as a result of local opposition, had turned out to be a fruitless commitment.

O'Donnell's Liberal Union (*Unión Liberal*) Party sought to appeal more widely for support but, in 1863, he was pushed out and Queen Isabella instead established a conservative government under the Marquis of Miraflores, and then Narváez. O'Donnell then returned to power. In 1866, General Juan Prim, a Progressive, tried to seize power, but this revolution was suppressed by O'Donnell.

Unpopularity combined with economic strains led in 1868 to rebellion, another *pronunciamiento*, the victory of revolutionary forces under Francisco Serrano at Alcolea, and the overthrow and exile of the maladroit Isabella in what was to be termed the Glorious Revolution. She had expended her personal and political capital. This was an overthrow of the monarch and not merely a change in ministry.

The resulting 'six revolutionary years', as they became known, saw constitutional experimentation, political division, rebellions in Spain and Cuba, assassinations including of Prim in Madrid while prime minister in 1870, and the search for a viable monarch. A general in the Carlist War, Serrano had played a key role in the military politics of the early 1840s, and was an ally of O'Donnell whom he succeeded as head of the Liberal Union Party after O'Donnell's death in 1867. Commander of the revolutionary forces in 1868, Serrano became prime minister and then regent.

SPANISH HISTORY IN THE NINETEENTH CENTURY: THE CUBAN VIEW

The Communist regime that took power in Cuba in 1959 extensively memorialised the two major insurgencies against Spanish rule that occurred in the nineteenth century. The first, in 1868, was linked to the crisis caused by the overthrow of Isabella in Spain. In trying to suppress the insurgency in Cuba, the Spaniards found the mountainous terrain difficult, but benefited greatly from ethnic, geographical and social divisions among the Cubans and from the willingness of many, in part as a result, to support Spain. In particular, from 1870, Cuban whites increasingly rejected what they now saw as a black-run revolution focused on opposition to slavery. Spanish forces also employed harsh measures, including the killing of rebel families and the forced relocation of the rural population so as to create free-fire zones and to prevent the rebels from gaining access to civilian aid. Once civil war in Spain ended in 1876, twenty-five thousand troops were sent to Cuba, and control was restored in 1878. The unsuccessful independence struggle had seen the partial abolition of slavery in rebel areas, which encouraged the move for gradual abolition in the island as a whole.

The insurgency resumed in the mid-1890s, and the Spanish army, while achieving considerable success, was affected by guerrilla attacks, disease, hostile weather and rainy seasons. In response, the Spaniards forced people from the countryside to the towns where, surrounded

by barbed wire, they were hit by disease and food shortages. Due in particular to yellow fever, 150,000 to 170,000
Cubans died in the camps. Successful American intervention in 1898 led to the end of Spanish rule.

Religious change was a major element. Prefiguring the situation under the Second Republic of 1931–6, the revolutionaries
proved anti-clerical, and certainly sought to expand freedom of
religion. The liberal constitution of 1869 embraced freedom of
religion: it still accepted Catholicism as the state religion, but
the toleration of other religions was regarded as unacceptable by
many Catholics, as were such measures as civil marriage and the
campaign against church bells. These measures clearly clashed
with Spanish 'deep history', in the shape of identity and traditions. Within towns, the destruction of convents to make way for
new streets was both symbolic and a cause of outrage. Clerical
interests and religious issues became heavily politicised, forshad-
owing the situation in the 1930s.

After a difficult and lengthy period of selection, Amadeo of
Savoy, the younger son of Victor Emmanuel II of Italy, was elected
king as Amadeo I in November 1870. Against an extremely difficult background, which included army mutinies, the standard
means by which troops expressed political beliefs, Amadeo failed
even to maintain his own position, although he survived a major
assassination attempt in 1872 in the Via Avenal in Madrid when
the royal carriage was shot at. His was not to be a successful
new dynasty as the Habsburgs had been in 1516 and, even more
clearly, the Bourbons had been in 1700.

In February 1873, Amadeo, who had found it difficult to get on
with his ministers, notably Serrano, abdicated and a republic was
proclaimed. This was in line with the declaration of republics
in France after the overthrow of Louis-Philippe in 1848 and the
defeat of Napoleon III in 1870. It was, however, a breach with the

pattern of Spanish history and with the general nature of rule in Europe in this period. Amadeo told the *cortes* that the Spanish people were ungovernable. He returned to Italy, resuming the title Duke of Aosta.

The republic was declared a federal one, as it encompassed Cuba, Puerto Rico and the Pacific archipelagos. The republic, however, also could not stop disorder, which included the declaration of self-governing 'cantons' in 1873. The radical, anti-centralist, Cantonalists suffered from disunity and reliance on the militia. They were quickly suppressed everywhere apart from Cartagena, which fell only in 1874 after being blockaded by land and sea. In Alcoi/Alcoy, in southern Valencia, the 'Petroleum Revolution', so-called because the workers carried petroleum-soaked torches, took place in 1873. The workers seized control of the city and declared themselves independent, only to be suppressed by the army. This was a major break between the republicans, who controlled the army, and the anarchists.

Separately, another Carlist war, the second if that of 1846–9 is not treated as a distinct conflict, or the third if it is, broke out in 1872. This was far less serious than the First Carlist War because support for the Carlists was largely restricted to the north, especially Navarre and upland Catalonia, although Carlist groups caused problems elsewhere. The Carlists were also affected by disunity, by the opposition of the major towns, and by the lack of an adequate supply base or administration, of foreign support and of good commanders. The Carlist siege of Bilbao in 1874, the crucial year in the war, ended with the relief of the city. In November 1875, Catalonia was regarded as pacified, and the Carlists were driven back to Navarre and the Basque provinces. At that point, it was estimated that the Carlists had thirty-five thousand volunteers and the Spanish army one hundred and fifty-five thousand men. The last Carlist field army was crushed at Montejurra in 1876 and the war came to an end. An annual celebration of the Carlist cause is still held at the site.

With republicanism identified by many, crucially the army, with anarchy, and certainly political failure, military leaders staged a coup in December 1874. They imposed first conservatism and then the Bourbon monarchy in the shape of Isabella's son, Alfonso XII (1857–85, r. 1874–85), who had been educated in Britain at Sandhurst. The widespread wish for stability both encouraged support for a solution and then gave it a degree of longevity. Constitutional monarchy appeared the best outcome. The effective 1876 campaign against the Carlists, in which Alfonso took part, led to their final defeat. Isabella had abdicated in favour of Alfonso in 1870. After an unimpressive exile spent in luxury and squabbling, she died in Paris in 1904.

AN IMAGE OF SPAIN: *CARMEN*

One of the most popular of all operas, Georges Bizet's *Carmen* (1875) was based very loosely on a 1845 story of that title by the French writer Prosper Mérimée, who had travelled extensively in Spain in 1830 and may have heard the story there. The opera is set in Seville and the nearby hills in about 1820, with the first act set outside the large eighteenth-century tobacco factory where Carmen and other women roll cigars. That factory can now be visited as it survives as the university. The bullring outside which the last act is set can also be visited. The opera presents the Spaniards as emotional and lawless, depicting a tavern brawl, smugglers, fortune-telling and the sound of the offset bullfight. The story and the opera were both in French, and reflected the extent to which Spain was presented from outside, notably with the femme fatale Carmen. The British, American and Russian premieres were in 1878, and the Spanish one, in Barcelona, in 1881, was a great success.

Visiting Spain

Spain only became familiar to British artists and the British public after the painter David Roberts's travels in the early 1830s. Roberts (1796–1864) achieved success with his *Interior of Seville Cathedral* (1834), produced a series of Spanish illustrations in 1835–6, and published them in *Picturesque Sketches in Spain* (1837). His high-end portfolios of engravings spread images of Spain. David Wilkie (1785–1841) was also important. He was influenced by his visit to Spain in 1827–8, and by the paintings he saw there. His later paintings accordingly had a richer tone, stronger use of colour and engagement with historical themes. Wilkie became Painter in Ordinary to King William IV in 1830. His Spanish works included *The Maid of Saragossa*, *The Spanish Podado*, *A Guerrilla Council of War*, *The Guerrilla Taking Leave of his Family*, *The Guerrilla's Return to his Family*, *Two Spanish Monks of Toledo* and *Columbus in the Convent at La Rabida*.

In mid-century, the notion of Spain as colourful and exotic was popularised by the artists John Burgess (1829–97) and John Phillip (1817–67). Burgess travelled in Spain regularly from 1858, taking an interest in the Spanish peasantry. His first major success, *Bravo Toro* (1865), was followed by such works as *A Little Spanish Gipsy* (1868) and *Licensing Beggars in Spain* (1877). Phillip, nicknamed Spanish Phillip, produced pictures of Spanish life after a trip there in 1851, returning in 1856 and 1860. His *The Letter Writer, Seville, Prayer* (1859), *The Promenade* (1859), *The Early Career of Murillo* and *La Gloria: A Spanish Wake* (1864) are among his better known works. His *The Prison Window* (1857) juxtaposed love with a Spain of imprisonment and religion.

Alhambrismo was triggered in art. This was encouraged by Washington Irving's *Tales of the Alhambra*, the 1832 first version of which was entitled *The Alhambra: a series of tales and sketches of the Moors and Spaniards*, which was written while he stayed there in 1829. Irving (1783–1859), American Ambassador to Spain from 1842 to 1846, had first travelled there in 1826–9, going to live in the Alhambra in 1829, He was a major interpreter of Spain and wrote a biography of Christopher Columbus (1828), followed by his *Chronicle of the Conquest of Granada* (1829) and *Voyages and Discoveries of the Companions of Columbus* (1831).

Owen Jones (1809–74), a Welsh architect, was another key figure. His detailed studies in the early 1830s of the decoration of the Alhambra played a crucial role in his work, and led to his *Plans, Elevations, Sections and Details of the Alhambra* (1836–45), which also represented a major advance in colour printing by means of chromolithography. One of the Superintendents of Works for the Great Exhibition of 1851 in London, Jones drew on the Alhambra for his colour scheme for the interior ironwork, and, when the Crystal Palace was re-erected in Sydenham, Jones within it recreated the Alhambra in the Alhambra Court. He also drew on the Alhambra in his *The Grammar of Ornament* (1856), and in his designs for wallpaper, textiles, carpets, mosaics and tessellated pavements.

BARCELONA

In the eighteenth century, the city eased overpopulation on its medieval site by reclaiming marshland and creating a housing development called La Barceloneta, a triangular spit of land in the old harbour. The industrial age added greatly to pressures on space, with the walls demolished in 1859 to enable the city to expand. Ildefons Cerdà, an engineer, was commissioned to produce a plan by which this process could be managed. He provided for both public transportation networks and open spaces by using a geometric grid pattern in his scheme for Eixample Garden City. *Eixample* means 'extension' or 'expansion'. The area is readily identifiable today beyond the dense old city and bordered to the north by the long thoroughfare of Calle Barcelona (now Avenida Diagonal). It was in this modern showcase area that Catalan Art Nouveau architects, such as the innovative Antoni Gaudí (1852–1926), were able to realise their designs, though many of the envisaged green spaces were not created. This part of Barcelona remains part of the city's charming palette of different neighbourhoods.

A New Political Order

Antonio Cánovas del Castillo, the new prime minister, was a politician who had risen by merit, energy and determination. He sought to replace the instabilities of military intervention and popular revolution with a stable party system on the British model, with Liberal and Conservative parties willing, in a system known as *el turno pacífico* (the peaceful turn), to alternate in power and accept the other in government. This constitutional monarchy was designed to exclude radicals and rested, as in Italy, on manipulation of the electoral process and political system, especially on behalf of existing patronage networks. As in Italy, the monarch had a major role. The constitution of 1876, which lasted until 1923, established joint sovereignty between king and *cortes*, with the former able to decide when it was appropriate to change the government, but having to appoint ministers who were responsible to the *cortes*. As in Britain, the king had a veto over legislation but did not use it. In 1881, however, after Alfonso refused to agree a law under which ministers were to remain in office for a fixed term, Cánovas del Castillo resigned. He was replaced by Práxedes Mateo Sagasta, the Liberal leader, with whom he then alternated power under the *turno pacific* until the assassination of Cánovas del Castillo by an Anarchist in 1897.

Political stability greatly assisted economic growth, which itself helped strengthen stability. The weak state of Castilian agriculture had limited the potential for urban expansion, and technological change was unable to overcome this until well into the nineteenth century. Nevertheless, there was improvement in the economic situation in its latter decades. For example, there was a significant development of metallurgy in and near Bilbao that was based on local iron ore.

CRITICISM

In much of Europe, there was criticism of Spain as a reactionary power, criticism that drew on long-established prejudices rather than responding to the difficulties of the situation or to reform attempts. Thus, the London barrister Edward Quin (1794–1828), in his posthumous *Historical Atlas* (1830), wrote of Latin America:

> Those beautiful countries were at length wrested from a cruel misgovernment and debasing dominion of Spain, but a great majority of their inhabitants had been too long familiar with oppression, and associated with bigotry and ignorance, to be fit to enjoy suddenly the blessings of freedom, and to rank among the settled communities of the civilized world.

There was also an attempt to widen backing for the political system, with universal male suffrage introduced in 1890. As in Italy, however, the engagement of the population as a whole was limited and politics was widely seen as a factional activity. At the same time, it worked to represent local interest and was presented in particular as a way to support the interests of the propertied. This was both a stabilising factor and a system of manipulation and corruption. These elements were especially present in municipal politics.

In part, criticism of the parliamentary democracy of these

years, both in Spain and Italy, for lacking popular support or, indeed, relevance, rests on a set of later assumptions about engagement that may have only a limited basis for this period. In particular, there was no necessary linkage between this lack of support and either the rise of Mussolini or the success of Franco. Instead, events played a key role. In Italy, it was to be a sense of failure and disillusionment after the First World War. In Spain, failure in the colonies was a key element – political, economic and psychological.

Serious rebellions in Cuba and the Philippines were transformed by American intervention. In the resulting Spanish-American War of 1898, Spain was totally defeated, and rapidly so. The key failure was that of the badly run navy, but the Spanish force in Cuba was also defeated in large part because it had been unable to dispute the American landing near Santiago. The Spanish army was in poor shape. It had been intensely politicised for decades, and this affected both the quality and the quantity of command: there were far too many officers. The determination to restrict expenditure ensured that the army lacked training. Like the American army, it was also short of recent experience. The climate and terrain of Cuba created problems for the Americans. Fortunately for them, despite a major manpower advantage, as well as good rifles and artillery, the Spaniards fought badly at the operational level, retiring into a poor defensive perimeter round Santiago and not attacking American communications. Santiago surrendered on 17 July. In the Treaty of Paris of 1898, Puerto Rico, the Philippines and Guam were surrendered to the United States, while Cuba became independent as an American client state. In 1899, Spain sold the Caroline and Mariana archipelagos in the Pacific to Germany.

In what was called *El Desastre*, Spanish prestige was shattered and there were demands for regeneration. The twentieth century came in with Spain a weak power, and Spanish politics, culture and thought newly febrile, on the part of some, notably the 'Generation of 1898', with a willingness to envisage radical transformation that extended more widely than it had done pre-war. That Spain had been defeated by the United States led to a counterpointing of that 'real nation' with Spain, a state without, to its critics, true nationhood. To some critics this was the fault of monarchy and Catholicism, to others of a regionalism that sapped the nation. The state could be seen as too strong or too weak, or both.

Spain's imperial ideology was now redundant, although there were to be attempts to cling to it in Morocco, indeed to strengthen it there. In some respects, the subsequent history of Spain was to be a matter of adjusting to its post-imperial status, not least in dealing with elements, especially the army and the social groups on which it drew, that no longer had a clear role or means of prestige. This transition was more difficult than was to be the case for, say, Britain after 1945 because, as yet, there was no general international move towards decolonisation, while Spain, unlike Britain, did not have the salve of victory in an equivalent of the Second World War. Precisely, indeed, because imperialism, which had been crucial to Spain's destiny since the fifteenth century, remained highly significant politically, economically and culturally on the world scale at the end of the nineteenth century, Spanish failure appeared more striking. It was also more rapid.

Moreover, the call for national regeneration seemed more necessary. This call was linked, as was politics more generally, to the presentation of certain accounts of the past. In particular, there was a tendency to claim the pedigree of a supposed return to the stability and unity of the reign of Philip II (1556–98). This was yet another iteration of the longstanding argument that Spain has always existed as an inherently Christian identity, at worse held at bay by external oppression and internal challenges. In practice, this was an account most suitable for Christian Castilians, and less so for other Spaniards.

THE DUKE OF PLAZA-TORO

A Spanish grandee was the most memorable character in Gilbert and Sullivan's highly successful operetta *The Gondoliers* (1889). The lyrics, by William Schwenck Gilbert (1836–1911), presented a conceited, bankrupt, proud coward very much concerned about his social position:

> In enterprise of martial kind,
> When there was any fighting,
> He led his regiment from behind
> (He found it less exciting).
> But when away his regiment ran,
> His place was at the fore, O-
> . . .
> No soldier in that gallant band
> Hid half as well as he did.
> He lay concealed throughout the war,
> . . .
> When told that they would all be shot
> Unless they left the service,
> . . .
> He sent his resignation in,
> The first of all his corps, O!

The target was the British aristocracy as much as its Spanish counterpart, but the use of the latter reflected a more general social contempt for Spanish pretension.

CHAPTER TEN

A Post-imperial Age, 1899–1935

Failure in 1898 led to demands for change across the range of Spanish opinion and politics, from protests against modernity and the supposed abandonment of historical destiny, to demands for a democratic republicanism that would support workers' rights. That, however, proved an easier argument in industrialised cities, notably Barcelona, than elsewhere. The Casamarona textile factory (1911) in Barcelona survives as a legacy of this period. It is also useful to visit the Catalan Museum of Science and Technology, which is located in a Modernist steam works factory (1909) in Terrassa.

Regional nationalism also gathered force in Catalonia, where the *Lliga Regionalista* (Regionalist League) was founded in 1901. It was designed to win autonomy and then regenerate Spain. The Basque National Party was established in 1894. The Spanish Socialist Party had been founded in 1879, while a more violent tone was provided by the Anarchists who sought to overthrow capitalism. A highly dramatic attack was that in Madrid in 1906 on the wedding day of Alfonso XIII (r. 1886–1931) and Victoria Eugenia, granddaughter of Queen Victoria. Twenty-four people were killed by the bomb and the bride was splattered in blood, but neither she nor her husband were killed.

A willingness to turn to violence was most clearly seen in Barcelona. Its economic growth increased its political significance. In 1893, an Anarchist threw two bombs during a performance in the opera house, leading to the death of twenty people. In 1909, in response to a call-up of reservists for service in Morocco, worker demonstrations turned violent and were then bloodily crushed by the army, which had already been used against striking miners in Catalonia in the 1890s. 'Tragic Week', which saw church burning in Barcelona, led to the resignation of the prime minister, Antonio Maura, a Conservative, in 1909.

Matching Giovanni Giolitti's attempt in Italy, the Liberal José Canalejas then sought to ease social divisions as an aspect of a 'revolution from above', but he was assassinated in 1912 by an Anarchist. Such a loss of political talent was detrimental for Spanish leadership, not least because Canalejas, like Maura, was a moderniser. Maura also pursued national regeneration, although the definitions of that goal varied greatly, as did ideas about implementation.

Politics, meanwhile, was made more unstable and difficult by divisions among the Conservatives and Liberals, combined with the difficulties posed by the new political movements, the Republicans, Socialists and regionalists. Each of the latter drained legitimacy from the political system, in part by attacking it as élitist and corrupt.

Neutrality in the First World War (1914–18) brought economic opportunity, notably for Catalan textile factories and Spanish agriculture, and with Spanish timber exported to provide props for Anglo-French trenches on the Western Front, although the last led to deforestation. The ability to move goods overland by train to France was important in evading German submarine attacks. The sea route from Barcelona to Marseille was also essentially safe. Neutrality was divisive: the Conservatives, under Eduardo Dato, prime minister in 1913–15 and 1917, pro-German, and the Liberals, notably Álvaro de Figueroa, closer to the Allies.

The major increase in exports, however, proved inflationary, and led workers to press for more money. A general strike was called in 1917, but was suppressed by the military, although that, in turn, was affected by discontent. The Bolshevik Revolution in Russia in 1917 proved a divisive example that helped encourage violence, notably in Barcelona. In Andalusia, landless peasants pressed for change and many turned to Anarchism.

Tension increased after the war. The army and the Civil Guard were widely employed against strikers and Anarchists in 1918–21, while employers organised their own forces. Supported by strikes, Catalan demands for autonomy were resisted by Madrid. Coalition governments could not bring stability, let alone enthusiasm, and the explicit and implicit agreements of the earlier period of two-party rule frayed. In March 1921, Dato, the prime minister, was assassinated by three Catalan Anarchists.

Meanwhile, long-term trends continued. Thus, the display of popular religious devotion led in 1918–20 to a number of apparitions in which life-size images of the crucified Christ were seen to move their eyes. Limpias was the key site, and seemed a possible Spanish Lourdes. Pilgrims began to congregate. Alfonso XIII visited, as did the prime minister, Antonio Maura. At once a response to economic uncertainty and a site of religious devotion, they were an aspect of Spanish life that should not be written out. The early decades of the century saw the Church attempt to 're-Catholicise' the population. Catholic activism, however, not only took an anti-modern stance, but was also an aspect of the Church's failure to reconcile itself to liberalism as well as its inability to mobilise more than a section of the working class, and notably the urban working class. Instead, the Church's devotional culture proved more effective for the conservative middle class. This difference looked ahead to the situation during the Franco years.

In contrast, there was major development as a result of new technology, notably electricity. The spreading use of electricity affected infrastructure, particularly with public transport in Madrid where the trams were electrified in 1898. Spain's cities saw an expansion of the urban infrastructure. This was particularly true of major public buildings, as well as pleasure gardens.

Moreover, within middle-class houses, comfort was expressed in terms of consumer goods.

Meanwhile, as with 1898 at the hands of the Americans, military defeat proved a political blow. At Annual in Morocco in 1921, a large force was crushed by Moroccan opponents. This caused an upsurge of criticism. Two years later, General Miguel Primo de Rivera, the Captain-General of Barcelona, staged a *pronunciamiento*. In response, revealing the weakness of liberal parliamentary practice, as well as his own acquiescence, Alfonso XIII dissolved the *cortes* and made Primo chief of a military directorate. As with Victor Emanuel II and Benito Mussolini in Italy the previous year, the monarch was a key figure in the collapse of parliamentary politics, little realising that such politics had become the guarantee of constitutional monarchy. Primo was backed by military action in Zaragoza and Valencia, but the majority of the military did not act in his favour. Nor, however, did they block him.

Using the language of fatherland, Church and monarchy, and offering a traditional nationalism, Primo sought regeneration by authoritarianism. This response to the rapid rate of change and, specifically to the challenge of mass politics in an age of swift modernisation, captured the attempt to reinforce the authoritarian duality of state and family, and to reposition it in a volatile world. The Communist Party, strikes and the Catalan regional government were all banned, the Constitution of 1876 suspended, political activity and the press restricted, and a statist approach to the economy adopted, one of public investment, high import tariffs and state monopolies.

Success was mixed. Social welfare in the pattern of Mussolini's changes was introduced, and there was a measure of growth as the world economy improved after the First World War. In Morocco, in cooperation with France in 1925–6, the Riff War was brought to an end. Spain used large quantities of mustard gas, dropped by air on civilians and fighters alike: heavy casualties resulted. The Spanish amphibious assault in the Bay of

Alhucemas (al-Hoceïma) was also significant. Francisco Franco led the first battalion ashore and wrote a first-hand account of the operation that was published. In practice, French assistance was more significant in overcoming opposition.

In Spain, it proved impossible to produce a political solution acceptable to those excluded from power, and there was growing hostility within the army to Primo's attempt to base promotion on merit, not longevity, and to get rid of some of the large number of superfluous officers in the top-heavy force. There was nearly a coup against him in 1926. Meanwhile, Catalonia continued to be a centre of opposition, and neither the Pedralbes Palace built in Barcelona for Alfonso in 1919–29 nor the International Exhibition of 1929 held in the Montjuïc area of Barcelona could disguise the situation, although the vast Plaça d'Espagna, and its Neoclassical fountain, left an impressive legacy. More generally, Primo ran out of support, with Alfonso now worried about not only his minister's but also his own growing unpopularity. In 1930, the prospect of another coup led Alfonso to force the exhausted Primo out.

His successor, Dámaso Berenguer, another general, had been High Commissioner of Spanish Morocco from 1919 to 1922 and Military Chief of the Royal Household from 1923. He sought a constitutional solution, but found that abandoning Primo's unpopular policies was not enough to win support in a divided society. Berenguer reversed some of Primo's more oppressive measures, which led to his government being called, in contrast, the soft dictatorship. Political problems stood in the way of creating a viable and popular government, a process made difficult by inherent differences. Moreover, the severe economic strains of the 1929 slump and the subsequent Depression hit hard.

Berenguer resigned in February 1931, to be replaced by Admiral Juan Bautista Aznar-Cabañas. Republicanism, meanwhile, became more potent politically, while the government was divided between absolutist and constitutional monarchists. The latter failed to reach an agreement with the Republicans, and the success of the Republican parties in the April 1931 municipal elections led Alfonso to abdicate in the face of crowds in the streets of Madrid, but in a peaceful transfer of power. In a key moment in Spanish history, the royal family went into exile. The military did not oppose the step. Other aspects of the old order were ended, the military orders being dissolved in April.

Monarchy had fallen victim not so much to inevitable contradictions but to the interplay of contingencies and individuals. Alfonso's manifest lack of ability was an important factor. To point out that the system had few defenders, while correct, is to neglect the degree to which this was also the case for most constitutional systems and political arrangements. It is apparent, however, that the monarchy did not enjoy great support.

The Second Republic was declared and Niceto Alcalá-Zamora became prime minister. The elections to the *cortes* in June 1931 led to a major victory for the parties of the Republican–Socialist coalition. Hopes of social reform, however, were handicapped by the acute economic problems stemming from the Depression, as well as the divisions among the governing coalition. The new constitution of December 1931 sought to entrench democracy, including by granting the vote to women and declaring full religious freedom. Moreover, wages were raised.

The new republic was not an effective force for stability. The anti-clericalism of the new government and constitution, notably the separation of Church and state which made possible the dissolution of the religious orders, angered the devout and indeed led Alcalá-Zamora to resign as prime minister, although he was then elected president. Anti-clericalism as well as the unwillingness of the powerful Socialist Party to commit to constitutional procedures in order to ground its policies, helped alienate and mobilise the right, and gave it a popular resonance that government attacks on élite economic interests could not do. The right was also offended by the government's support for Catalan self-government.

The Falange Party was founded in 1933 by José Antonio Primo de Rivera (1903–36), the eldest son of the dictator. Willing to endorse violence, it was bitterly against regional separatism, and also sought to regain Portugal and Gibraltar. The Falange attacked Jewish-owned department stores in 1935.

Meanwhile, as part of the flux of ideas and institutions in the period, a Catholic priest, Josemaría Escrivá de Balaguer, having experienced a vision in Madrid, founded the Opus Dei movement designed to foster Catholic holiness. It was to benefit greatly from the Franco regime.

Under growing threat from the right, there was pressure for more radical change from the radical left, which wanted social revolution without seeking Catholic support. Agrarian reform proved a particular source of division, and led to conflict between anarcho-syndicalists and Civil Guards. The latter were widely used in the early 1930s, and in July 1931 artillery was deployed against Anarchist strikers in Seville.

In November 1933, general elections proved successful for the Confederación Española de Derechas Autónomas (CEDA, Spanish Confederation of Autonomous Rightist Parties), led by José María Gill-Robles, and the centrist Republican Radicals, and a failure for the Socialists and the leftist Republicans. The Republican Radicals formed the new government, but the left proved unwilling to cooperate. Anti-clerical legislation was repealed and a general strike was violently suppressed in June 1934. In October 1934, the CEDA was taken into the government.

In response, the left called a general strike, while Catalonia's regional government proclaimed independence. The government, however, used the army to maintain control. Lluís Companys, the President of Catalonia, was sentenced to thirty years in prison.

In Asturias, the ability of the coal miners to unite, seize weapons from depots and arms factories, and defeat the local police, provoked a military response, partly planned by Franco, which was brutal. The air force bombed and strafed rebel-held towns and positions, demoralising the defenders who lacked anti-air-craft defences. The cruiser *Libertad* shelled the town of Gijón. The government deployed twenty-six thousand troops against about ten to twelve thousand rebel fighters. The rebels fought hard but the deployment of the Spanish Foreign Legion under Franco ensured that they faced good, well-trained troops with high morale, the last necessary for the room-to-room fighting required to retake Oviedo. After the rebellion had been defeated with much damage to the city, there was serious looting and widespread killing of prisoners as well as of civilians.

As the implications of the events of 1934 were digested during 1935, tensions were becoming obvious that would pit one section of society against another. The polarisation was to be tested in a crucial election for the Republic in February 1936. In this atmo-sphere of growing polarisation and violence, too few politicians and commentators across the political spectrum were willing to accept the essence of democracy: a willingness to welcome results that benefited opponents. Instead, violence became more persistent and the threat of violence even more pervasive.

Living Standards

The conditions of life were poor for much of the population, whether urban or rural. Housing was often overcrowded, as well as damp and insanitary. Wages were low, and this was made worse by the taxation of consumer goods and the rise in prices and rents from the late 1890s. As a result, living standards were greatly under pressure. Social welfare was extremely limited and periodical unemployment or underemployment a major issue.

The worldwide Great Depression that began in 1929 hit hard and exacerbated already difficult living standards. This was particularly so, as the economic growth of the 1910s had been followed in the 1920s by much foreign investment in the context of easy credit. The Depression cut off this source of credit and activity.

A WORLD OF LIGHT: THE MUSEO SOROLLA

Amid the grandeur of Madrid it is wonderful to visit a museum in which the paintings are bathed in light and suffused with intimacy. Many of Joaquín Sorolla's paintings can be visited in the pleasant house built for him in 1910 and fronted by a charming garden inspired by those of Granada. Born in Valencia, Sorolla (1863–1923) was not so much an Impressionist but rather a more varied painter. The orphaned son of a tradesman who was inspired by the paintings in the Prado before doing his military service and training in Rome and Paris, Sorolla ranged widely in his subjects, not least with Orientalist themes and portraits, as well as with his vivid *Sad Inheritance* (1899), a presentation of polio-crippled children bathing in the sea at Valencia (which had earlier been hit by polio) under the supervision of a monk.

Honoured in Paris, Sorolla was invited to exhibit in the United States in 1909 and 1911 and painted a series of portraits including one of President Taft. His major work of the 1910s was a series of fourteen massive murals on the 'The Provinces of Spain' that is exhibited in the Manhattan headquarters of the Hispanic Society of America.

Sorolla also painted Impressionist beach scenes that are masterly studies of colour, the paint brilliantly offering fluidity, iridescence and charm. These are much in evidence in the Sorolla museum, along with *Walk on the Beach* (1909) and *The Horse's Bath. My Wife and Daughters in the Garden* (1910) brilliantly brings together his interests in portraiture and light. It is a charming museum that is a wonderful foil to the heaviness of so many museums and much art.

CHAPTER ELEVEN

Civil War, 1936–9

A group of senior army officers, who called themselves the Nationalists, sought to seize power in 1936, in a rebellion that began in Spanish Morocco on 17 July and on the Spanish mainland on 18–19 July. They were opposed to the modernising policies of the left-leaning Republican government. They were also concerned about the possibility of a Communist seizure of power via the *Frente Popular* (Popular Front), a coalition of left-wing parties, after the Front's narrow victory in the hard-fought elections of 16 February 1936. The army's attitude to politics explains the rebellion by much of it. Claiming that the government had lost control (which in practice was due to right-wing as well as left-wing violence), the rebellious army units were really against the Republic itself, and, with it, democracy and freedoms.

The Nationalists, however, achieved only partial success in 1936. They conspicuously did not take control of Madrid, let alone Barcelona. Moreover, the failure of any attempt by the rebels to negotiate a settlement led to a bitter civil war, which only ended on 28 March 1939 when the Nationalists seized Madrid.

The Spanish Civil War is commonly seen as a harbinger of the Second World War, and the ideological division between the two sides is stressed. Indeed, the Nationalists, who very much emphasised religious themes, depicted the Republicans as the servants of the Antichrist. Caution is required in seeing the Civil War as a harbinger of the world war, while the ideological dimension was scarcely new. It had played a role in the civil war aspect of the Peninsular War of 1808–13, and even more in the Carlist Wars.

Although there was a naval side, the Spanish Civil War was essentially fought in mainland Spain. As a result of the nineteenth-century loss of most of the Spanish Empire, the overseas dimension of the rising was slight, although there was initial fighting in Spanish Morocco, with Republican resistance in the town of Larache being overcome after hard fighting.

As far as land conflict was concerned, the Spanish Civil War was different from the Western Front in the First World War, as well as from the initial campaigns in the Second World War. In contrast to the former, there was no density of defensive positions, so that, as a well-developed system, the front line was only episodic. This made it possible to break through opposing fronts relatively readily, but, contrary to the German successes in 1939–41, it proved to be very difficult to develop and sustain offensive momentum. As a result, following the pattern of the First World War, exploitation was inadequate; a pattern seen in the failure of Republican attacks in the battles of Brunete (1937), Belchite (1937), Teruel (1937–8) and the Ebro (1938), and of Nationalist attacks at Jarama (1937) and Guadalajara (1937).

This failure was a product of the nature of the Republican and Nationalist armies, which were poorly trained and inadequately supplied, but also of a lack of operational art, seen particularly in inadequate planning. This lack helped give an attritional character to the war, much of which did not involve fast-moving manoeuvres, which were a dimension of the Russian and Chinese civil wars of the 1920s. The mountainous relief of much of Spain contrasted with the relatively flat, open terrain in Russia where the fronts could move very rapidly. In Spain, the transport infrastructure was also very limited. Moreover, the sheer physical size of Russia meant lower unit density and thus thinner lines, which ensured that, once a line was broken, it was difficult to reconstruct it.

The attritional character of the struggle in Spain underlined the importance of resources, including foreign support. It also meant that much value accrued to the side that was better able to manage its economy, maintain morale and retain political cohesion. On all three heads, the Nationalists proved more effective. The Republicans were particularly unfortunate in the timing of the conflict because, if it had occurred during the Second World War, the Western Allies probably would have provided them with support in response to the German backing for the Nationalists.

Instead, Britain was not willing to help the Republicans, while French military assistance was small-scale and, in 1937, the US Congress banned the sale of arms to either side. The British government did not like the idea of France having right-wing dictatorships on three of its borders, but was unclear as to what could be done without jeopardising Britain's international position. The government, which was not only Conservative-dominated but also greatly concerned about Spain becoming a strategic partner of its Soviet supplier, tried to stop British volunteers taking part, a measure that damaged the Republicans, who benefited most from such volunteers. The Civil War also fed into the left–right ideological rivalry in British society.

The initial Nationalist rising was successful in some areas but elsewhere, notably in Madrid, Catalonia and Valencia, Republican positions were preserved by worker militias or by loyal regular forces. Political ideology was a key definer of sides, but so was individualism in terms of the responses of particular officers, troops and civilians. The rebel generals had failed to carry the whole of the military.

Areas of control were consolidated on both sides during July 1936 as flying columns sought to suppress local opposition. This suppression involved large-scale violence, with those judged unacceptable murdered. In Republican areas, this had a quasi-revolutionary character, not least in the killing of clergy. At least eight thousand civilians were executed in Madrid in the first year of the war. The killings and repression were conducted by all the Popular Front groups. The Falange leader, Primo de Rivera, was executed by the Republicans in Alicante, which freed Franco from a rival he despised. The Nationalists also killed in accordance with their own vision of order, and did so in a less disorganised fashion. The British diplomat G. H. Thompson was to find 'the same repression, the same terror', on both sides.

In practice, each side was guilty of terrible crimes and policies, not least because violence towards those judged opponents was a means of establishing control, while the victors had more of an opportunity to enforce their new order in, and through, blood. The practice of military violence was well established in nineteenth-century Spain, as in Portugal and Latin America. In part, this was a baleful consequence of the destabilisation wrought by the Napoleonic conquest in 1808. Against this background, the twentieth century offered a new iteration of old themes and methods, a situation also seen in the Balkans. Extreme violence was employed, as by the Nationalists in Seville in 1936, irrespective of the degree of violence required to achieve specific goals. General Francisco Franco's Army of Africa was notably violent, and repression employing disproportionate force continued after particular places had been captured and, indeed, after the war.

By the end of July 1936, Spain was divided into two zones, with the Republicans controlling the capital, Madrid, and the bulk of the population and industry, and backed by the navy and most of the air force; the Nationalists, supported by most of the army's combat units, dominated the more rural areas. Hardened by operations in Morocco, the Army of Africa was a particularly experienced unit, and the role of German intervention in helping Franco, from 29 July, to transport close to fourteen thousand troops by air from Morocco was highly significant. The blockade by the Spanish navy was thus circumvented. The Nationalists also called up reservists where they could and organised the right-wing militias into army units.

As the Second Republic was dismantled, the Republicans found it far harder to organise an effective army, partly because of political differences, but also because they, and especially their militias, lacked the necessary planned organisation and discipline. Those of the military who remained loyal were challenged by the role of Socialist, Anarchist, regional and other militia volunteers. The military rebellion, the arming of workers and the major role given to militias all encouraged this situation. These issues compromised training and affected fighting quality. The militias were also short of equipment. The Communists favoured a more centralised outcome with the militias organised into a regular army.

Republican divisions became more pronounced in May 1937 when, in what is sometimes called the May Events, fighting began in Catalonia, especially in Barcelona, over the stance, within the Republican camp, of the Anarchists. The fighting included the destruction of church interiors. In the event, the Anarchists were brutally suppressed by an alliance of the Communists and the Catalan nationalists. In a parallel to the purges in the Soviet Union, Stalin, who very much directed the Spanish Communists, was determined to destroy alternative views, and those holding them were murdered. He wanted to drive non-Comintern (Communist International) Marxists from power. To his opponents, Stalin was trying to thwart social revolution, and to his supporters he was seeking to keep a popular front, anti-Fascist, approach.

HOMAGE TO CATALONIA, GEORGE ORWELL

Published in April 1938, this book was based on Orwell's military service in 1936–7 with the militia of POUM, the Workers' Party of Marxist Unification, an anti-Stalinist force banned by the Republicans in June 1937. The NKVD (Soviet Secret Police) set out to eliminate POUM, and Orwell only narrowly escaped the murderous purge in Barcelona in June 1937. The ad hoc Anarchist fortresses, notably the Telephone Exchange, were all stormed. Earlier, Orwell had been shot through the throat by a sniper. His book, an attempt to set down the truth, was trashed by what Orwell termed 'the Communism-racket'. This account captured the location of the presentation of the war not only in Cold War rivalries but also in those within the left.

As a consequence of their difficulties, notably their lack of a striking force, the Republicans lost the initiative in the opening stages of the war in 1936 and were unable to capitalise on the early problems faced by the Nationalists. Instead, Franco used the Army of Africa to overrun western Andalusia and to link up with Nationalists further north, storming the city of Badajoz on 14 August. The untrained worker militias were unable to mount effective opposition. Franco's success enabled him to gain predominance over his military colleagues and, on 21 September, he was made *Generalisimo* of the rebel armies, and, on 1 October, *Caudillo*, or head of state.

Although Franco was able to fight his way close to Madrid by early November 1936, he was blocked, in the assault on 8 November, by the strength and determination of the resistance in and around the capital. Subsequent frontal attacks conquered part of the city, but were stopped. On 23 November, Franco called off the assault. This check resulted in the war becoming both longer and more wide-ranging in its intensity, which increased the likely value of foreign help to both sides while also putting a premium on the resilience of the Spanish combatants. Under the pressure of necessity, both sides had proved able to adapt to circumstances. In his advance towards Madrid, Franco had successfully motorised his force, using buses and trucks that he had seized, and was therefore able to outflank larger Republican forces.

Conversely, helped by Franco's decision to move first, in late September, to relieve the besieged Nationalists in the Alcázar (fortress) of Toledo, the Republicans had been able to improvise an effective defence of Madrid, and, supported by larger numbers of troops, guns and armour, to block the Nationalist attack, before obliging the overstretched Franco and his tired forces to abandon it in late November. The Republicans controlled the air because Soviet aircraft went into action at that time. Despite its limitations, air power was important as aircraft served as a substitute for artillery.

Notwithstanding Franco's failure to capture Madrid, Germany and Italy recognised his government on 18 November, which committed them to Nationalist victory. Ideological issues were coming to the fore in the international response to the conflict. In November, Hitler sent twelve thousand men, as well as tanks and aircraft, but he proved unwilling to do much more. In December, Mussolini agreed to dispatch two brigades of troops. In the end, Mussolini was to send eighty thousand troops and Hitler fewer than nineteen thousand. This joint contribution greatly furthered the alliance between Germany and Italy, so that, by the end of 1936, Mussolini was talking of a Rome–Berlin Axis. Some Spanish commentators today see the conflict as the first stage of the Second World War.

Operations in Spain enabled the Germans and Italians to test out weapons, tactics and doctrine, notably of air attack. There was spectacular terror bombing of cities, notably Madrid (1938), Guernica (1937), Barcelona (1938) and Cartagena (1936 and 1939) by German and Italian aircraft. These were civilian targets, but more was at stake: attacks on Cartagena and Barcelona, both port cities, were aspects of the attempt to prevent the Republicans from importing arms. The German destruction of Guernica on 26 April 1937 was intended to destroy the morale of the Republican Basques and thus weaken their resistance to the Nationalist advance. Concerned about the world response to the bombing of Guernica, the Germans and Nationalists sought to deny responsibility. The bombing of the town probably affected the resistance mounted when the Nationalists moved on to take Bilbao in June. The bombing of refugees became an Italian speciality, notably those fleeing from Málaga in February 1937 and towards Barcelona in the winter of 1938–9. The Italians sent 759 aircraft to Spain, the Germans about 700 and the Soviets 623.

THE MURDER OF TALENT: THE KILLING OF LORCA

Federico García Lorca (1898–1936), a noted poet and playwright, was a member of the Generation of '27, a Spanish group well-attuned to Modernism and cosmopolitan cultural tendencies. His *Romancero Gitano* (Gypsy Ballads, 1928) was based on popular Andalusian ballads, and brought him much fame. His major plays, such as *The House of Bernarda Alba*, questioned established social norms. Completed in 1936, that play, which explored practices of repression and family control by a callous matriarch who is concerned only with public reputation, tradition and chastity, was not performed until 1945 at all and then in Buenos Aires. The play can stand as a critique of Spanish society. A Socialist and a homosexual, Lorca was murdered by Nationalist militia in August 1936.

Lieutenant-General Walter von Reichnau told a meeting of Nazi leaders in 1938:

the experience of the Spanish war has made it easier for us to abandon the wrong path we were treading as regards tanks. The war in Abyssinia [the Italian conquest in 1935–6], where the Abyssinians lacked all means of countering tanks, had established the reputation of the light tank ...

We neglected the building of heavy armoured tanks. On the Spanish battlefields it turned out that it was precisely the heavy tanks with their steel armour plates that proved far away the more efficient.

Once operational mobility had been lost, the Nationalists discovered the intractable nature of position warfare in the face of a numerous opponent. Attempts to recover mobility in November 1936 by outflanking Madrid only overstretched the Nationalists and exposed them to attack. Franco tried again in February 1937, when he sought to cut off Madrid from Valencia, thus rupturing a key supply route, but the larger Republican force thwarted him in the battle of Jarama.

The nature of the war excited considerable foreign attention, being widely seen as a test case for the changing character of war – it was 'Aldershot on the Ebro', in the words of one contemporary referring to where the British army trained. J. F. C. Fuller, then a retired British major general and a newspaper correspondent, displayed marked sympathies with Franco, but this does not detract from the value of his military observations. Having visited Franco's army, he sent a report to British Military Intelligence in March 1937 that drew attention to its deficiencies:

It is in no sense a great war, a trench war or even a guerrilla war . . . a city war . . . main strength of the Reds was in the towns . . . had Franco a highly organised army and plenty of transport he could take Madrid. But he has not. For instance, General Queipo de Llano [a prominent Nationalist] told me himself that, when he launched his advance against Málaga, he had only 28 lorries . . . Nothing like the full manpower has been called up, in fact it cannot be, as the military organisation is not able to absorb more men.

Fuller also drew attention to the nature of the fighting sphere, and its relation to the limited tempo of the conflict:

> though the nominal front is immense . . . its garrisons are minute . . . The front is totally unlike the fronts in the [First] World War. Not only is it in no way continuous, but, generally speaking, hard to discover, and during my journey, so far as I know, at times I may have been in Red territory . . . The villages normally are natural fortresses, generally walled all round, and whichever side holds them 'holds' the intervening gaps as well. Immediately west of Madrid, and of course in other places also, actual trenches do exist. I visited the Madrid ones which were very sketchy . . . Though I was in this frontline for an hour and a half only two Red shells were fired and a few rifle shots were heard.

Interested in tank warfare, Fuller was disappointed by what he saw:

> Of tanks I saw few: on Franco's side the Italian light tank is an indifferent and blind machine . . . Tank tactics are conspicuous only through their absence. Machines are generally used singly, or, if in numbers, they split up over a wide front. The result is that they are met by concentrated fire . . . In fact, there are no tactics, no proper training or maintenance. One of Franco's officers told me that the largest number so far used in an attack was 15! I do not think we have to learn from either tanks or anti-tank weapons in this war, because the basis of tactics is training, and this is mainly a war of untrained men with a sprinkling of foreign mercenaries.

Fuller's view was too critical, not least because there were many experienced men in the Spanish armies, but he was correct about the emphasis on infantry and the difficulties of developing effective mass armies given the lack of sufficient time, training and resources. There were similarities with the problems that had faced the British in 1915-16 and the Americans in 1918 during the First World War. The context, however, was far more difficult for both sides in Spain, not only because resources were lacking and the front line very spread out, but also because there was not a cohesive and effective state organisation for either side.

In the absence of a rapid Nationalist victory, different strategies were proposed. The Italians, who had about fifty thousand troops in Spain at this stage, as well as aircraft, sought to emulate their success in conquering Ethiopia in the spring of 1936, and proposed rapid advances. These included a converging drive on Valencia, the seat of the Republican government, from Málaga (captured on 8 February) and Teruel, that would quickly have split the Republican zone into a number of areas. Victory would enable the Italians to redeploy their forces to pursue other opportunities. The Germans, who like the Italians had expected and wanted a quick war, backed the same plan, but Franco rejected it. He was more concerned to fit strategy and operations into a structure and, in particular, to adopt a cautious approach. This has led to claims that his approach was essentially attritional and that he wanted to destroy the Republicans accordingly.

The deficiencies of motorised forces, which the Italians did not know how to use according to British and German theories, were displayed in March 1937. Then, an Italian advance east of Madrid towards the city of Guadalajara became overly dependent on the few roads in the region, lost momentum and logistical support in poor weather, and was finally driven back in a successful counter-attack that began on 18 March. Franco had failed to provide the Italians with necessary support. He was opposed to the Italians playing an independent role as they had done both in the capture of Málaga and in the Guadalajara offensive. The outcome of the latter helped persuade Franco to decide not to resume his attack on Madrid.

Franco then turned north to conquer the Cantabrian littoral and its industrial resources, capturing the port of Bilbao on 19 June 1937. The divided and poorly commanded Republicans in the north were badly trained and lacked air power. To take the pressure off the north, the Republicans counter-attacked in the centre, especially in the battle of Brunete, west of Madrid, on 6 July. The Republicans broke through the weak Nationalist line, but Franco sent reinforcements including German and Italian aircraft. The Republicans proved unable to maintain their impetus, a general problem in military operations, and their troops lost more heavily. Brunete revealed their deficiencies, not least poor coordination between the arms and, related to this, an inexpert use of the available artillery and tanks. The Republicans also lacked sufficient air power. The Soviet decision in July 1937 to dispatch aid to the Guomindang party in China against Japanese attack greatly reduced the amount available to help Spain, while Stalin became increasingly uninterested in the Spanish struggle.

The intractability of the conflict, however, led Franco in August 1937 to press for Italian help against Soviet shipments of arms to the Republicans. Mussolini rapidly complied in the Mediterranean, and submarine attacks were soon launched.

Defeated at Brunete, the Republicans were unable to prevent the Nationalists capturing the port of Santander on the northern coast on 26 August, while San Sebastián fell on 13 September. The loss of ports reduced the possibility of obtaining foreign supplies and, indeed, of counting internationally. Similarly, a Republican offensive near Zaragoza in late August revealed the same problems as Brunete and failed to prevent the Nationalists overrunning Asturias in October. This success gave the Nationalists an important industrial zone, and freed their troops and warships to operate elsewhere against the divided Republicans. As in the Russian Civil War, the relationship between the fronts was readily apparent for both sides. So also was the cumulative nature of success.

The desire to gain the initiative was understandable, but repeated offensives had already weakened the Republicans and the next, launched on 15 December 1937, only did the same. The Republicans captured Teruel. Instead of this success leading to hoped-for peace negotiations, however, an effective Nationalist counter-offensive regained the town on 22 February 1938 and inflicted heavy casualties in fighting during the bitter winter.

Foreign commentators continued to be critical about the character and quality of the war-making, which is not an approach appreciated within Spain. In April 1938, the British Assistant Military Attaché in Paris commented, after visiting Nationalist Spain:

Even a short visit brought out very clearly a number of singular features which characterise this war, a war in which the majority of the participants are almost entirely untrained, a war in which comparatively small forces are strung out on a vast length of front, a war in which modern weapons are used but not on the modern scale, and, finally, a war in which there have been more assassinations than deaths in battle . . . In view of these singularities, it will be obvious that the greatest caution must be used in deducing general lessons from this war: a little adroitness and it will be possible to use it to 'prove' any preconceived theory . . . To anyone with experience of the Great War, the almost complete absence of warlike activities in all three sectors of the front visited was most striking . . . It seems that the battle only flares up intermittently, and then only on small portions of the front; for hundreds of miles the enemy is out of rifle shot . . . no attempt is made by either side to harass the other in his business of living and feeding . . . the paucity of the artillery when an action does take place

... very soon the full fury of the fight dies down; and the end is either a stalemate in the same positions or rapid advances.

The Assistant Attaché went on to ascribe recent Nationalist successes principally to 'their ability to concentrate in secrecy a large preponderance of field artillery in the sector selected for the break-through'. He noted that, in general, tactics were 'largely based on Great War principles', with creeping barrages and trenches. He also commented on deficiencies, including 'an incomplete and ad hoc organisation', poor transport and roads, and the conduct of the war 'in an utterly haphazard way'.

These strictures were overly harsh. Franco had followed up his success at Teruel, where the leading Republican units were destroyed, rather as the Guomindang ones had been in Shanghai in 1937, by overrunning the region of Aragón and driving on to the Mediterranean, which was reached on 15 April 1938. The Nationalists benefited from superior numbers of artillery and aircraft, on the whole supplied when and where needed by Germany and Italy. Republican Spain was now divided in two and morale was low. Nevertheless, Franco did not exploit his success by turning on Barcelona at once, despite German pressure to do so. Concern about the possibility of French entry on the Republican side was a factor, as was a determination to crush his opponents.

Franco's delay gave his divided opponents an opportunity to regroup. Indeed, the ability of the Republicans to generate and deploy considerable forces was clearly demonstrated by their surprise counter-attack on the River Ebro in July 1938. This operation, however, also indicated the problems of mounting breakthrough attacks, as initial Republican successes were contained by Nationalist reinforcements. The Republicans did not have the skills to profit by their early success. Ultimately, Franco's better logistics and supply of aircraft and artillery gave him the edge. The battle continued until November as an attritional struggle, with both sides suffering heavily. This was more serious for the Republicans as it was not easy for them to acquire fresh armaments, especially heavy guns. In contrast, Germany and Italy provided plentiful supplies to the Nationalists.

In late December 1938, the Nationalists turned against Catalonia with greatly superior equipment and numbers. Initially, but only very briefly, their attack was held, but the campaign showed the possibility of a rapid advance, as the Republican front collapsed, in part due to stronger Nationalist firepower. Many Republicans fled across the frontier into France. On 26 January 1939, Barcelona fell with scant resistance. On 27 February, Britain and France recognised the Nationalist government.

On 5 March Segismundo Casado López, the commander of the Republican Central Army, staged a coup within the weakened Republican government with the backing of Julián Besteiro, a prominent right-wing Socialist. They claimed that Juan Negrín, the prime minister, was planning a Communist takeover. This attempt led to fighting for several days in Madrid, but the coup's opponents were defeated. The coup leaders were determined to force through negotiations with Franco, but he insisted on unconditional surrender. At the end of the month, the Nationalists, meeting scant resistance, overran the remaining Republican areas, Madrid falling on 28 March. This led to the end of the republic. At least three hundred thousand Spaniards had been killed in the war. Many fled abroad, Negrín to France and Casado to Venezuela. There had been much damage, most famously in Guernica, but also to cities and settlements across Spain, for example the cathedral at Sigüenza and the Alcázar in Toledo.

Despite having the state apparatus, the Republicans could not feed their population, raise revenue and control inflation. This affected military logistics, with the army short of food. In contrast to the Russian Civil War, the side that held the central position lost, while that which benefited from most external support and military experience won. This contrast underlines the need for caution in the analysis of reasons for victory.

CONTESTING THE CIVIL WAR

Whereas during the war both sides were vicious, after the war the victor continued the reprisals. Moreover, the memorialisation of the war was very important to the Franco regime. In the Valle de los Caidos (Valley of the Fallen), Franco spent two decades and about £200 million on building the basilica in which he was buried, as well as a monastery and a towering crucifix. The vast edifice, readily visible 30 miles (48 kilometres) away, was designed as a monument to the Nationalist dead in the Civil War and a 'national act of atonement', Franco declaring, 'The stones that are to be erected must have the grandeur of the monuments of old, which defy time and forgetfulness.' Some of the ex-Republicans used as forced labour in harsh conditions for the building died. Officially inaugurated in 1959, the monument was intended as a revival of Juan de Herrera's architecture under Philip II, as seen in the Escorial, which was also part of the landscape of memorialisation close to Madrid.

Franco prevented critical accounts of the Civil War. Thus, a Basque translation of George Steer's *The Tree of Gernika: A Field Study of Modern War* (1938) had to be published by Spanish exiles in Caracas in Venezuela in 1963.

Spain's trauma in the 1930s remains an issue that greatly troubles its collective account of the past. Those who see themselves as the heirs of the combatants exchange blame, notably over atrocities and over whether there was justice in the cause then. In focusing on the right's responsibility for launching the Civil War in 1936, the left largely ignores the extent to which their unsuccessful uprising against the republic in 1934 also challenged democracy and was not somehow necessary to stop Fascism, as was sometimes argued.

In contrast, post-Francoist research revealed the extent to

which, in pursuing political goals, Franco's regime was responsible for the large-scale killing of prisoners and civilians, only, in
turn, for this work to produce a reaction. Similarly, after the fall
of Franco, nationalists on behalf of regions with a strong separatist tradition, notably Catalonia, produced accounts that found
historical support for their case, only for the right to emphasise
the longevity of a reality of Spain. This is a tension that continues
to the present.

After Franco's death in 1975, the Civil War could be discussed
more freely. Initially, there was a setting aside of the war in order
to help foster national reconciliation. There was a determination to move beyond his legacy as an aspect of the creation of a
new, democratic Spain. This was *el Pacto del Olvido* (the Pact of
Forgetting), and it was maintained during the centrist government of 1976–82, and its left-wing and right-wing successors
of 1982–97 and 1997–2004 respectively. As a result of the 1977
Amnesty Law, there were no prosecutions. In addition, the 'Day
of Victory' was renamed 'Armed Forces Day', and the mausoleum
in the Valley of the Fallen was not used for official occasions.
Franco's palace, the Pardo, a historic royal palace with an impressive park where he hunted, was not opened to visitors. José María
Aznar's government of 1997–2004 in particular tried to present
a consensus view of the past. There was also a failure of novelists
and filmmakers to consider the Civil War, especially in the 1970s.
The anniversaries of key events in the 1930s were left to private
discussion rather than public memorialisation.

There were, however, cracks in the edifice. An anti-Francoist
intellectual consensus developed with, for example, a discreet revolution in the Spanish universities in the 1980s. Moreover, a Civil
War archive in Salamanca was opened in the 1980s. Ironically,
most of the material was originally by Republicans and had been
compiled under the Francoists in order to try Republican leaders. The opening or, at least partial opening, of foreign archives
was also instructive. The end of the Cold War and the fall of

the Soviet Union were important, as this clarified much about Stalin's policy, not least his manipulation of the Republican government, although much of the intelligence material remained closed. There was also an opening up of non-Soviet material, including in Italy.

From the 1990s, pressure built up to confront the true character of the war and in the 2000s, the uneasy consensus within Spain about the Civil War collapsed. In part, this collapse was a result of political pressure, especially from the regions striving for a proto-nationalism, particularly Catalonia. The more general assault on the centralised account of Spanish history helped lead to the reconsideration of the Civil War, not least because of the prominent role of Catalonia in the resistance to Franco until the end of the war, although many non-Catalans were just as involved.

There was also an attack in Spain at the popular level on the 'Pact of Forgetting', an attack that proved that there was some loss of control by the politicians in a more democratic society. The Asociación para la Recuperación de la Memoria Histórica (ARMH), established in 2000, sought to recuperate the historical memory of the Republicans. Novelistic accounts of the large-scale slaughter of Republicans during, and after, the Francoist takeover were published in the 2000s in what became a widespread cultural movement. These books became popular, and many were published at the local level. Moreover, the internet was extensively used in order to discuss the issue.

Much of this discussion and pressure focused on the bodies in the large number of mass graves across Spain that contained those murdered for holding unacceptable views. The families of Republicans were insistent that their forbears be exhumed, identified and reburied. This pressure coincided with advances in DNA testing and forensic science that made such identification a stronger prospect. Furthermore, the age of the children of the victims lent a sense of urgency to the situation, with pressure for the identification of their parents before they themselves died. The grandchildren proved the main champions. The first exhumation occurred in 2000 and, by 2003, there were exhumations at Francoist concentration camps.

The search for truth was linked to memorialisation, with plaques now explaining how people had died. This process paralleled that in France where plaques came to emphasise the role of Vichy in the fate of France's Jews. As with similar campaigns elsewhere in the world, there was also in Spain pressure for restitution of property and for the return of children who had been seized. After the Civil War, such children had been given to the families of Francoist officers, as also happened in Argentina under an authoritarian conservative military rule in the 1970s.

Politics played a role. The Aznar government opposed what it saw as left-wing pressure for action, not least for a judicial process to investigate the cause of all deaths. After the government fell in 2004, its replacement in 2004–11, under the Socialist José Luis Rodríguez Zapatero, was keen not only to reverse Aznar's policies but thereby also to win political capital. There was a willingness to engage with the issue of the large numbers killed as the Nationalist forces repressed opposition and secured their position. Funds, political backing and legal support were provided for the ARMH. In October 2007, the government passed an Historical Memory Law, which recognised the victims of both sides of the Civil War, formally condemned the Franco regime, ordered the removal of Francoist symbols from public buildings, provided state help for the exhumation of victims of Francoist repression, prohibited political events at the Valley of the Fallen, and granted Spanish nationality to surviving members of the International Brigades. The Popular Party voted against this legislation, arguing that the measure weakened the political consensus of the transition to democracy, while the Republican Left of Catalonia voted against it on the grounds that the measures did not go far enough. In 2009, the Valley of the Fallen monument was closed, and in 2010 the basilica there was closed for Mass. It was reopened for Mass after the change of government in 2011.

Left-wing pressure also led to a backlash from the right, with writers who restated the old Francoist view and attacked the re-evaluation of the history of the 1930s finding an eager public. In 2006, 30 per cent of the respondents in a poll in the newspaper *El Mundo* argued that the Francoist rising of 1936 had been justified. Thus, the recall of history reflected, and sustained, persisting cleavages in Spanish society and, indeed, beyond.

The Civil War, moreover, continued to be part of the vocabulary of Spanish politics. In 2007, Jesús de Polanco, the head of the media empire Grupo Prisa, accused the opposition of wanting 'to go back to the Civil War', because of its criticism of left-wing media opinions. This reference to the past provided an easy way to say that something appeared unacceptable, and was a more general tendency in Spain's treatment of its history. The comparison was misguided, however, not least because Spain was in a very different situation to that in the 1930s, in part because, in the 2000s, it was integrated into international systems, most obviously the European Union.

The bitter debate continued into the 2010s, with revisionism on behalf of Franco criticised from the left. Tales of atrocities by both sides were recounted in a partisan fashion. Foreign writers did not help with emotive titles such as 'Spanish Holocaust', a term that greatly misrepresents both Spanish history and, by comparison, Hitler's policies. Indeed, although not intended as such, the use of such a term could be held to constitute Holocaust diminishment. In 2012, the UN High Commissioner for Human Rights pressed for the repeal of the 1977 Amnesty Law on the grounds that there is no statute for limitations for crimes against humanity under international human rights laws. The Spanish government disagreed: the conservative government of the Popular Party, in power from 2011, restricted help given for exhumations.

Controversies in Spain are, at once, as is common elsewhere in the world, an instance of the truth and reconciliation process and also an example of present politics. The first has become normative as a result of what is held to be the positive instance of such a process in post-apartheid South Africa. The political dimension, however, operates in part as a cross-current to that of truth and reconciliation, as political capital is sought, although this process can also be regarded as central to the entire idea of truth and reconciliation.

In Spain, the role of politics was seen in 1998 when a Spanish judge arranged for the arrest of General Augusto Pinochet, dictator of Chile from 1973 to 1990. This was a move very much opposed by the Aznar government, which was keen on reconciliation within Spain as well as being anxious to preserve good relations with Chile. Pinochet was regarded on the left as a substitute for the dead Franco. Contradiction in Spain between the impossibility of arresting any member of the Franco government, and the possibility of acting against Pinochet, was brought into the open in a way intended to embarrass the Aznar government.

The complex process of marking Spain's recent past was seen in 2014 when the anniversary of an attempted right-wing military coup in 1981 was honoured. Lieutenant-Colonel Antonio Tejero Díez of the Civil Guard was dismissed for organising an unauthorised lunch at a Civil Guard barracks for his father, Antonio Tejero Molina, the leader of the attempted coup, and other plotters. The Catalan crisis of 2017–18 saw separatists there repeatedly compare the attitudes, policies and moves of the national government to those of Franco.

At the end of 2015, 317 streets with Franco's name still exist. Some cities have changed street names and removed statues, but others take a different view.

CHAPTER TWELVE

Dictatorship, 1939–75

THE FRANCO DICTATORSHIP

Until 1973, when he appointed a prime minister, Francisco Franco, the *Caudillo* (leader), was both head of state and head of the government. Created in the Civil War as a nationalist military state, this was a right-wing dictatorship. The state was based on the theory of 'organic democracy', allegedly a representation of the true interests of society, rather than the 'inorganic democracy' of universal suffrage, which was presented as inherently selfish and dominated by a lack of understanding of truth. The *cortes*, established in 1942, was an advisory body, and was dominated by the government, while, by the Law of the Principles of the Movement of 1958, Spain was defined as a monarchy that was Catholic and traditional as well as representative. The emphasis on a monarchy reflected the strength of monarchism, notably in army circles. It was agreed, however, that the monarch would not be restored until after Franco died, an event expected long before he actually died in 1975. The Organic Law, which followed in 1967, confirmed Franco's personal legislative powers. Franco appointed and chaired the Council of Ministers, the key governmental body and a place for factional struggles.

In contrast, public meetings were closely controlled, as was the media. Regarded as a threat, regional separatism was treated as another justification for strong government and its means to provide 'unity of power'. Lluís Companys, who had declared Catalan independence in 1934 and taken shelter in France, was arrested by the German occupiers in 1940 and handed over to the Francoist authorities who mistreated him before he was shot.

In the aftermath of the Civil War, in 1939, large numbers suspected of opposition sympathies, let alone activity, were executed

– at least twenty thousand in three years – with Franco personally signing many death sentences. The military and paramilitary became the key defences of the regime. Republican guerrillas continued to resist, for example in the Axarquia and in the mountains of the Alpujarra until 1942. Although state terror became less murderous with time, with executions tapering off from 1942, the extended state of war helped make civilian life brutal, notably in the 1940s. For example, teachers considered disloyal were imprisoned, exiled, executed, sacked or made to undergo re-education. Censorship was supported by fear of denunciation. The black market was dominant. Poverty was widespread and the period become known as the *años del hambre* (hunger years).

THE SECOND WORLD WAR

In 1940, Hitler was interested in the idea of a league of Germany, Italy, Spain and Vichy France, but his commitment to the interests of the last two was greatly limited. Spain's entry into the war could have led to an attack on Gibraltar, which would have destroyed the British ability to operate in the western Mediterranean, not least as the Germans would also have gained air bases in southern Spain. Furthermore, such an alliance would have given the Germans submarine bases on Spain's Atlantic and Mediterranean coasts and in the Canaries. Hitler met Franco at Hendaye on 23 October 1940.

Although Franco, who had signed a Treaty of Friendship with Germany in 1939, was a keen supporter of Hitler's cause, a point greatly played down after the war, Spain stayed out of the conflict. Francoists later pretended that Spanish neutrality during the war was a result of Franco's brave and adept rejection of Hitler's pressure. In practice, Franco, was a firm opponent of democracy, and a sharer in Hitler's belief that Judaism, Communism and cosmopolitanism were linked and threats, and that Jews were responsible for the alliance against Germany. Franco did not want Spain to shelter Jews. A decree of 11 May 1939 prevented entry of 'those of a markedly Jewish character', and another of 23 October 1941 banned the passage of Jews to the New World on Spanish ships. Few Jews were given shelter.

To Franco, Hitler was bound to win. This likelihood apparently provided an opportunity to gain control of Gibraltar, Morocco and even Portugal, a traditional ally of Britain. Within Spain, there were calls for such gains, notably from the Falange. In June 1940, Franco had already occupied the international zone of Tangier.

Franco's demands for territorial gains from French North Africa, particularly Morocco, were seen as excessive by Hitler, and as likely to weaken Vichy France, which, with its empire and fleet, was regarded as more important politically and militarily. The demands for food, raw materials, manufactured goods and armaments were also unacceptable. To Hitler, Spain was largely inconsequential, a source of minor advantages that were not worth major effort, not least due to the clear weakness of the Spanish economy. Indeed, due to the Allies' sea blockade, Spain was dependent on the Allies for fuel and food. The multiple problems posed by alliance with Mussolini discouraged Hitler from taking on Franco, and the latter was believed to offer little bar distraction from the goal of war with the Soviet Union. Franco anyway claimed that Spain was exhausted, and that war with Britain or giving German forces transit permission to attack Gibraltar would lead to British attacks on Spanish overseas possessions. Spain was a self-declared 'non-belligerent'.

Nevertheless, Franco actively collaborated, for example providing bases for German reconnaissance aircraft and Italian human torpedo units, facilitating German espionage and propaganda, and refuelling U-boats. Franco also provided not only raw materials, but also the volunteer 'Blue Division' that fought on the Eastern Front against the Soviet Union in what was presented as a crusade against Communism. About forty-seven thousand Spaniards fought in the division. The División Española de Voluntarios was known as the Blue Division because many of the early volunteers were Falange militia who had that shirt-colour. This was not a regular force but it was justified as a response to Soviet intervention in the Civil War, although Franco did not declare war on the Soviet Union. There was a shortage of volunteers, so that by late 1942 even anti-Fascists were being recruited. The division fought bravely and well.

The regime itself was divided. There were tensions within the government, within the army, within the Falange and among the right as a whole. In 1942, in the Basilica of Begoña episode in Bilbao, Falangists and Carlists clashed, with grenades thrown, and a subsequent punishment of Falange leaders. Franco's brother-in-law, Ramón Serrano Suñer, the leader of the Fascist Falange, was strongly anti-Allies when he was Foreign Secretary from 1940. He was replaced in 1942.

In turn, when the war started to go very badly for Germany, and notably after Sicily was invaded and Mussolini overthrown in July 1943, the Franco regime became more accommodating to the Allies. The Allied conquest first of Vichy Morocco and Algeria in November 1942, and then the defeat of Axis forces in Tunisia, had already made Spain appear vulnerable, even though the German occupation of Vichy France in November 1942 increased the German presence on Spain's northern border. In 1943, Portugal also moved towards the Allies, allowing them to establish air bases in the Azores. As the war continued to look less good for the Axis powers, the Franco regime tried to make itself look less Fascist. For example, Franco became more sympathetic to Jewish refugees.

The 'Blue Division' was run down in size, and withdrawn in 1943; 1,500 men remained as the Spanish Legion, but were ordered home in February 1944. Under the pressure of the threat of the United States cutting off oil supplies, Franco, in May 1944, agreed to hand over all interned Italian ships, to expel all German agents, and largely to cut off the supply of tungsten to Germany. In October 1944, Spain recognised the government of Charles de

Gaulle in France. Diplomatic relations with Germany, however, were not cut until April 1945, while intelligence aid to Germany was provided until the close of the war. Moreover, German and Vichy French figures were sheltered at the end of the war, and some were helped in their flight to South America.

As with Thailand, the process of wartime change prepared the way for the postwar myth of neutrality, a myth that facilitated Franco's military cooperation with the USA during the Cold War. The Spanish rewriting of the Second World War since 1975 has been clearly linked to political trends and is subordinate to dissension over the Civil War.

THE COLD WAR

The Cold War would have been much more difficult for the West if the Communists had won the Spanish Civil War and thus gained Atlantic bases, notably for both warships and aircraft. Earlier, Spain, in the event of such a victory in 1936–9 and of the Nazi–Soviet pact of 1939–41, would have been a German ally anyway in 1939–41.

In contrast, thanks to its clear and sustained post-1945 anti-Communism, Spain, a Fascist dictatorship, was eventually brought into the Western alliance. Initially, the situation was less easy for Spain. In early 1945, Britain and then the United States informed Franco that Spain's wartime policy and Fascism meant isolation. As a result, Spain was not invited to the United Nations founding conference in 1945, and was not admitted to the UN until 1955. Indeed, many people in Spain assumed that the Allies would invade in 1945.

In response, in the summer of 1945, Franco sought to improve Spain's reputation. It was declared a monarchy and domestic constitutional rights were supposedly improved, while an Axis sympathiser was dropped as Foreign Minister. In March 1946, however, Britain, France and the United States declared that good relations were impossible as long as Franco remained in power.

The UN pressed for firmer action. Nevertheless, when this crisis passed, Western coexistence with the Franco regime developed, and this persuaded Don Juan de Borbón, the Pretender to the Spanish throne, to move towards reconciliation with Franco.

Portugal, another authoritarian right-wing dictatorship, had been a member of NATO (the North Atlantic Treaty Organization) from the outset, in large part because the American air bases established in 1943 in the Azores were regarded as important to the USA's global strategy. Air bases were crucial both to the resupply of American forces in NATO, notably those in Italy and the eastern Mediterranean, and in providing strategic depth in the event of a Soviet advance overrunning much territory. In 1953, the USA and Spain signed an agreement giving the Americans rights to establish air bases, although Spain did not join NATO until 1983, by which time it was a democracy. Under the 1953 agreement, Franco received money and recognition, including eventually a meeting with President Eisenhower.

Meanwhile, in an episode that is still somewhat overlooked, there was a major attempt to challenge the Franco regime, an attempt that bridged the Civil War, the Second World War and the Cold War. The insurrection was at its height in 1944–8, with up to ten thousand guerrillas in action. In addition to Civil War Republican soldiers hidden in the mountains, the government faced guerrillas operating from the French border in the Pyrenees, and they became more active against the Franco regime after the German occupation of France ended in 1944. In October 1944, an invasion by about 2,500 men was launched through the Val d'Aran. The Spanish Republican flag was flown over places taken, but the Francoists were ready and the invasion failed. There had been a wave of strikes in Spain the previous month, but there was little support for the insurrection. In 1944, anxious to focus on Germany, both the United States and Britain pressed the new French government not to let the situation in Spain get out of hand.

The Spanish government defeated the remaining Republican rebels in the late 1940s and early 1950s, in part through a ruthless policy of hunting down the rebels, backed by very punitive action against any sign of local support. It also benefited from divisions within the opposition between Communists and anarchists; from popular exhaustion with conflict after the travails of the Civil War; from its use of food rationing in order to influence popular support; from the strength of Francoist support in some areas close to the Pyrenees, especially Navarre; and from the extent to which the French, initially sympathetic to the insurrection when its government was a post-war coalition containing Communists and Socialists, became more hostile to the insurrection from the end of 1946. In the 1950s, Spanish Republican activities in France were closed down and activists arrested. Because the reliability of the conscripts in the Spanish army was doubted, Franco's government used the Civil Guard against the rebels. The appropriate tactics, doctrine and brutal forcefulness had been developed in the Civil War. Those captured were usually shot at once. About five thousand guerrillas were killed. The insurrection, according to the government, officially ended in 1951, although it continued at a low level thereafter.

Spain continued to be a police state, with surveillance of critics, notably of the Communists. Much is still unclear, notably as the archives of the Secret Police await study. Nevertheless, it is difficult to consider the period without understanding this dimension, and that the 'undercurrent' of state surveillance and violence was mainstream and apparent. Regional separatism was blocked. Indeed, Catalan autonomy was abolished in 1938. The Catalan language was treated as a dialect, while Catalan names were banned, as was the national dance.

Spain was still an imperial power in the Spanish Sahara, officially the Overseas Province of the Spanish Sahara, resisting an independence movement although eventually accepting that self-determination would be the long-term outcome. Moreover,

Spain returned to Morocco the border province of Tarfaya in 1958 and the enclave of Ifni in 1960. In 1968, having tried partial decolonisation since 1960 in an attempt to keep it in the Spanish system, Spanish Guinea was granted independence as Equatorial Guinea. In 1970, the Spaniards, in what has been called the *Zemla Intifada* (Zemla Uprising), suppressed independence demonstrations in Spanish Sahara. In 1973, however, Spain agreed to hold a plebiscite in early 1975.

Meanwhile, Gibraltar, where a 1967 referendum had overwhelmingly rejected Spanish sovereignty, was blockaded by means of police and customs harassment, notably with the closure of the border gate, telephone lines and postal communications in 1969. This harassment only entrenched hostility to Spain there. Moreover, the British government proved unwilling to yield. The blockade, which had hit the economy of neighbouring parts of Spain, came to an end in 1985, years after the death of Franco.

IDEOLOGY AND POLICY

The Franco dictatorship, which lasted until his death in 1975, was Fascistic, but its key theme was a conservative authoritarianism led by a general enjoying military support and also drawing on the widespread backing from sections of society, as seen in the Civil War and sustained thereafter. The support particularly came from the smallholding peasantry, but also from much (although by no means all) of the middle class. The authoritarianism included a strong role for the family, one at once patriarchal but with a powerful ideology of motherhood and a repression of women and certainly of female independence. This helped cement the Catholic Church's support for Franco. The female section of the Falange, which claimed 580,000 members in 1939, sought not passive piety, but an active religious participation in the needs of society. As with much of 'Francoism', the section was also conservative, with its leaders mostly from the social élite. The police interrogated couples caught kissing in cars. Rival authoritarianism, notably that of the Communists, was banned. So also were independent trade unions, which were replaced by those acceptable to the state.

There were other trends as well. Nazi Germany and Fascist Italy affected Franco's domestic policies, encouraging the attempt to pursue a modern, mobilising dictatorship, a policy particularly associated with the more radical sections of the Falange. This attempt was limited, however, by the consequences of war, repression and ideology, notably the destruction of human capital and institutional factors.

The results were very varied. As a testimony to the Church's backing for Franco, church-building was an important aspect of the new-model Spain being constructed as the concrete was being poured. In 1940, work resumed on Antoni Gaudí's Church of the Holy Family in Barcelona. State engineers sought to plan a new national political economy that would produce an effective and fair society able to provide a grounding for Catholic renewal and political stability.

Implementation, however, was more difficult than conception, in part due to administrative rivalries. The hydroelectric dams built before 1956 took longer to build, were not so high, and their spillways were smaller than those of the 1930s. The capture of Madrid in 1939 was followed by schemes to transform the city but, in the wake of the war, these plans fell victim to a lack of money.

As a separate strand, Christian nationalism, as with Russia today, was a key element of the regime's ideology. The regime pursued a programme of state-sponsored social conservatism, indeed a version of Christian non-democracy. For example, under the General Law of Education (1970), free compulsory education was presented as a goal, although it was still not in place in 1980. The general approach to cultural innovation was that of Philistinism.

SPANISH SURREALISM

A filmmaker from the 1920s to the 1970s, Luis Buñuel (1900–83) was a key figure in Spanish Surrealism. He was born to a comfortable background in Calanda in the province of Teruel in Aragón, a town he later described as where 'the Middle Ages lasted until World War I'. His education at the University of Madrid was transformative. Buñuel became close friends with Lorca and Salvador Dalí (1904–89), and, with finance from his mother, made *Un Chien Andalou* (1929), a surrealist film shocker with Dalí. Rejecting Catholicism and, in 1931, joining the Communist Party, Buñuel made a film *Las Hurdes: Tierra Sin Pan* (1933), an account of peasant poverty in Extremadura, that, while initially critical of the Republic's neglect of rural life, was then used in anti-Fascist propaganda that was banned by Franco. Supporting the Republicans during the Civil War, Buñuel thereafter lived in the United States and then Mexico, becoming a Mexican citizen.

Born in Catalonia to a comfortable family, Dalí studied art in Madrid, where he experimented with Cubism, and then became a Surrealist working in Paris. He refused to commit himself during the Spanish Civil War, and spent the troubled years of mid-century in safe New York, returning to Spain in 1948. His willingness to live there during the Franco years displeased those who stayed in exile, as did his praise for the dictator. Increased Catholic devotion was another difference. In 1982, Dalí was made a Marquis by King Juan Carlos, a fan. The *Teatre-Meseu Dalí* in his birthplace, Figueres, is a surrealist fantasy house in a one-time theatre.

FRANCOIST ARCHITECTURE

The visitor to modern Spain can see many instances of the architecture favoured under Franco, and especially so in Madrid. There was both an indigenous retro-style, in the shape of looking back to Golden Age Spain, and notably the architecture of the Escorial, and also a Fascist Modernism that drew on Italian and German models. The shared characteristic was that of mass, as in the Ministerio del Aire, the Museo de América and the church of San Francisco de Borja.

SIGNS OF CHANGE

Francoism is generally divided into two periods, the first of repression, the second of transition. The latter, focusing on the 1960s and early 1970s, is described in terms of liberalisation, economic growth and social change. There is much to say for this interpretation, for example with the liberalisation of censorship by the Press Law of 1966, but it also has limitations. Each period saw attempts at state-directed, corporatist economic growth, notably thanks to the Stabilisation Plan of 1959, with bureaucrats playing key roles in governance, a process aided by the lack of democracy. Moreover, the context in the 1960s and early 1970s remained that of state control. Thus, the industrial take-off in the 1960s was in part dependent on the availability of a pliant, cheap and largely migrant workforce that had its origins in the Civil War and its aftermath. This situation had also been seen in the Soviet Union and China.

At the same time, it is a mistake to take too insular an approach. The more general economic 'Long Boom' of the period was significant in providing export markets, investment capital and new technology. Car culture spread. Increased trade made autarkic self-sufficiency less desirable and less necessary. Yet, due to the isolation that stemmed from Spain's political position, this boom was largely delayed in Spain until the 1960s.

Economic growth greatly accentuated regional divisions. It

benefited most clearly the cities, where manufacturing was concentrated, especially in Catalonia. Much of the business élite there backed Franco. In contrast, on a longstanding pattern, the rural interior did badly, both relatively and absolutely. This was particularly so of eastern Andalusia, most of Galicia and much of the Castilian Meseta. To profit, agriculture modernised, notably the mechanisation offered by tractors, but this led to rural unemployment and to large-scale migration from the interior, and encouraged the decline of former market towns. Andalusia and the Meseta lost population heavily, particularly to Barcelona, Madrid and jobs abroad. This was on a pattern more generally seen in Europe.

The escape from rural misery was increasingly linked to the quest for economic opportunity and social mobility, a quest expressed in terms of new housing estates such as the *Barrio del Pilar* in Madrid. The population of Madrid rose from 950,000 in 1930 to three million by 1970, a proportionate rise much exceeding that of the Spanish population. New churches were built in the neighbourhoods constructed under Franco.

These changes greatly hit established social and economic patterns, and tested the Catholic nationalism of the regime. Indeed, the latter, with its essentially conservative character and reactionary stance, became increasingly redundant in the 1960s. This was not least because the impact of television took even further the earlier questioning offered by cinema. There was control over the media by the government, but also a support for consumerist values. Moreover, there were more specific critiques and challenges, notably the Communism of the trade unions and the liberalism or Marxism of many intellectuals and students. Although strikes were illegal, they became more common from the start of the 1960s. Police repression did not end strikes. *Comisiones Obreras* (Workers' Commissions) offered clandestine trade unions and helped create an example for activism elsewhere, as with student protests. The net effect was to encourage opposition to Franco, and certainly the circulation of a set of different values. Residents' associations played a role, notably in response to concerns about public services.

With its cult of unity, Francoism had thus come to preside over, rather than direct, a society that included very disparate tendencies that could not be coerced, as had appeared possible in the 1940s and even the 1950s. The difficulties of directing this society was indicated by student, worker and other initiatives, protests and activities from the late 1960s. Moreover, many clerics became critical. Across the country, progressive parish priests offered their congregations, most of whom were conservative, criticism of the system in their sermons. The resulting tension within the Church was replicated in many families.

One aspect of diversity was *Euskadi Ta Askatasuna* (ETA; Basque Homeland and Liberty), a movement founded in 1959 in order to support Basque culture, which became a Marxist terrorist group that was responsible for killings from 1968. The first assassination was that, in 1970, of the torturing chief of the Secret Police in San Sebastián. ETA also tried and failed to assassinate Franco, part of a series of unsuccessful attempts.

FRANCOIST HISTORY

As in Italy with Mussolini from 1922, the authoritarian, right-wing Nationalist Franco regime that gained power in Spain thanks to success in the Civil War both commemorated victory and also adopted an historical reference point that marked a return to a past age of greatness, as well as drawing on an analysis of what had supposedly led to this greatness. In a parallel with what was presented as the expulsion of anti-Christian foreignness, in the shape of the Nationalists' left-wing, secularist Republican rivals, the regime looked back to the medieval Reconquista of Spain from the Muslims. The Francoist approach to Spain's past had nothing in common with the post-Francoist engagement with al-Andalus. In particular, there was a focus on the reigns of Isabella of Castile and her husband, Ferdinand of Aragón, under whom the Muslims had been finally defeated, the Jews expelled, Catholic purity safeguarded and the New World claimed for Spain. Philip II's reign provided an image employed by Franco's regime of a religiously united country and people. In contrast, the Spain of the eighteenth-century Enlightenment and of nineteenth-century liberalism was ignored, and the latter in particular was not much covered in teaching.

In his *Atlas historicó éspañol*, published in Madrid in 1941, Gonzalo Menéndez Pidal, for example, essentially ignored the nineteenth and twentieth centuries. Modernisation and domestic politics were denied in this book, in favour of a more heroic and united past. The Reconquista received much attention. A page was devoted to industry and commerce in Habsburg Spain, another to maps of the journeys of four saints, and several pages to early-modern cultural history. The Jews and the Moriscos were ignored: a racist statement by omission. This atlas remained important after the Second World War.

As with most examples of the use of the past, the Francoist hankering back to past greatness had a longer provenance. It had been used as a comparison by those who focused on Spain's abject failure at the hands of the USA in the war of 1898. Nevertheless, as again with most examples of the use of the past, there were important differences in tone and usage, not least, in this case, the degree of government support. The devout Catholicism, territorial expansionism, and racialism of Ferdinand and Isabella, all apparently served as a suitable model for Franco. An imaginary history based on clearly ideological positions was powerfully advanced.

As in Fascist Italy, the rejection of liberalism under Franco also drew on a number of currents, some of which had a stronger historical imagination and mythos than others. Franco disliked all whom he held responsible for Spain's earlier weakness and current problems. In international relations, this approach meant a hatred of France and Britain, both of which had weakened Spain as an imperial power. That they were also tolerant democracies contributed to his attitude. Modern history was downplayed under Franco in favour of a past of Spain as a great imperial power and one stronger than France and Britain. Meanwhile, the Spanish government presented its colonial position, cooperating with the Instituto de Estudios Africanos to produce the *Atlas Histórico y Geográfico de Africa Española* (1955).

At the same time, other views circulated and were presented. The Catalan historian Jaume Vicens Vives produced an *Atlas y sintesis de Historia de España* (published in Barcelona in 1944), which was more vivid than that of Pidal. Due to the Franco regime, Vicens had to be cautious in what he tacked politically, but his atlas eventually covered crucial episodes of Spanish disunity – the Carlist Wars and the Civil War – and was more willing than Pidal to present Spanish history in its European context. There were also no maps of the travels of saints in his atlas. Vicens proved particularly interested in social and economic history and in links with French scholars. He founded Estudios de historia moderna (1951). Other historians followed suit. An interest in historical materialism led to, and was encouraged by, Marxist perspectives.

THE END OF DICTATORSHIP

Dictatorship in Spain was very much focused on Franco and started to unravel with his death in 1975. This, however, was a death that came very slowly and with Franco holding onto religious relics as he died. The situation was different to, and more benign, than that in Portugal where the authoritarian government established by António Salazar, dictator from 1932, survived his death in 1970, only to end in 1974 with a coup that led to a period of instability that lasted until 1976.

Franco firmly did not want to see any transition to democracy after his death. He was a proponent of *continusimo*. In ETA's

Operación Ogro, however, Admiral Luis Carrero Blanco, his keen supporter and prime minister, and a potential strongman successor, was blown up (along with two bodyguards) in Madrid in December 1973: the car was catapulted high into the air by the force of the bomb, which had been placed under the road surface. The government replied with tougher anti-terrorist measures, while ten of those involved in the conspiracy were convicted and executed.

Implacably against democratic change, Franco made Juan Carlos (r. 1975–2014), grandson of the last king, swear an oath that he would uphold the values of the Francoist National Movement. Franco claimed that he had left everything 'all tied down, well tied down', but the struggle to keep him alive suggested how ill-prepared Spain was for a successor. Moreover, Franco did not reckon with significant members of the political and economic élites who saw that the structures of Francoism were in decay, nor with the consequences of Spain becoming increasingly urban and bourgeois.

THE TOURIST INDUSTRY

The Franco years saw Spain become a key tourist destination. The package industry, jet aircraft and the rising disposable wealth of northern European industrial workers in the 'Long Boom' produced massive demand. Lax planning controls and the cheap price of land were key enablers and a series of tourist resorts took off, sometimes, as with Benidorm on the Costa Blanca, from modest fishing villages. Helped by the climate, the sandy beaches and the development of jet aircraft and package holidays, tourism grew rapidly from the 1960s. In 1959, limits on foreign investment were taken off. The number of tourists rose from four million in 1959 to fourteen million by

1964. It then continued to rise. In 2015, Spain was the most common tourist destination in the EU for non-nationals; 270 million nights were spent in tourist accommodation, which was 21.3 per cent of the EU total. Tourism provides about 10–11 per cent of Spain's GDP and in 2016 Spain was the third most visited country in the world. In 2016, the largest category of visitors arriving in Spain on a short-term basis were from Britain (17.8 million), France (11.4) and Germany (11.2). There were 75.6 million international visitors, compared to 68.2 million in 2015. Tourism served as a way to redefine Spain by making traditional regional names irrelevant. In 1964, the renaming and reconfiguring of much of Spain by coasts, notably the Costa Brava and the Costa del Sol, began. New towns came to prominence such as Marbella, the leading resort on the Costa del Sol. On Majorca, Palma became a key resort. The Canary Islands are also a major tourist destination. Barcelona took off as a tourist destination as a consequence of the 1992 Olympics. Before that, it had seen fewer than one million tourists a year, but, by 2016, the number was over eight million.

CHAPTER THIRTEEN

Democratic Era, 1976–

'Españoles, Franco ha muerto.' Prime Minister Carlos Arias Navarro's announcement on TVE (Televisión Española), the national television channel, on the day of Franco's death, meant a journey to a new Spain, but what that would entail was unclear. The transition to democracy was by no means inevitable and there were a number of forces, especially the army, the Communists and ETA, that could have thrown a spanner in the works. Moreover, once a democratic succession was determined and took effect after Franco's death, it was uncertain whether former Francoists would cooperate with it. The prospect of another coup, like that in which Franco had himself seized power in 1936, was a concern, however improbable that might seem today.

Power continued for a while to be held by Francoists, while the monarchy was reintroduced, under Juan Carlos, the king from 1975 until his abdication in 2014. The relatively orderly transition to a democracy in which there was a considerable amount of continuity was very much a shift encouraged by the USA, which wanted to ensure that Spain did not experience the instability seen in Portugal, with the opportunities provided for a left-wing takeover. Juan Carlos, crowned two days after Franco died, proved important to the shift. Grandson of Alfonso XIII, he was the son of Don Juan de Borbón (1913–93). Franco had declared Spain a monarchy in 1947 but, in 1969, passed over Don Juan, whom he feared (wrongly) would be too liberal, in favour of Juan Carlos whom he thought (wrongly) more amenable to continuing the Francoist state. Don Juan, whose independence was also unwelcome to Franco, did not renounce his claims on the throne until two years after Juan Carlos had become king.

The new king in practice proved willing to support

democratisation. He took an active role, helping to encourage Francoists and the military, which looked to his leadership, to accept the new order. Under Franco, there had been no independent political parties and no free press, and, outside the small group that ran the state, scant political life at a national level, and no capacity for organised change. As a consequence, against the background of dissident movements and political prisoners campaigning for change, it was the new king and the small group of Francoists that played the key role in what Spaniards term the 'Transition'.

Franco's last prime minister, Carlos Arias Navarro, who had been a deadly public prosecutor for the Nationalists in Málaga during the Civil War, was kept in office until 1976 when he fell due to the king replacing him. This was because the illiberal Arias had sought to keep the old system in place by arresting the heads of the newly constituted Democratic Coordination of banned parties of the left. Although the Transition was relatively orderly, political killings were rife in the late 1970s. For example, in January 1977, in the Atocha massacre, five Communist labour lawyers were shot dead and four seriously wounded by far-right assassins, members of a group calling itself the *Alianza Apostólica Anticomunista* (the Apostolic Anti-Communist Alliance). Allegedly Italian neo-Fascists played a role. Another left-wing activist had been murdered by the AAA two days earlier. The funerals became occasions for large-scale gatherings. The events were presented in the film *Siete dias de enero* (Seven Days in January) by Juan Antonio Bardem, a Communist who had produced *Muerte de un ciclista* (Death of a Cyclist, 1955), a powerful social realist account of society's hypocrisy. There is a monument for the murdered lawyers in Antón Martín Square in Madrid.

Juan Carlos replaced Arias with Adolfo Suárez González, a member of the Francoist system and the General Secretary of the Francoist official party, but one willing to see through change, rather like some of the ex-Communists who would hold power in eastern Europe in the 1990s. Indeed Suárez had told Franco that democratisation was inevitable. Suárez created a political party, the Centre Democratic Union (*Unión de Centro Democrático*, UCD), and secured a national referendum for universal suffrage for a bicameral parliament, a measure overwhelmingly passed on 15 December 1976. The following spring, he legalised the Spanish Socialist and Communist parties, trade unions and the right to strike, while the Francoist National Movement, once headed by Suárez, was disbanded. The Atocha massacre contributed to this change.

FOOTBALL

See a pleasant-looking café or small restaurant across Spain? Well, be warned. Sitting outside might be nice, but all-too-often a television inside will be devoted to the religion, notably for many men, of football. This religion centres on local loyalties. One of the strongest is that focused on Real Madrid, which was founded in 1902 as Madrid Football Club. From its white home kit, it is known as *Los Blancos* and, since 1947, has played in the Santiago Bernabéu Stadium with its massive capacity of eighty-one thousand. Identification is strengthened by the members owning and operating the club. The *Real* (Royal) title was given to the club by Alfonso XIII in 1920. Financially highly successful, the club has repeatedly been successful on the pitch too, both in Spain and in Europe, winning the European Cup every year between 1956 and 1960.

FC Barcelona, usually known as Barça, is the major rival. Matches between the two are known as *El Clásico*. Founded in 1899, the club is regarded as crucial to Catalan identity, and is owned and operated by its supporters. Like Real Madrid, it is wealthy and frequently successful, both in

> Spain and in Europe. In 1925, the crowd at Barcelona jeered the Royal March, in 1936 the club president was murdered by Falangists, and, after the Civil War, the team was identified with the opposition to Franco and Real Madrid with the regime.

The elections, the first Spanish ones since 1936, held in June 1977, gave Suárez's moderate party just under half the seats, and the new Assembly drafted a constitution, which was confirmed in December 1978 by a referendum delivering 88 per cent support. This constitution added social and cultural reform to the institutionalisation of a parliamentary monarchy; the death penalty was abolished, the voting age was reduced to eighteen, and there was to be no state religion. Proportional representation and bicameralism were seen as ways to promote a moderation lacking in the pre-Francoist Second Republic. In an important break with the centralising practices of the Francoist state, the constitution recognised regional autonomy and, under the Statutes of Autonomy, such autonomy indeed followed for all of Spain, although the central government reserved key powers including foreign policy. The constitution also declared the 'indivisible unity of the Spanish Nation', which was a block to separatism and became a major issue in the politics concerning Catalonia in 2017.

The abandonment of radical Marxism by the Socialist Party, which did well in the 1977 election, was also significant to the success of the Transition. So too was the lack of a significant far-right party. Suárez won re-election in 1979, but tension increased with newfound rights for strike action and regional autonomy, creating unease. The 1979 Statute of Autonomy of Catalonia was unwelcome to traditionalists. In 1979, Córdoba elected a Communist council. Both unemployment and inflation were high. ETA activity, which became more deadly in

1978–80, encouraged the sense of instability. As a result, in January 1981, Suárez was forced out by his party. As an instance of the old order, he was made a hereditary duke by Juan Carlos following his resignation, just as Arias had been made a hereditary marquis.

Paranoid anxieties on the right, or, looked at differently, a response, drawing on a genuine hatred of democracy and on nostalgia for old ways, to the destruction of the Francoist order, led to an attempted coup on 23 February 1981. Lieutenant Colonel Antonio Tejero of the Civil Guard, with two hundred armed Civil Guards, took over the *cortes*, while General Jaime Milans del Bosch, the head of the Valencia military region, called a state of emergency, put tanks on the streets and pressed Juan Carlos to establish a military government.

This coup was very much a make-or-break moment for democratic Spain, and led to many fearing that there would be a return to a Francoist past, or at least instability in an echo of Primo's seizure of power in 1923. Juan Carlos, however, rejected the idea from his confidant, General Alfonso Armada (possibly a member of the plot), that Armada head a 'salvation government'. Juan Carlos used television to broadcast his affirmation of the constitution and democratic rule. His stance ensured that most of the army, notably that in Madrid, did not support the coup, which then collapsed. There had been no casualties. The public demonstrated its support for democracy. The military conspirators were imprisoned.

There are many conspiracy theories about the coup, notably about larger plans for action, about the role of the king, who can be seen as waiting to see which way the wind was blowing, and about the relationship between the fall of Suárez and the coup. The key point, however, is that the new system held. In Poland, in contrast, in 1981, the army suppressed the Solidarity movement at the behest of the Communist government and the Soviet Union.

Juan Carlos was also significant in that he did not seek power for himself. Instead, he proved a successful constitutional monarch in a country that, despite the situation prior to 1923, did not have a recent tradition of such a monarchy. This serves as a reminder of the diversity of types of government in late twentieth-century Europe. By contrast, the monarchy did not return when military rule ended in Greece, and there was no prospect of its return in Portugal.

The failure of the 1981 coup helped to further break the logjam of the past. The divided military, especially the army, was now weaker and the military budget was reduced. The military also became increasingly professionalised rather than politicised, and membership of NATO meant that officers' horizons shifted hugely, so that combating 'the enemy within' no longer became its primary purpose.

This development was a key aspect of a more long-term departure by Spain from the alignments and issues of the 1930s. It was a departure that, to a considerable extent, had been carried out under the last years of Franco's regime. In part, this was due to the strength of Franco's position and the success of his policies, with anarcho-syndicalism and violent anti-clericalism both ceasing, as a result of Franco's repression, to play a role in Spanish politics. Neither revived in the 1970s in part because a general weariness of oppositional politics existed.

More significant was the social and economic transformation centred on the rapid move of people from the land, with all the resultant social changes. In addition, affected by the Second Vatican Council, the Catholic Church by the 1970s was more willing to consider change, while its new-founded democratic credentials ensured that it was not the target for political action.

As a consequence of the 1981 attempted coup, more social change could be pushed through, in the shape, in particular, of the legalisation of divorce. As another sign of change, Spanish politics could more closely be approximated to those of other western European countries. Turning away from dreams of Francoist return, the right consolidated itself within the democratic political system, backing the People's Alliance (*Alianza Popular*, AP), a party founded in 1976 and led by Manuel Fraga. This backing reduced the range of manoeuvre for the UCD even though the uneasiness with change that had caused tension in the run-up to the attempted coup remained strong on the right. The AP was to be refounded in 1989 as the People's Party.

For tourists, one legacy of change was the sale by the marquises of Viana of their Córdoba palace. It is now open to the public, who can see on the tour a Franco portrait. A different legacy was the closure of railway lines, such as that of the *Tren de Aceite* (olive oil train), as road culture took over, leading to the establishment of attractive walking routes.

Added difficulties arose from economic problems. The Francoist regime had not been best placed to respond to the serious economic shocks of the early 1970s and, instead, had exacerbated the situation by trying, like eastern European governments or, for that matter, Britain's Labour governments of 1974–9, to manipulate the situation in order to win popularity. Control over the currency encouraged such manipulation. This, however, had led to high inflation, fiscal problems and a major rise in unemployment, which produced doubts about the future of Spain, doubts exacerbated by the problems stemming from the renewed oil-price shock of 1979.

The response was a corporatist one, the Moncloa Pacts of 1977 and their successors up to 1984. In these, the government brought employers and trade unions together to agree on measures to contain fiscal problems and reform the economy. There was a parallel with developments in much of Europe including Britain's experiment with a social compact.

GOLF AND SEVERIANO 'SEVE' BALLESTEROS

Born in Cantabria, Seve Ballesteros (1957–2011), a key figure in the golfing world from 1976 to 1995, was important as a leader in the revival of European golfing through the success of the European Ryder Cup team in the 1980s and 1990s. He won the Open Championship three times and the Masters twice. He was also significant to the growth of golf courses as a business in Spain. Indeed, golf became a key form of theme tourism in Spain and notably so in the south. The Costa del Sol is noted for its golf courses and, in 2017, there were 349 courses in Spain.

Despite the Moncloa Pacts, tensions in Spain continued because economic problems remained serious. These tensions strained the social and political fabric, with strikes and with the Communist Party unhappy that the Pacts did not ease hardship. In October 1982, helped by the 1981 attempted coup, there was a political transformation, rather like that in France the previous year. The Socialist Party won an absolute majority in Parliament, while the Communists were routed. There were also changes on the right, with the divided UCD destroyed electorally, while the People's Alliance won just over a quarter of the vote and became the major opposition party.

As with François Mitterrand's Socialists in France in 1981, the Socialist Party under Felipe González won in part by exploiting populist hunger for change and widespread concern about the consequences of capitalism and, as in France eventually from 1982, there was in practice to be a more prudential and pragmatic governance. Relatively deflationary policies intended to ensure fiscal stability were continued under González, who remained prime minister until he lost the 1996 election. There was major

economic growth in the 1980s and considerable social liberation, although, less positively, politics was in part run as a spoils
system.

As an aspect of the crucial international contexts, Spain
anchored itself more widely, joining in 1986 the EC (now EU).
International recognition was seen in 1992 when the Olympics
were held in Barcelona and Expo in Seville. Unlike Portugal and
Greece, which had been longstanding members of NATO, Spain,
despite approaches under Franco, for example in 1975, only joined
it in 1982, a decision reaffirmed in 1986 with the support of 57
per cent of the votes cast in a referendum, and membership of
NATO and the EC prefigured the same route that was to be taken
by most of the states of former Communist Europe. The EC provided a route to much more foreign investment and economic
growth, in both agriculture and industry.

The domestic political situation was different because the left
was more politically powerful and popular in Spain in the 1980s
than in much of eastern Europe in the 1990s after the fall of the
Communist regimes. Indeed, in 1982, the Spanish Socialists had
campaigned on a plank of leaving NATO, while there was also a
strong Marxist plank to the party. González's breach with this
stance, one that followed that of the German Social Democrats
and prefigured that of British Labour, was important to the more
general transition of the Spanish left, and also to the developing
character of the EC at this juncture. He won absolute majorities
in the elections of 1982, 1986 and 1990, creating a crisis for the
parties of the right, although, as a result of losing his absolute
majority in the 1993 election, from 1994 he had to rely on Basque
and Catalan nationalists. In some respects, González was a
Spanish version of Tony Blair, although the countries and periods
of control were different, and González did not take Spain to war.
He was hit, however, by an economic downturn in 1993 when
Spain could not support its currency within the Exchange Rate
Mechanism, and by a series of corruption scandals that overtook

the Socialists. They had used power to reward their areas of particular support, especially Andalusia and notably Seville.

In the 1990s and 2000s, Spain coped with change and crisis more successfully than Italy. In the 1990s, rapid economic growth was accompanied by an absence of a sense of malaise. There was a peaceful transition of power from the tired Socialists to the conservative People's Party under José María Aznar in 1996. Each party drew on the deeply entrenched nature of patronage in Spanish society, but also sought to respond to new social forces. More generally, the influence of Catholic civic society declined, but without any pronounced sense of crisis.

Focusing its foreign policy on the EU and on Latin America, Spain ceased to play a major military role, although it remained a member of NATO and continued to deploy some impressive warships. In 1993, Spain decided that it could not contribute a brigade to the United Nations forces in Bosnia as conscripts could not be expected to serve and there were insufficient regular troops. Politics was crucial. Under the conservative Aznar government, Spain joined in the Iraq War in 2003, although this was essentially a political, not a military, role, and there was much popular opposition even to that.

The 1996 election brought to an end thirteen years of Socialist rule. The conservative *Partido Popular* (People's Party, PP), founded in 1989 by Manuel Fraga, a former Francoist minister, which had already taken over Madrid city council in 1991, now won 37.6 per cent of the vote and 156 of the 350 seats, the largest number; the Socialists won 14 per cent. Aznar, the PP leader, who had survived an ETA assassination attempt the previous year, reached agreements with regional nationalist parties and 181 votes in the *cortes* backed him as prime minister. Determined to meet the criteria for Euro membership, and to distinguish itself from what it presented as Socialist extravagance and corruption, his government cut the deficit by means of spending reductions. This led to union-led protests. The privatisation of state-owned holdings was another policy. Areas of PP support enjoyed much largesse, especially Valencia, where there were highly ambitious building schemes. As with the Socialists, the largesse was accompanied by corruption, largely to the benefit of party political funds, although also for personal enrichment.

In the 2000 election, Aznar won an outright majority of seats, 183, based on 44.5 per cent of the vote. His managerialism chimed with much of the public, notably his distinguishing himself from the ideological legacy of the past. Thereafter, Spain did well economically in comparison to most of the EU. Optimism led to much building. It also encouraged bold projects such as the Universal Forum of Cultures Expo held in Barcelona in 2004, which involved the creation of the Diagonal Mar district. Earlier, the same process had been associated with the 1992 Olympics, which led to the waterfront development of Port Olímpic.

Spain, however, was hit by the global economic recession in 2002. Attempts to reduce unemployment benefits led to a general strike in that year. Alongside economic growth, there was inflation, notably in house prices, encouraged by loose money policies, as well as high unemployment. Although there was a marked degree of recovery in the mid-2010s, unemployment continued to be high. The rate in February 2018 was 16.1 per cent, and that despite a growth rate in Gross Domestic Product of 3 per cent.

Aznar's support for the 2003 Gulf War resulted in criticism. On 11 March 2004, three days before the general election, ten bombs killed 191 people in Madrid train bombings. The government initially blamed ETA despite increasing evidence of Islamist involvement. This blaming led to public criticism of the government, and the opposition won the elections by 164 to 148 seats, although the extent to which this victory was due to the response to the bombings is controversial.

The new prime minister, the Socialist José Luis Rodríguez Zapatero, held office until 2011, also winning the 2008 elections.

He withdrew Spanish troops from Iraq in 2004, legalised same-sex marriage in 2005, reformed the abortion law to the fury of the Church and raised the minimum wage, as well as granting amnesty to migrants.

RAFAEL NADAL: TENNIS STAR

Born in the Balearic Islands in 1986, Rafael Nadal, 'the King of Clay', is a great clay-court player who, in 2017, returned to the top of the world rankings. He has won sixteen Grand Slam singles titles and earned over $90 million in prize money. He is aggressive and athletic, and good at top-spin groundstrokes. His lengthy 2008 Wimbledon victory against Roger Federer is generally seen as the most impressive Wimbledon final. That year, Nadal won the world no. 1 ranking, and he returned to no. 1 in 2010, a year in which he also won Wimbledon again. At the time of writing, Nadal has won twenty-three of his thirty-eight games with Federer, and seventeen of his twenty-four with Andy Murray.

The Basque situation had become more complicated in the 1980s as government agencies backed the *Grupos Antiterroristas de Liberación* (Anti-terrorist Liberation Group, GA) in a 'dirty war' against ETA in 1983–7. ETA itself went on killing more people, notably when they blew up a shopping centre in Barcelona in 1987, slaughtering twenty-one. ETA also killed journalists. Violence and ceasefires continued to alternate until a permanent ceasefire was negotiated in 2011, ending a conflict in which over eight hundred people had been killed. The Spanish government had benefited both from French support in closing Basque safe havens and from the international move against terrorist organisations during the War on Terror that had begun in 2001. A 2017 poll by the University of Deusto found 29 per cent content with the existing level of Basque self-rule, 38 per cent in favour of more autonomy, and 17 per cent supporters of independence. In the 2016 regional election, Bildu, a pro-independence party, won 21 per cent of the votes cast.

Economic problems became more pressing from 2007 both as a consequence of a worldwide fiscal crisis and as a product of the bursting in 2008 of a loose-money credit bubble. Much of the money had been spent on speculative building projects. Unemployment rose to 27 per cent, the highest in the EU. Debt escalated. In the aftermath of the crisis, house prices fell by an average of a third, and the remains of unfinished building projects are still scattered across Spain.

A sense of crisis contributed to the Socialists' loss of power in 2011 and their replacement by the PP, which had been headed since 2004 by Mariano Rajoy. The PP won a landslide in the November 2011 election: 186 out of 350 seats in the lower house of the *cortes*, the largest majority since the restoration of democracy. An austerity plan introduced in December 2011 froze the salaries of public workers, ended rent assistance for young people, froze the minimum wage and increased income tax, among other measures.

The position of the PP, however, was challenged by revelations of secret funding, including of politicians. Rajoy, who had been treasurer of the PP, was a particular focus of the scandal, as of a separate one of politicians receiving subsistence allowances for lodgings despite having residences in Madrid. Rajoy resisted popular and political pressure to resign, and delayed the 2015 election until 20 December, the last day on which it could be held. The PP won the most votes in a heavily fragmented Parliament, but lost 64 of its 187 seats.

Another political element was provided by the rapid rise of a new political party, Podemos, which was established in March 2014 as a left-wing populist party against austerity and corruption.

In the elections on 20 December 2015, Podemos received 20.65 per cent of the vote and won 69 of the 350 seats, compared to 28.7 per cent for the PP and 22 per cent for the Socialists. The political impasse led to another general election, held on 26 June 2016, in which the PP gained more seats, but still no overall majority. The crisis was only alleviated when most of the Socialist representatives abstained on 29 October, which allowed the reappointment of Rajoy.

Meanwhile, immigration slowly affected the character of Spain, notably southern Spain, with large numbers seeking entry from Africa, and concern grew over a possible Islamic challenge. In 2010, calls for Muslim worship in the cathedral of Córdoba, earlier a major mosque, or for the cathedral to be signposted as a cathedral-mosque, led to contention in which themes from the Reconquista were echoed. Anxieties about the extent to which immigration from North Africa was affecting the character of Andalusia gave a current focus to the politics of the issue. Al-Qaeda called for the withdrawal of non-Muslims from what it termed *al-Andalus*. In 2017, a terrorist attack in Barcelona increased concern about Islamic fundamentalism.

In response to immigration, Spain, in 2017, strengthened its border fences and frontier posts at the African outposts of Ceuta and Melilla, which constitute the only land border between Africa and the European Union. The Canary Islands were a more significant and longstanding point of entry. Would-be migrants cross from north-west Africa in crowded open boats and seek asylum, with traffickers making money from transportation under inhumane conditions. For example, in the year from August 2005 to August 2006, twenty thousand African refugees arrived in the Canaries, and up to three thousand are thought to have died in the dangerous crossing. The Spanish navy seeks to intercept the boats and block the immigration which, due to the more tumultuous Atlantic waters, is more dangerous than that across the Mediterranean from Libya to Italy. Spain also leans on Morocco, which has a border with Ceuta and Melilla, to try to limit migration.

Regionalism continued to be a key issue, as it remains to the present. After Franco died, regional political movements, notably in Catalonia, accepted autonomy under the 1978 constitution and did not tend to seek independence, although in 1982 there were protests in Catalonia against attempts to limit autonomy. Jordi Pujol, the founder of the Convergence and Union, the Catalan nationalist party, who governed Catalonia from 1980 to 2003, supported greater autonomy but a Catalonia within Spain as part of a Europe of the regions.

The Aznar government was not forthcoming on separatist issues, but its Socialist successor, which sought a solution, in 2006 agreed a Statute of Autonomy with the Catalan parties that expanded the authority of Catalonia's government. This was approved by a Catalan referendum in 2006 with 73 per cent support from the 49 per cent of the electorate who voted, but was opposed by the PP, which challenged the statute before the Spanish Constitutional Court or Tribunal. The Court intervened in 2010, by a six to four majority, to rewrite and interpret the statute, which was effectively emasculated. This led to a mass demonstration of over a million people in Barcelona with the slogan 'We are a nation. We decide'. The Court's intervention was seen as politically partisan.

ANOTHER CATALAN CONTRIBUTION: ELBULLI

Ferran Adrià, who was the head chef of elBulli, a restaurant in Roses, is regarded as one of the leading chefs in the world. Born in 1962, he refers to his cooking as 'deconstructivist' in order, through transforming established means and responses, to provide unexpected contrasts of flavour, temperature and texture. His unusual dishes have included liquid olives, paella with Rice Krispies, and white garlic and almond sorbet, and there was a more general use of culinary foam. The restaurant closed in 2011 and was reopened as an innovation centre. Adrià argues that cooking and art is coextensive, a controversial view. There has also been criticism of his cooking for using additives.

The controversy encouraged pressure for independence, which was endorsed by the Catalan government in 2012. An election in Catalonia resulted in a majority for independence and to the passage, in 2013, of the Catalan Sovereignty Declaration which stated that the Catalan people had the right to decide their own political future. The Constitutional Court blocked an independence referendum in 2014, but a non-binding 'consultation', held on 9 November 2014, saw 81 per cent of the 35 per cent who voted opt for independence. As an attempted historical reference point, Catalan nationalists transformed the commemoration of the end of the War of Spanish Succession in 1714 into an attempted denunciation of 'Spain against Catalonia'. In turn, another election in September 2015 saw pro-independence parties win a majority of seats, although not of votes, and the new Catalan parliament began steps for independence.

The Catalonian regional government claimed in 2017 that it had a democratic mandate to hold an independence referendum, but the measure was ruled illegal by the Constitutional Court and the public prosecutor ordered the investigation and prosecution of all measures to that end. The country's constitution, which forbids secession, was publicly defended by the prime minister, Mariano Rajoy, an opponent of greater autonomy, by King Philip VI (r. 2014–present), who took a somewhat partisan stance, and by the Socialists. In practice, the constitution had already been revised, both with previous changes to regional autonomy and as a result of entry into the EU.

The issue reflected both a strong traditional sense of separate identity and more specific recent concerns, notably the
consequences of the constitution's principle of 'solidarity
between regions'. Catalonia is responsible for 16 per cent of
Spain's population, 19 per cent of its GDP, 25.6 per cent of
its exports and 20.7 per cent of foreign investment; albeit
heavily indebted, Catalonia (unlike the Basque Country) was
paying a disproportionate share of taxation and was receiving
insufficient benefit from government expenditure. Two rival
nationalisms were in collision. The Spanish government failed
to deliver on its promise to stop the vote and, on 1 October
2017, 43 per cent of those eligible voted despite large-scale
intimidation. Criticism of the brutal use of the Civil Guard
led to its withdrawal. Pressure from businesses willing to relo-
cate to Madrid proved more effective in limiting backing for
independence. In October–December 2017, over three thousand companies moved their headquarters outside Catalonia,
including Catalonia's two largest banks and Planeta, the largest Spanish-language publisher. Some of the self-employed
also left. Hotel bookings in Barcelona fell.

Moreover, over 20 per cent of Spaniards have stopped buying
Catalan products, while hostility to Catalonia was encouraged by
PP spokesmen who claimed, for example, that Spanish speak-
ers in Catalonia were discriminated against. In practice, Spanish
nationalism is a collective agreement to keep the country together
that coalesced after the death of Franco. Spain is a composite that
entails mutual respect for the constitution.

Catalan nationalism also suffered from a marked lack of
international support. The Catalan government sought international recognition and EU mediation of the dispute with Madrid,
but neither was forthcoming. Instead, in a marked rejection of
the earlier idea that the EU would be a Europe of the regions, the
EU backed the existing situation, in part because it was fearful
that Catalan independence would begin a disintegration of the

EU. There was scant evidence for this view, but the net effect was a marked support for the existing situation.

The contrast with French support for Catalan independence in the 1640s and with British backing for Catalan autonomy in the 1700s was readily apparent. This contrast underlined the role of historical conjunctures and contingencies in the development of what otherwise might appear an inevitable part of the political structure. Here, the clear contrast was with the very different destiny of Portugal despite Spanish attempts to take it over, and success in doing so from 1580 to 1640. There was also a longer tension between the view of the birth of Spain through the uniting of kingdoms, principalities and seigneuries that predated the Spanish nation, which therefore was inherently pluralist, and the alternative that emphasised a nation-state.

For Madrid, there were key questions of governability, and the fear that Catalan nationalism, if successful, would encourage similar pressures in other areas, notably the Basque Country and Galicia, but even including Andalusia, where, in 2007, a new charter of autonomy declared that it had a 'millennium-long' history and a 'nationality'. The tensions of a federal system were consistently illustrated by national referenda. For example in the 1986 referendum on Spain remaining in NATO, 56.85 per cent of the votes cast had been yes, but the majority in the Basque Country, the Canary Islands, Catalonia and Navarre had all been against staying in, with 67.55 per cent of the votes cast in the Basque Country being no. In 2017, however, the Basque regional government failed to back its Catalan counterpart. Its head, Iñigo Urkullu, who is from the Basque Nationalist Party (*Partido Nacionalista Vasco*, PNV), claimed that the Catalan referendum was neither legal or binding. He has been able to improve the Basque region's autonomy and financial system: unlike the Catalans, Basques do not pay more in taxes than is spent on their region. The PNV is a key ally of the PP, swapping this support for improved terms, but failed to prevent the PP from taking a harsh approach towards Catalan politicians, just as it was unable to persuade Catalonia not to declare independence.

In October 2017, in response to the declaration of direct rule by the Spanish government, the Catalan parliament voted for independence. In response, Madrid acted firmly but harshly. The Catalan government was sacked and its parliament dissolved in preparation for new elections that December. Rajoy declared he would end 'separatist havoc'. Catalan politicians were then arrested by the national government on the charges of rebellion and sedition, and remanded without bail. This led to large-scale demonstrations in Barcelona, demonstrations mirrored on a smaller scale in Bilbao. Prior to the provincial election on 21 December, the national government made clear that any recurrence of a vote for independence would lead to the same consequences. Soraya Sáenz de Santamaría, the deputy prime minister, declared, 'Secessionists don't have leaders today because they have been decapitated', by which she meant arrested, adding that the PP would 'continue liquidating the independence movement'. In the provincial election, which was called by the national government, separatist parties. Together for Catalonia, Republican Left of Catalonia, and Popular Unity held a slim, reduced majority of seats (seventy in place of seventy-two), although, with 25.3 per cent of the vote and thirty-seven seats, the Citizens Party, which wants Catalonia to remain a semi-autonomous part of Spain, is the single largest party. The division of Catalonia remains as pronounced as ever, with a strong support for independence in small towns and villages, while in Barcelona a majority supports remaining with Spain. In total, 48 per cent of votes were for the pro-independence parties and 52 per cent for unionist parties. The PP recorded its worst ever result, winning only 3 of the 135 seats.

IMAGES OF THE PAST

The Spanish presentation of the past was very much affected by political changes. This was not just a matter of the content of scholarly research and publication. For example, Spanish historical atlases of the post-Franco period were more innovative in their cartography and bolder in their projections than their predecessors had been. Juan Roig Obiol's *Atlas de Historia Universal y de España* included information on the Spanish parliamentary elections of 1931, 1933 and 1936, and a page on those of 1977, including details of the Basque and Catalan parliaments. In contrast to the views of the Franco regime, this atlas was not an overly centralised account of Spanish history. Similarly, the *Atlas Histórico, Edad moderna* (1986) of E. Martínez Ruiz, A. Gutíerrez and E. Díaz Lobon did not disguise the depth of the crisis in Spanish power in the seventeenth century.

Aside from the general treatment of the past, there are more specific historical divisions, and not solely due to the Civil War. For example, history continues to be a key issue in the case of discussion of Catalan nationalism. Historical identity was also cited by Rajoy when he lifted the ban on live bullfights on state-run television. The location of artistic treasures also involves politics, as in the decision that Picasso's *Guernica* should stay in the Reina Sofía museum in Madrid, and not go to the Guggenheim museum in Bilbao, the nearest major museum to Guernica.

ECHOES OF THE PAST

In September 2017, efforts to stop a Catalan independence referendum led to frequent references to the past. Protestors repeatedly decried what they saw as a repetition of the Franco years. In contrast, the government referred to the post-Franco 1978 constitution as its justification, a constitution in many senses defined by the attempt to win the support of Francoist elements. On 20 September 2017, Carles Puigdemont, the Catalan president, described the Spanish state as authoritarian and stated that Catalonia would never accept 'a return to the darkest times'. Pablo Iglesias, leader of the Podemos, a national opposition party, declared it was 'shameful' to return to an era with 'political prisoners'. The Civil Guard, the national force used to carry out arrests, were associated by many with the Franco years.

In turn, also on 20 September 2017, Alfonso Dastis, the foreign minister, drew attention to Franco having organised two referenda and claimed that some separatists were using a 'Nazi' approach of intimidation. A PP spokesman referred to the fate of Lluís Companys who had declared Catalan independence in 1934 only to be shot by a Civil Guard firing squad in 1940. Companys has a potent legacy in Catalonia, where streets, squares and the main stadium used in the 1992 Olympics are named after him, and there is a monument to him in Barcelona (1998).

Deeper history was also in contention. Some Catalan separatists wished to remove the Columbus monument in Barcelona because they saw it as too Spanish.

There are also historical parallels in the discussion about Islam in Spain today. Indeed, many current questions about identity and alleged threat repeat those made at the time of the expulsion of the Moriscos in 1609. The possibility and character of assimilation, and the prospect of multiculturalism come to the fore.

POST-FRANCO LIBERALISATION

The transition experienced by Spain after the demise of its dictator, as also by Greece and Portugal, was considerable. It may appear not to have matched that of the former Communist states of eastern Europe, but a comparison of Spanish society and politics in 2018 with that forty years earlier might suggest otherwise. The common note was of a liberalisation, however, that was not solely political, and this was also to be the case with eastern Europe. Economic liberalisation was also a problem as free trade within the EU threatened the viability of uncompetitive sectors of the economy, which had serious social consequences. The most important example was the challenge to traditional agriculture, especially to peasant producers.

Spain, Portugal and Greece also witnessed large-scale social and cultural liberalisation, which was politically prominent because the earlier conservative dictatorships in each country had closely identified themselves with opposition to such liberalisation, an opposition seen as affirming moral worth. The subsequent liberalisation can be seen in terms of the crucial importance of governmental change, but it can also be argued that this analysis exaggerates the importance of governmental action, and that, in practice, a major transformation was already taking place, not least because the young were responding to trends elsewhere in Europe. This was particularly true of Spain, where the Francoist regime became less rigid in its last years although it still had an oppressive system including a police force used to impose morality.

CHAPTER FOURTEEN

Conclusions

The environment with which we started the book suggests immutable factors in Spanish history, notably those of geology and climate. In practice, however, choices were repeatedly present for Spaniards and their governments, and counterfactuals (what ifs?) are therefore valid. In *Historia virtual de España, 1870–2004: Qué hubiera pasado si?* (Virtual history of Spain, 1870–2004: What if?) 2004, contributors discussed what would have happened if Spain had avoided war with the United States in 1898, if the Republican parties had been united in the 1933 elections, if Spain had entered the Second World War, if Carrero Blanco had not been murdered by ETA in 1973, and if Spain had not joined the Iraq War in 2003. One of the chapters considered whether the Civil War would have been avoided had the Socialist Indalecio Prieto accepted the premiership in May 1936, concluding quite possibly so, and thus drawing attention to contingencies and leadership.

The impact of the Civil War and of Franco in the Spanish imagination, and on recent Spanish history, are such that the majority of the chapters related directly or indirectly to one or the other. Counterfactualism offered a way to address these issues and this impact. In 1976, the year after Franco's death, two books, *El desfile de la Victoria* by Fernando Díaz-Plaza and *En el día de hoy* by Jesús Torbado, offered counterfactuals based on Republican victory in the Civil War. Indeed, civil wars tend to encourage counterfactual thought.

Looking further back, there is the question of what would have happened had the Reconquista been completed soon after the fall of Toledo in 1085. Also what would have happened but for the Protestant Reformation in the sixteenth century. The Hispanic world would have been more powerful both had there been no Dutch revolt and had Philip II's dynastic alignment with England been maintained and produced an heir, either to his marriage with Mary or, once she had died, to Elizabeth I, had she accepted a proposal from Philip. Continued dynastic unity with Portugal, rather than the rift in 1640, would also have been highly significant, certainly in the international sphere and possibly also domestically. The futures possibly offered by Philip II's eldest son, Don Carlos, represent other counterfactuals. For the eighteenth century, the foremost questions are those of a continuation of the Spanish Habsburg dynasty in 1700, and of a competent successor to Charles III in 1788, rather than the baleful Charles IV.

Thereafter, the avoidance of the Napoleonic takeover in 1808, or the success of Joseph I (Joseph Bonaparte), invite reflection. Each focuses attention on the impact of international power politics on Spanish developments. The counterfactuals relate not only to France but also to the wider international context. For example, was Spanish history in the nineteenth century ultimately dependent on Napoleon's defeat outside Moscow in 1812? Did this at least in part explain why one French dynasty was successfully imposed from 1700, but another was not from 1808? The total mishandling by Ferdinand VII in the 1810s and 1820s of Spanish American demands for autonomy also invites consideration, notably with different policies and events in Spain and Spanish America, and with Britain adopting a different stance. This mishandling is an instance of the baleful impact of the monarchy on many occasions in Spanish history. To some, this can be widened out to include the question of the role of the Church and of religious commitment.

The subsequent political history of the nineteenth century is shot through with counterfactuals, notably with reference to the First Carlist War, the political crises of 1868–74, and the outbreak of war with the United States in 1898. In Cuba, as, very differently, in Catalonia, there was an inability to search for an effective compromise and a determination to preserve central control. Looked at in another counterfactual light, Catalonia remained with Spain, unlike Ireland and Hungary with Britain and Austria respectively.

Thus, the counterfactuals of the last ninety years, which focus on the Civil War but also include, for example, no Madrid train bombings in 2004 and the possible consequences for the general election of that year, sit in a longer tradition, one that richly deserves attention. Certainly, there is no reason to argue for inevitability in the past, present or future.

The Catalan crisis of 2017 saw counterfactualism about Catalonia's past, alongside what, to critics, were accounts tainted by ethnic parochialism, historical mysticism and rhetoric. To supporters of Catalan independence, their nationalism drew on a history that included a need to understand that other developments had been possible, and had simply been prevented by force. The latter is certainly correct as with Philip V's victory in the War of the Spanish Succession; although what that entails for the present and the future is far from clear. This is very much part of the living history of Spain, one that is even more potent than the environment.

Counterfactualism can contribute to the debates about Spanish 'difference' and failure, until late, to achieve modernity. These debates are, in part, misplaced because they neglect the extent to which there is no common European path from which Spain supposedly diverged. Instead, the emphasis should be on multiple pathways and inherent differences, differences to which Spain contributes invigorating examples. There is a tendency to treat Spain as part of a simple, uniform narrative of European and world history, and notably so with the Spanish Civil War. The parallels and contexts are frequent, for example of the Reconquista and the Crusades, and of the American and Latin American wars of independence. This is a helpful approach but, in every case, there are also not only specific elements in the Spanish situation, but also the need to locate this case in relation to longer-term developments in Spanish history. Thus, the Reconquista looked back to the eighth century in a way that the Crusades did not. The Civil War can be located not solely in the ideological rivalries and moves against democracy of the 1930s, but also in a longer-term pattern of military intervention in Spanish politics. And so also with future events: they will have to be understood in the pattern of Spain's past.

Selected Further Reading

Alvarez-Junco, José, *The Emergence of Mass Politics in Spain: Populist Demagoguery and Republican Culture, 1890–1910* (Brighton, 2002).

Amelang, James, *Parallel Histories: Muslims and Jews in Inquisitorial Spain* (Baton Rouge, LA, 2013).

Barton, Simon, *A History of Spain* (London, 2009).

Boyd, Carolyn, *Historia Patria: Politics, History, and National Identity in Spain, 1875–1975* (Princeton, NJ, 1997).

Campbell, Jodi, *At the First Table: Food and Social Identity in Early Modern Spain* (Lincoln, NE, 2017).

Camprubí, Lino, *Engineers and the Making of the Francoist Regime* (Cambridge, MA, 2014).

Carr, Matthew, *Blood and Faith: the Purging of Muslim Spain, 1492–1614* (London, 2017).

Edwards, John, *Ferdinand and Isabella* (London, 2005).

Elliott, John, *Imperial Spain* (London, 1963).

—, *Empires of the Atlantic World: Britain and Spain in America, 1492–1830* (New Haven, CT, 2006).

Esdaile, Charles, *Fighting Napoleon: Guerrillas, Bandits and Adventurers in Spain, 1808–1814* (New Haven, CT, 2003).

—, *The Peninsular War: A New History* (London, 2002).

Gilmour, David, *The Transformation of Spain* (London, 1985).

Graham, Helen, *The Spanish Republic at War, 1936–1939* (Cambridge, 2002).

Graham, Helen (ed.), *Interrogating Francoism. History and Dictatorship in Twentieth-Century Spain* (London, 2016).

Kamen, Henry, *Empire: How Spain Became a World Empire* (New Haven, CT, 2004).

—, *Imagining Spain: Historical Myth and National Identity* (New Haven, CT, 2008).

—, *Philip II of Spain* (London, 1997).

—, *Philip V of Spain* (New Haven, CT, 2001).

—, *The Spanish Inquisition: A Historical Revision* (New Haven, Conn., 1993).

Lawrence, Mark, *The Spanish Civil Wars: A Comparative History of the First Carlist War and the Conflict of the 1930s* (London, 2017).

Mancing, Howard, *The Cervantes Encyclopaedia* (Westport, CT, 2004).

Miller, Montserrat, *Feeding Barcelona 1714–1975: Public Market Halls, Social Networks, and Consumer Culture* (Baton Rouge, LA, 2015).

Minder, Raphael, *The Struggle for Catalonia: Rebel Politics in Spain* (London, 2017).

Moreno-Luzón, Javier, *Modernizing the Nation: Spain During the Reign of Alfonso XIII, 1902–1931* (Brighton, 2012).

Parker, Geoffrey, *Imprudent King: A New Life of Philip II* (New Haven, CT, 2014).

Sarrión, Guillermo Pérez, *The Emergence of a National Market in Spain, 1650–1800* (London, 2016).

Seidman, Michael, *Republic of Egos: A Social History of the Spanish Civil War* (Madison, WI, 2002).

—, *The Victorious Counterrevolution: The Nationalist Effort in the Spanish Civil War* (Madison, WI, 2011).

Stein, Stanley and Barbara, *Silver Trade and War: Spain and America in the Making of Early Modern Europe* (Baltimore, MD, 2000).

Tardió, Manuel Álvarez and Fernando del Rey Reguillo (eds), *The Spanish Second Republic Revisited: From Democratic Hopes to the Civil War, 1931–1936* (Brighton, 2012).

Thomas, Hugh, *The Golden Age. The Spanish Empire of Charles V* (London, 2010).

Tone, John, *The Fatal Knot: the Guerrilla War in Navarre and the Defeat of Napoleon in Spain* (Chapel Hill, NC, 1994).

Townson, Nigel (ed.), *Is Spain Different? A Comparative Look at the Nineteenth and Twentieth Centuries* (Brighton, 2015).

Index